D0464774

NO FUTURE FOR YOU

NO FUTURE FOR YOU

Salvos from *The Baffler*

EDITED BY JOHN SUMMERS,
CHRIS LEHMANN, AND THOMAS FRANK

BAFFLER BOOKS
The MIT Press
Cambridge, Massachusetts
London, England

Book design by Phoebe Flynn Rich.
Cover design by The Flynstitute.
Cover photograph by James Griffioen.
This book was set in Hoefler Text by The Flynstitute, Madison, Wisconsin.
Printed and bound in the United States of America.

MIT Press books may be purchased at special quantity discounts for business or sales promotional use.
For information, please email: special_sales@mitpress.mit.

The Baffler Foundation Inc., PO Box 390049, Cambridge, MA, 02139
thebaffler.com
MIT Press, One Rogers Street, Cambridge, MA 02142

Library of Congress Cataloging-in-Publication Data is available.
ISBN: 978-0-262-02833-2

10 9 8 7 6 5 4 3 2 1

Also from ***The Baffler***

Boob Jubilee: The Cultural Politics of the New Economy (2003)
Commodify Your Dissent: Salvos from The Baffler (1997)

This book is dedicated to
the memory of Aaron Swartz
(1986–2013).

CONTENTS

INTRODUCTION

PART ONE: THE FUTURE, RECYCLED

PART TWO: THE ARTS OF REGRESSION

PART THREE: POSITIVE THINKING

PART FOUR: QUIET ROOMS, DEAD ZONES

Introduction

JOHN SUMMERS, CHRIS LEHMANN,
AND THOMAS FRANK

This book of salvos from *The Baffler* magazine comes with a smile and a simple message: *There's no future for you.*

We mean this with only a slight dash of metaphor, since our goal is to enlighten, not depress. The forces presiding over our country's disintegration have already robbed a generation of jobs and money, ruined our private aspirations, and sunk collective confidence, on which, we are often told, depends the vibrancy of the market itself.

All too true, alas and uh-oh.

This book, though, offers a different perspective, one that also bears a gleam of hope. Our current economic depression and stratification follow materially from the great financial crash of 2008. But it was the erosion of belief in the future in the years *leading up* to it that's made the slump so difficult to imagine transcending now—long after we've discovered the full scale of damage done to our institutions by a greedy and fraudulent leadership class posing as defenders of individual liberty and general prosperity.

For a quarter of a century following America's victory in the Cold War, our most celebrated executives, theorists, politicos, and pundits enjoyed a virtually unchallenged monopoly over the future, which, they insisted, belonged to the manifest destiny of the market—and which, in practice, extended not much further than the next business cycle. It was their magical thinking that drew our pensions, mortgages, and careers past the gates of the celestial city, perched so invitingly high above history and politics. So long as we chose well from life's opportunities, exercised the requisite mental determination, elbowed aside the competition, and went shopping a lot, we were sure to flourish.

The achievement of the market consensus was to produce a mental world in which alternatives to capitalism did not seem conceivable—much less attainable. The key, it seems, was to make the principles of rapacity and plunder into a new catechism for economic policymaking, and then to watch our culture collapse into miniature idols and our technology shrink from prosthetic gods to prosthetic pals. Cutting taxes for the rich and slashing social spending, downsizing workers and deregulating financial speculation, *how can we help you disrupt and exploit, mister marketplace?*—this cruel tic was once, in the recesses of the mid-twentieth century, the provenance of crackpots, and it's always had principled opponents. But its cultural power has become so concentrated among our leaders that it's produced a nearly unbroken fog over the past twenty-five years, shrouding a tiny elite from the disasters inflicted on the rest of us.

The Baffler, born in ye olde 1988, was present at the uncreative destruction of American thought and culture. We declined back then to bow before the golden calves of the one-and-only future, freshly polished and hosannahed by the cyber-prophets, and generally greeted the messaging campaign of the boom years with a chorus of derisive horselaughs. And when the gilded swindle finally collapsed from the weight of its own sleaziness and the country embarked on its present course of jobless recovery, progress-free innovation, and unparalleled corporate profits, we heard the call. Consensus-makers from both parties woke up in 2008 long enough to rescue the perpetrators of the fraud, then fell promptly back to sleep while the banks went back to business and we began writing the salvos you now have lodged between your eyeballs.

To anyone who's stayed awake to observe the weakness of liberal and progressive reform as it conducts its lockstep dance with the Right, it's been a bloodshot sight to behold. To a magazine devoted to blunting the cutting edge, the partisan skirmishes that fill the news and opinion cycles are a case study in missing the point. The inability

RENÉ MAGRITTE, *The Castle of the Pyrenees*, 1959. The Israel Museum | Bridgeman Art Library of *any* of our leaders to offer an alternative to this wreck of dogmas and miseries—a future worthy of the name, fundamentally different from the present—might very well rank with the sorriest examples of learned idiocy in the whole dreary chronicle of America's business civilization. The overall effect has been uniformly conservative, and by design and default, much to the benefit of the entrenched political class. Well, we have seen their future, and it doesn't work.

No Future For You, like our two previous collections, *Boob Jubilee* (2003) and *Commodify Your Dissent* (1997), gets a great deal of mileage simply out of listening to the way that certain Americans in positions of power avoid talking about class. Proceeding from this simple method, plus an ardent desire to smash the icons and pet utopias of the 1 percenters, we piece together a counternarrative from within the country's three main power centers of stagnation.

Welcome to Washington, D.C., with its armies of hireling blowhards and donor-directed research groups, legacy liberal media providing ammunition and endless cover stories in the center.

Welcome to New York and its bicoastal culture trust—the trophy art collectors, the painters of pretty light, the foundation grandees hustling after vibrancy, the publishers of sadomasochistic fantasy fiction for the hard of feeling.

And welcome to Silicon Valley, home to a corps of nerds, popes, and gurus, whose revolutionary improvements in the technique of living always seem to come packaged in the disciplines of the office park.

Along the way, we hope to smash in a space for alternatives, for those whose time has come. Don't expect marching orders to fall from between these pages, though. Those you will have to think up on your own. We set out neither to sell you a Replacement Concept on the secondary market of ideas nor to unlock the secret of history, and least of all to flatter the ladies and gentlemen who serve as the standard-bearers of correct liberal and left opinion. How is it possible to reform a society that no longer recognizes itself? How can we mobilize a collective sense of agency when our life chances are subcontracted to the market? Somehow, the great questions that once preoccupied our traditions have become distressed intellectual properties, fallen into receivership and snapped up by the culture trust.

Criticism bearing our abrasive tone and uncompromising stance is sometimes derided as lowdown or (worse yet) easy. But the truth is, this kind of criticism is the hardest thing in the world to produce if you happen to live in a culture ruled by the dicta of positive thinking and dread of the existential crime of *being negative*. Ordinary complaining is permitted; it might even be a virtue from time to time. But your compliance is ultimately expected, and the enterprise of criticism in America has to contend with a culture of consensus that reduces conflicts over values to matters of individual attitude.

And so we present this third collection of writing from *The Baffler* with the usual leap of confidence and act of faith, plus a dedication.

You may recognize the name Aaron Swartz from the outpouring of spontaneous grief that followed his 2013 suicide, at age twenty-six, after a two-year prosecution for downloading scholarly journals without permission. Aaron was a genius computer programmer and democracy activist who seemed to have the most brilliant of futures ahead of him, and when we resumed regular publication of this magazine and began firing off these salvos, he was handy in lighting fuses.

The irony was inspiring. Printed magazines like ours were supposed to have laid down arms and withdrawn quietly from the scene eons ago, along with the rest of the traditional culture. And young technologists endowed with Aaron's gifts typically came programmed with orders to betake themselves to Silicon Valley, where they were expected to, you know, start networking companies, optimize things, and maybe even affect to save the world.

In the end, there was no future for Aaron. But in his memory, let us dedicate our own gleam of hope.

PART ONE

THE FUTURE, RECYCLED

Too Smart to Fail

Notes on an age of folly

THOMAS FRANK

The "sound" banker, alas! is not one who sees danger and avoids it, but one who, when he is ruined, is ruined in a conventional and orthodox way along with his fellows so that no one can really blame him.

—JOHN MAYNARD KEYNES

In the short hapless years of the present millennium, we have looked on as three great bubbles of consensus vanity have inflated and burst, each with consequences more dire than the last.

First there was the "New Economy," a millennial fever dream predicated on the twin ideas of a people's stock market and an eternal silicon prosperity; it collapsed eventually under the weight of its own fatuousness.

Second was the war in Iraq, an endeavor whose launch depended for its success on the turpitude of virtually every class of elite in Washington, particularly the tough-minded men of the media; an enterprise that destroyed the country it aimed to save and that helped to bankrupt our nation as well.

And then, Wall Street blew up the global economy. Empowered by bank deregulation and regulatory capture, Wall Street enlisted those tough-minded men of the media again to sell the world on the idea that financial innovations were making the global economy more stable by the minute. Cen-

From *The Baffler*, no. 19

tral banks puffed an asset bubble like the world had never seen before, even if every journalist worth his byline was obliged to deny its existence until it was too late.

These episodes were costly and even disastrous, and after each one had run its course and duly exploded, I expected some sort of day of reckoning for their promoters. And, indeed, the last two disasters combined to force the Republican Party from its stranglehold on American government—for a time.

But what rankles now is our failure, after each of these disasters, to come to terms with how we were played. Each separate catastrophe should have been followed by a wave of apologies and resignations; taken together—and given that a good percentage of the pundit corps signed on to two or even three of these idiotic storylines—they mandated mass firings in the newsrooms and op-ed pages of the nation. Quicker than you could say "Ahmed Chalabi," an entire generation of newsroom fools should have lost their jobs.

But that's not what happened. Plenty of journalists have been pushed out of late, but the ones responsible for deluding the public are not among them. Neocon extraordinaire Bill Kristol won a berth at the *New York Times* (before losing it again), Charles Krauthammer is still the thinking conservative's favorite, George Will drones crankily on, Thomas Friedman remains our leading dispenser of nonsense neologisms, and Niall Ferguson wipes his feet on a welcome mat that will never wear out. The day Larry Kudlow apologizes for slagging bubble-doubters as part of a sinister left-wing trick is the day the world will start spinning in reverse. Standard & Poor's first leads the parade of folly (triple-A's for everyone!), then decides to downgrade U.S. government debt, and is taken seriously in both endeavors. And the prospect of Fox News or CNBC apologizing for their role in puffing war bubbles and financial bubbles is no better than a punch line: what they do is the opposite, launching new movements that stamp their crumbled fables "true" by popular demand.

The real mistake was my own. I believed that our public intelligentsia had succumbed to an amazing series of cognitive failures; that time after time they had gotten the facts wrong, ignored the clanging bullshit detector, made the sort of mistakes that would disqualify them from publishing in *The Baffler*, let alone the *Washington Post*.

What I didn't understand was that these were moral failures, mistakes that were hardwired into the belief systems of the organizations and professions and social classes in question. As such they were mistakes that—from the point of view of those organizations or professions or classes—shed no discredit on the individual chowderheads who made them. Holding them accountable was out of the question, and it remains off the table today. These people ignored every flashing red signal, refused to listen to the whistleblowers, blew off the obvious screaming indicators that something was going wrong in the boardrooms of the nation, even talked us into an unnecessary war, for Chrissake, and the bailout apparatus still stands ready should they fuck things up again.

Keep on Dancing Till the World Ends

My aim here isn't to take some kind of victory lap or to get in the granite faces of our eternal pundit corps one more time—honestly, who really wants to read a twenty-part takedown of the social philosophy of, say, Jim Cramer?

Nor is it to blame Republicans for our problems. It is true that, from the scandal of CEO pay to the scandal of lobotomized regulators, each of the really monumental mistakes of our time arose from the trademark doctrines of the political right. And, yes, it was the Bush administration that installed as national archivist a scholar much criticized for his questionable research methods, that muzzled government scientists, and that declared war on organized intelligence in a hundred other ways.

But the problem goes far beyond politics. We have become a society that can't self-correct, that can't address its obvious problems, that can't pull out of its nosedive. And so to our list of disasters let us add this fourth entry: we have entered an age of folly that—for all

BILL LEWIS

our Facebooking and the twittling tweedle-dee-tweets of the Twitterati—we can't wake up from.

Besides, the reign of corruption has taken plenty of right-wing scalps, too. In fact, one of the most interesting comments on the machinery that is making us stupid came from the libertarian Doug Bandow of the Cato Institute, after he had temporarily lost his job (he got it back a little while later, don't worry) for puffing clients of Jack Abramoff in exchange for the lobbyist's largesse. But what was the big deal? fumed Bandow in a 2006 cri de coeur called "The Lesson Jack Abramoff Taught Me." Living in Washington was expensive; and besides, everyone was basically on the take:

> Many supposedly "objective" thinkers and "independent" scholar/experts these days have blogs or consulting gigs, or they are starting nonprofit Centers for the Study of…Who funds their books, speeches or other endeavors? Often it's those with an interest in the outcome of a related debate. The number of folks underwriting the pursuit of pure knowledge can be counted on one hand, if not one finger.

Bandow had been caught, yes, but he wasn't the only culprit, he insisted—with some accuracy. All opinions are paid for. Everything written in this city, everything in this land that is thought and tweeted and toasted with a hip hip hooray . . . is Abramoffed. We are all slaves to the market; there is no way to stand outside that condition.

I can remember the contempt I felt when I read Bandow's essay, back in 2006. Of course there was a place where ideas weren't simply for sale, I thought—it was called the professions. Ethical standards kept professionals independent of their clients' gross pecuniary interests.

These days, though, I'm not so sure. Money has transformed every watchdog, every independent authority. Medical doctors are increasingly gulled by the lobbying of pharmaceutical salesmen. Accountants were no match for Enron. Corporate boards are rubber stamps. Hospitals break unions and, with an eye toward future donations, electronically single out rich patients for more luxurious treatment.

And consider the university, the mothership of the professions. For-profit higher education is today a booming industry, feeding on the student loans handed out to the desperate. Even the traditional academy, where free inquiry nominally lives, has become a profit center, a place where exorbitant tuition somehow bypasses the adjuncts who do the teaching but makes for lavish executive salaries; where economists pull in fantastic sums for "consulting"; and where the prospect of launching the next hot Internet startup is a gamble that it is worth bending any rule to take.

One of Jack Abramoff's tricks, you will recall, was to hand intellectuals cash and trips to tropical islands in exchange for such intellectual services as might get the tycoons who owned the sweatshops in those paradises off the regulatory hook. And how different was the Abramoff model of enlightenment from the activities of the Cambridge, Massachusetts, consultancy called "Monitor," with its prominent Harvard connections? According to the *Boston Globe*:

> The management consulting firm received $250,000 a month from

> the Libyan government from 2006 to 2008 for a wide range of services, including writing [a] book proposal, bringing prominent academics to Libya to meet Khadafy "to enhance international appreciation of Libya" and trying to generate positive news coverage of the country.

"Trying to generate positive news coverage," by the way, included placing pro-Qaddafi stories by prominent scholars in *The New Republic*, the *Washington Post*, *Newsweek International*, and the *Guardian*—a record far more impressive than the Bush administration's suborning of syndicated columnist Armstrong Williams or Abramoff's own episodic triumphs on the op-ed page of the *Washington Times*.

Another thing Doug Bandow got right was one of the basic reasons for all this: for most Americans, the building blocks of middle-class life—four years at a good college, for example—are growing scarce and out of reach. For other people and other entities, though, they grow ever cheaper; they are baubles to be handed out as necessity requires. The result is exactly what our nineteenth-century ancestors would have expected. Think of Jack Grubman, the superstar stock analyst of the nineties, who famously upgraded AT&T's shares in exchange for getting his children into a ferociously competitive *preschool*. Or the congressional aides on Capitol Hill, surrounded by the inaccessible luxuries of Washington, D.C., who would do nearly anything for a lobbyist in exchange for a shot at a future job on said lobbyist's staff. Or the actual members of Congress who sold their votes in exchange for little bits of sushi or a blowout party in Hawaii or good seats at sporting events.

And as we serve money, we find that money wants the same thing from us: to push everyone it beguiles in the same direction. Money never seems to be interested in strengthening regulatory agencies, for example, but always in subverting them, in making them miss the danger signs in coal mines and in derivatives trading and in deep-sea oil wells. You can have a shot at being part of the 1 percent, money tells us, only if you are first committed to making the 1 percent stronger, to defending their piles in some new and imaginative way, to rationalizing and burnishing their glory, to exempting them from regulation or taxation, to bowing down as they pass, and to believing in your heart that their touch will heal scrofula.

So money gives us not only the bond-rating scandal of 2008, in which trash investments were labeled super-wholesome so that the rating agency in question could win more business from the manufacturers of said trash; and not only the Enron scandal of 2001, in which head-spinning conflicts of interest were overlooked by Enron's accountants in order to preserve the nice ka-ching those conflicts delivered to everyone involved; but also the analyst scandal of 2002, in which Wall Street insiders pushed certain corporate securities on their sappy middle-American clients in order to win those corporations' business—and then while it is corrupting all the watchmen, money also dashes off an enormous body of literature assuring those sappy middle Americans that they are in fact financial geniuses who can outsmart any possible combination of Wall Street insiders, because together the saps reflect the wisdom of crowds or some other such reassuring bullshit. And all of it—the airy populism of the market and its simultaneous complete negation by reality—is as determined by the current distribution of wealth as gravity is by the mass of the planet. Both of them will continue indefinitely regardless of the constant violence the one does to the other simply because that's the way money wants it, and every dollar in the nation will strain at its leash to ensure that financial naïveté persists on into infinity in complete ignorance of financial fraud.

If You're One of Us, Then Roll With Us

It's not that Americans revel in our folly: having been "right" about the debacles of recent years still seems to carry some modicum of value. The reason Newt Gingrich likes to claim that he warned his onetime client Freddie Mac of the dangers of the subprime lending market, for example, is because he believes that there is something honorable about having seen it coming, something that sets him apart from the wild-eyed politicians who shared the stage with him during the presidential primaries of 2012.

Of course, Gingrich's claim to the title is based on no verifiable historical data, and if what we know about Freddie Mac's relationships with its hired hands holds true in his case, the work for which Gingrich received his million-plus payday was not ringing the mortgage company's alarm bell but the opposite: helping to minimize resistance to the outfit's operations among his fellow Republicans—doing what money *always* wants "consultants" like him to do.

Still, there are others who might rightfully claim the laurels Gingrich covets: the economists who warned of a bubble in real estate prices and the handful of journalists who figured out that crazy retail lending practices were inflating the profits of the Wall Street banks.[1] Were society to honor these people, however, just think about who we would be lionizing: a handful of uncelebrated business reporters; economists like Dean Baker, who has spent much of his career deriding consensus economic wisdom; and out-of-the-way publications like *Mother Jones*, the *Pittsburgh City Paper*, and *Southern Exposure* ("Journal of the Progressive South") that stumbled across the big scoop because they happened to be interested in sweaty, wretched subjects like predatory lending.

That is why a more honest reaction, it seems to me, is to declare that there is in fact no value at all in having seen the catastrophe coming. If the honors can't go to the people who already wear the consensus seal of approval, it is better to declare that there is no prize for rightness in the first place.

This seems to be the reasoning behind one of the strangest comments on the epidemic of folly to appear in recent years, the meditation on pervasive wrongness by *Washington Post* columnist Ezra Klein that appeared in June 2011. In it, Klein remembers a boneheaded 2007 Michael Lewis essay in which Lewis mocked people who were worried about risky derivatives; Klein then declares that if a writer as good as Michael Lewis didn't see the problems mounting, it was either impossible to see the problems mounting or wasn't worth it to see the problems mounting. "[N]o explanation of the financial crisis that doesn't have room for Lewis to miss it is sufficient," Klein writes.

And so those worriers back in 2007—the ones who did get it right—were not only gratuitously insulted by Michael Lewis; they are now insulted all over again by Ezra Klein, who seems to believe that Lewis's awesomeness is so overwhelming—that our love for him is so great—that he must remain the polestar of intellectual legitimacy no matter how wrong he turns out to be, no matter how grievous the losses the world suffers, and no matter how dreadful the fate of those thrown out of work during the succeeding recession. The celebrity of the celebrated outweighs it all; the situation may change but the personnel must stay the same.[2]

Another way of putting this idea might be to say that the individuals who got things wrong—the ones who saw few problems in financial deregulation, anyone who thought derivatives eliminated risk, anyone who counted on markets to police themselves—were "one of us." There can be no consequences for them because they merely expressed the consensus views of the time. Like John Maynard Keynes's "sound banker," they might have failed, but they failed in the same way that the rest of "us" failed. To hold them accountable for what they said and did would expose the rest of "us" to such judgment as well. And obviously *that* can't happen.

A résumé filled with grievous errors in the period 1996–2006 is not only a non-problem for further advances in the world of consensus; it is something of a prerequisite. Our intellectual powers-that-be not only forgive the mistakes; they require them. You *must* have been wrong back then in order to have a chance to be taken seriously today; only by having gotten things wrong can you demonstrate that you are trustworthy, a member of the team. (Those who got things right all along, on the other hand, might be dubbed "premature market skeptics"—people who doubted the consensus before the consensus acknowledged it was all right to doubt.)[3]

Christopher Hitchens became the toast of Washington only after he had gone safely wrong on the Iraq War. Or consider the curious saga of *New York Times* op-ed columnist Joe Nocera, who was elevated to the most exalted post in American journalism in 2011, and who has, since then, done outstanding work exposing financial frauds and assessing the value of the old Glass-Steagall rules regulating banks. But there's a peculiar twist to this story. Before Nocera became an admirer of bank regulation, he played the opposite role: he was the journalist who told, in the 1994 book *A Piece of the Action*, the awesome and heroic tale of how the bankers blew Glass-Steagall apart.

Nocera has clearly seen the error of his ways and has changed course. (So has Michael Lewis, for that matter.) It would be churlish not to forgive and forget.

But what about the ones who have not changed? Here is the aforementioned economist Dean Baker, one of the few people who has attempted a grand theory of folly, in a 2011 interview published on the valuable blog *Naked Capitalism:*

> We have people who have literally been wrong about everything having to do with the economy over the last five years. They totally missed the $8 trillion housing bubble, the largest asset bubble in the history of the world.... Then they underestimated the severity of the downturn, telling us the economy was going to bounce right back. And then they got the interest rate story wrong. They told us that the large budget deficits caused by the downturn would lead the bond vigilantes to send interest rates through the roof. Instead they fell through the floor.

"So who gets listened to in national debates," Baker continues, "those who have been consistently right on all the key points, or those who have gotten things as wrong as you possibly can?"

Let us take the question a little further: it is not merely a matter of "who gets listened to" but *why* they get listened to. Recall in this connection the peculiar comment of White House press secretary Jay Carney in December 2011 as he scrambled to get the Obama administration off the hook for its tepid response to the slump: "There was not a single mainstream, Wall Street, academic economist who knew at the time, in January of 2009, just how deep the economic hole was that we were in."

Of course there were plenty of economists who knew how bad

things were. That one was easy to call. But if you limited your inquiries—as Carney is confessing the administration did—to the statements of economists who are "mainstream" and "Wall Street" you would not have encountered such economists. You would have been counting on the wisdom of people who had been "wrong about everything," as Dean Baker puts it.

On the other hand, you would also have been listening to the greatest names of professional economics. And this, we know, is in keeping with President Obama's deepest instincts: *trust the experts.*

But what happens when the experts are fools? What happens when their professions are corrupted, their jargon has become a shield against outside scrutiny, their process of peer review has been transformed into a device by which a professional faction can commandeer the discipline, excommunicate rivals, and give members of the "us" group endless pardons for their endless failures?

The economist James K. Galbraith, who was right about many of the disasters of our age but who is neither "mainstream" nor "Wall Street," once wrote that something very much like this had happened to his discipline:

> Leading active members of today's economics profession ... have formed themselves into a kind of Politburo for correct economic thinking. As a general rule—as one might generally expect from a gentleman's club—this has placed them on the wrong side of every important policy issue, and not just recently but for decades. They predict disaster where none occurs. They deny the possibility of events that then happen. ... No one loses face , in this club, for having been wrong. No one is dis-invited from presenting papers at later annual meetings. And still less is anyone from the outside invited in.

Where does this leave the premature market skeptics, the ones (like Galbraith) who were right all along? The answer is, by and large, nowhere. These people have remained at the out-of-the-way universities, the do-it-yourself blogs, and the impotent think tanks where they began.

They were ignored in 2008 and they are ignored today because an extremely convenient corollary to the reigning dogma of the consensus reminds us that it is impossible to see a disaster of the 2008 variety coming. Of course, there were plenty of people who did see it coming, but this corollary defines their work away as a series of lucky guesses, dismisses their methodology as not worth considering, and blows them off as not worth listening to—all of which "we" can prove using equations. "The main lesson we should take away from the E[fficient] M[arket] H[ypothesis] for policymaking purposes is the futility of trying to deal with crises and recessions by finding central bankers and regulators who can identify and puncture bubbles," announced Chicago school economist Robert Lucas from amid the ruins in 2009. "If these people exist, we will not be able to afford them."

And the main lesson we should take away from the Efficient Market Hypothesis for *our* purposes is the utter futility of economics departments like the one that employs Robert Lucas.

A second lesson: if economists—and journalists, and bankers, and bond analysts, and accountants—don't pay some price for egregious and repeated misrepresentations of reality, then markets aren't efficient after all. Either the gentlemen of the consensus must go, or their cherished hypothesis must be abandoned. The world isn't gullible enough to believe both of them any longer.

Or maybe it is. Maybe this state of affairs can go on for years. As you watch the anointed men of the Washington consensus shuttle through the CNN green room or relax comfortably at the $10,000 Halloween party the neighbors are throwing for their third grader, you begin to wonder what kind of blunder it will take to shatter this city's epic complacency, its dazzling confidence in its own stupidity.

We will assuredly find out soon. And when we do, we can be just as assured that the fools who let it happen will walk away once again without feeling any consequences.

NOTES

1 There were relatively few of these journalists, and their reporting dried up after the Bush administration preempted state-level predatory lending laws in 2003. See the painstaking summary by Dean Starkman in *Columbia Journalism Review*, May/June 2009.

2 As far as I know, Michael Lewis himself has never made such a preposterous claim. His own take on the grand folly of recent years, *The Big Short*, is that epidemic madness of the mid-aughts variety creates opportunities for really smart people to make really big profits. On all of this stuff see Yves Smith, "Ezra Klein Should Stick to Being Wrong About Health Care," a blog post from June 24, 2011, on *Naked Capitalism*.

3 A similar situation occurred in the red-hunting years after World War II, when the need arose to separate the righteousness of the just-concluded war against fascism from the ardent anti-fascists on the left, who had opposed fascism since the beginning but who now needed to be ridiculed, blacklisted, and otherwise ostracized. The phrase that was invented to do this job was "premature anti-fascist"—it meant someone who had opposed fascism before the consensus had determined that fascism was a thing Americans ought to oppose.

The Long Con

Mail-order conservatism

RICK PERLSTEIN

Mitt Romney is a liar. Of course, in some sense, all politicians, even all human beings, are liars. Romney's lying went so over-the-top extravagant by the summer of 2012, though, that the *New York Times* editorial board did something probably unprecedented in their polite gray precincts: they used the L-word itself. "Mr. Romney's entire campaign rests on a foundation of short, utterly false sound bites," they editorialized. He repeats them "so often that millions of Americans believe them to be the truth." "It is hard to challenge these lies with a well-reasoned-but-overlong speech," they concluded; and how. Romney's lying, in fact, was so richly variegated that it can serve as a sort of grammar of mendacity.

Some Romney lies posit absences where there are obviously presences: his claim, for instance, that "President Obama doesn't have a plan" to create jobs. Other Romney fabrications assert presences where there are absences. A clever bit of video editing can make it seem like Romney was enthusiastically received before the NAACP, when, in fact, he was booed. There are lies, damned lies, statistics—like his assertion that his tax cut proposal won't have any effect on the federal budget, which the Tax Policy Center called "not mathematically possible." That frank dismissal vaulted the candidate into another category of lie, an attempt to bend time itself: Romney responded by calling that group "biased"; last year, he called them "objective."

From *The Baffler*, no. 21

There are outsourced lies, like this one from deep in my files: in 2007, Ann Romney told the right-wing site Newsmax.com that her husband had "always personally been pro-life," though Mitt had said in his 1994 Senate race, "I believe that abortion should be safe and legal in this country." And then Ann admitted a few sentence later, "They say he flip-flopped on abortion. Well, you know what? He did change his mind."

And then there's the most delicious kind of lie of them all, the kind that hoists the teller on his own petard as soon as a faintly curious auditor consults the record for occasions on which he's said the opposite. Here the dossier of Mittdacity overfloweth. In 2012, for example, he said he took no more federal money for the Salt Lake City Olympic Games than previous games had taken; a decade earlier, however, he called the $410 million in federal money he bagged "a huge increase over anything ever done before."

There are more examples, so many more, but as I started to log and taxonomize them, their sheer volume threatened to crash my computer. (OK, I'm lying; I just stopped cataloging them, out of sheer fatigue.) You can look back at "Chronicling Mitt's Mendacity," Steve Benen's series for MSNBC's *Maddowblog*, for a tally. He was at Volume XXXIX as of this writing, with more on the way. Volume XXVIII, posted early in August 2012, listed twenty-eight *separate* lies. Then came the Republican convention, when Romney's designated fibbing-mate Paul Ryan packed so many lies into his charismatic introduction to the nation that a *Washington Post* blogger assigned by his editor to write a piece on "the true, the false, and the misleading in Ryan's speech" could find only one entrant for the "true" section, and even then his editor had to concede that "the definition of 'true' that we're using is loose."

Pundits—that is to say, the ones who aren't stitched into their profession's lunatic semiology, which holds that it's unfair to call a Republican a liar unless you call a Democrat one too—have been hard at work analyzing what this all says about Mitt Romney's character. And more power to them. But that's not really my bag. I write long history books that are published with photos of presidents and presidential aspirants on the covers. The photos are to please the marketers: presidents sell. But my subject is not really powerful people; biography doesn't much interest me. In my view, powerful men are but a means to the more profound end of sizing up the shifting allegiances on the demand side of our politics.

The leaders are easy to study; they stand still. We can amass reams on their pasts, catalog great quantities of data on what they say in the present. Grasping the shape of a mass public, though, is a more fugitive process. Publics are amorphous, protean, fuzzy; they don't leave behind neat documentary trails. Studying the leaders they choose helps us see them more sharply. Political theorist James MacGregor Burns's classic book *Leadership* explains that "leadership over human beings is exercised when persons with certain motives and purposes mobilize, in competition or conflict with others, institutional, political, psychological, and other resources so as to arouse, engage, and satisfy the motives of followers ... in order to realize goals mutually held by both leaders and followers." Watching charismatic people try to seize their attention and win their allegiance becomes the intellectual whetstone. As political psychologist Harold Lasswell once put it, a successful aspirant to leadership is one whose "private motives are displaced onto public objects and rationalized in terms of public interest." Watching those private motives at work, the public they seek to convince comes into focus.

All righty, then: both the rank-and-file voters and the governing elites of a major American political party chose as their standard-bearer a pathological liar. What does that reveal about *them?*

An Oilfield in the Placenta

In 2007 I signed on to the email lists of several influential magazines on the right, among them *Townhall*, which operates under the auspices of evangelical Stuart Epperson's Salem Communications; *Newsmax*, the organ more responsible than any other for drumming up the hysteria that culminated in the impeachment of Bill Clinton; and *Human Events*, one of Ronald Reagan's favorite publications. The exercise turned out to be far more revealing than I expected. Via the battery of promotional appeals that overran my email inbox, I mainlined a right-wing id that was invisible to readers who encounter conservative opinion at face value.

Subscriber lists to ideological organs are pure gold to the third-party interests who rent them as catchments for potential customers. Who better suits a marketing strategy than a group that voluntarily organizes itself according to their most passionately shared beliefs? That's why, for instance, the other day I (and probably you) got an advertisement by way of liberal magazine *The American Prospect* seeking donations to Mercy Corps, a charity that helps starving children in the Third World. But back when I was getting emails every day from *Newsmax* and *Townhall*, the come-ons were a little bit different.

> Dear Reader,
> I'm going to tell you something, but you must promise to keep it quiet.
>
> You have to understand that the "elite" would not be at all happy with me if they knew what I was about to tell you. That's why we have to tread carefully.
>
> You see, while most people are paying attention to the stock market, the banks, brokerages and big institutions have their money somewhere else ... [in] what I call the hidden money mountain ...
>
> All you have to know is the insider's code (which I'll tell you) and you could make an extra $6,000 every single month.

Soon after reading that, I learned of the "23-Cent Heart Miracle," the one "Washington, the medical industry, and drug companies REFUSE to tell you about." (Why would they? They'd just be leaving money on the table: "I was scheduled for open heart surgery when I read about your product," read one of the testimonials. "I started taking it and now six months have passed and I haven't had open-heart surgery.") Then came news of the oilfield in the placenta.

"Dear *NewsMax* Reader," this appeal began, leaving no doubt that whatever trust that publication had built with its followers was being rented out wholesale. "Please find below a special message from our sponsor, James Davidson, Editor of Outside the Box. He has some important information to share with you."

Here's the information in question: "If you have shied away from profiting from the immense promise of stem cells to treat disease because of moral concern over extracting stem cells from fetal tissue, pay close attention. You can now invest with a clear conscience. An Israeli entrepreneur, Zami Aberman, has discovered 'an oilfield in the placenta.' His little company, Pluristem Life Systems (OTCBB: PLRS) has made a discovery which is potentially more valuable than Prudhoe Bay."

Davidson concluded by proposing the lucky investor purchase a position of 83,000 shares of PLRS for the low, low price of twelve cents each. If you act now, Davidson explained, your $10,000 outlay

MARK DANCEY

"could bring you a profit of more than a quarter of a million dollars."

Not long after I let the magic of the placenta-based oilfield sink in, I got another pitch, this one courtesy of the webmasters handling the *Human Events* mailing list and headed "The Trouble with Get-Rich-Quick Schemes." Perhaps I'm a little gullible myself; for a couple of seconds, I believed the esteemed Reagan-era policy handbook might be sending out a useful consumer advisory to its readers, an investigative guide to the phony get-rich-quick schemes caroming around the right-leaning opinion-sphere. But that hasty assumption proved sadly mistaken, presuming as it did that the proprietors of outfits like *Human Events* respect their readers. Instead, this was a come-on for something called "INSTANT INTERNET INCOME"—the chance at last to "put an end to your financial worries ...permanently erase your debts...pay cash for the things you want... create a secure, enjoyable retirement for yourself...give your family the abundant lifestyle they so richly deserve."

Back in our great-grandparents' day, the peddlers of such miracle cures and get-rich-quick schemes were known as snake-oil salesmen. You don't see stuff like this much in mainstream culture any more; it hardly seems possible such *déclassé* effronteries could get anywhere in a society with a high school completion rate of 90 percent. But tenders of a 23-Cent Heart Miracle seem to work just fine on the readers of the magazine where Ann Coulter began her journalistic ascent in the late nineties by pimping the notion that liberals are all gullible rubes. In an alternate universe where Coulter would be capable of rational self-reflection, it would be fascinating to ask her what she thinks about, say, the layout of HumanEvents.com on the day it featured an article headlined "Ideas Will Drive Conservatives' Revival." Two inches beneath that bold pronouncement, a box headed "Health News" included the headlines "Reverse Crippling Arthritis in 2 Days," "Clear Clogged Arteries Safely & Easily—without drugs, without surgery, and without a radical diet," and "High Blood Pressure Cured in 3 Minutes...Drop Measurement 60 Points." It would be interesting, that is, to ask Coulter about the reflex of lying that's now sutured into the modern conservative movement's DNA—and to get her candid assessment of why conservative leaders treat their constituents like suckers.

The history of that movement echoes with the sonorous names of long-dead Austrian economists, of indefatigable door-knocking cadres, of soaring perorations on a nation finally poised to realize its rendezvous with destiny. Search high and low, however, and there's no mention of oilfields in the placenta. Nor anything about, say, the intersection between the culture of "network" or "multilevel" marketing—where ordinary folks try to get rich via pyramid schemes that leave their neighbors holding the bag—and the institutions of both evangelical Christianity and Mitt Romney's Church of Jesus Christ of Latter-day Saints.

And yet this stuff is as important to understanding the conservative ascendancy as are the internecine organizational and ideological struggles that make up its official history—if not, indeed, more so. The strategic alliance of snake-oil vendors and conservative true believers points up evidence of another successful long march, of tactics designed to corral fleece-able multitudes all in one place—and the formation of a cast of mind that makes it hard for either them or us to discern where the ideological con ended and the money con began.

Those tactics gelled in the seventies—though they were rooted, like all things right-wing and infrastructural, in the movement that led to Barry Goldwater's presidential nomination in 1964. In 1961 Richard Viguerie, a kid from Houston whose heroes, he once told me, were "the two Macs"—Joe McCarthy and General Douglas MacArthur—took a job as executive director for the conservative student group Young Americans for Freedom (YAF). The organization was itself something of a con, a front for the ideological ambitions of the grownups running *National Review.* And fittingly enough, the middle-aged man who ran the operation, Marvin Liebman, was something of a P. T. Barnum figure, famous on the right for selling the claim that he had amassed no less than a million signatures on petitions opposing the People's Republic of China's entry into the United Nations. (He said they were in a warehouse in New Jersey. No one ever saw the warehouse.) The first thing Liebman told Viguerie was that YAF had two thousand paid members but that in public, he should always claim there were twenty-five thousand. (Viguerie told me this personally. I found no evidence he saw anything to be ashamed of.) And the first thing that Liebman showed Viguerie was the automated "Robotype" machine he used to send out automated fundraising pitches. Viguerie's eyes widened; he had found his life's calling.

Following the Goldwater defeat, Viguerie went into business for himself. He famously visited the Office of the Clerk of the House of Representatives, where the identities of those who donated fifty dollars or more to a presidential campaign then by law reposed. First alone, and then with a small army of "Kelly Girls" (as he put it to me in 1996), he started copying down the names and addresses in longhand until some nervous bureaucrat told him to cease and desist.

By then, though, it was too late: Viguerie had captured some 12,500 addresses of the most ardent right-wingers in the nation. "And that list," he wrote in his 2004 book, *America's Right Turn: How Conservatives Used New and Alternative Media to Take Over America*, "was my treasure trove, as good as the gold bricks deposited at Fort Knox, as I started The Viguerie Company and began raising money for conservative clients."

Fort Knox: an interesting image. Isn't that what proverbial con men are always claiming to sell?

The lists got bigger, the technology better ("Where are my names?" he nervously asked, studying the surface of the first computer tape containing his trove): twenty-five million names by 1980, destination for some one hundred million mail pieces a year, dispatched by some three hundred employees in boiler rooms running twenty-four hours a day. The Viguerie Company's marketing genius was that as it continued metastasizing, it remained, in financial terms, a hermetic positive feedback loop. It brought the message of the New Right to the masses, but it kept nearly all the revenue streams locked down in Viguerie's proprietary control. Here was a key to the hustle: typically, only 10 to 15 percent of the haul went to the intended beneficiaries. The rest went back to Viguerie's company. In one too-perfect example, Viguerie raised $802,028 for a client seeking to distribute Bibles in Asia—who paid $889,255 for the service.

Others joined the bonanza. Lee Edwards, a YAF founder who today works a nifty grift as "Distinguished Fellow in Conservative Thought" at the Heritage Foundation writing credulous hagiographies of conservative movement figures and institutions (including, funnily enough, the Heritage Foundation), cofounded something called "Friends of the FBI." This operation's chief come-on was a mass mailing of letters signed by the star of TV's *The FBI*, Efrem Zimbalist Jr., purportedly to aid the families of fallen officers. The group raised $400,000 in four months—until Zimbalist abruptly withdrew his support. The TV star said he'd looked at the organization's books and seen how much was going to the fundraisers—and claimed he'd been the victim of "fraud and misrepresentation."

In 1977 Democratic congressman Charles H. Wilson of California proposed timid regulations to inform donors exactly how much of their money was going to the cause they thought they were supporting. The Heritage Foundation raced forth with an "issues bulletin" announcing that any such rule changes would subject "church leaders" to "vicious" attacks, and would "increase the paperwork on every Christian organization ... inevitably lessening the funds each charity can use for its stated purpose." (Christianity itself being the obvious target of this Democratic subterfuge of "reform.") And just to give the cause the imprimatur of elected office, a favorite congressman of the Christian right, John Conlan of Arizona ("He's never been honest," Barry Goldwater once said about him), was drafted to explain that the high overhead of direct-mail campaigns was a *boon* to the charity-customers: it represented start-up—"prospecting"—costs that would permit organizations to raise yet more money down the line. ("Defends charities against Big Government," read the caption beneath a picture of Conlan in *Conservative Digest*—the magazine Richard Viguerie published.)

Here's the thing, though: as is the case with most garden-variety pyramid schemes, the supposed start-up costs never seemed to stop.

And conservative groups that finally decoupled their causes from Viguerie's firm found their fundraising costs falling to less than fifty cents on the dollar. Viguerie would point out his clients didn't *feel* ripped off. At that, maybe some were in on the con, too—for instance, his client Citizens for Decent Literature, an anti-smut group, took in an estimated $2.3 million over a two-year period, with more than 80 percent going to Viguerie's company; the group's principal was future S&L fraudster Charles Keating.

It all became too much for Marvin Liebman, the Dr. Frankenstein who had placed the business model in Viguerie's palpitating hands. Liebman told conservative apostate Alan Crawford, author of the valuable 1980 exposé *Thunder on the Right*, that Viguerie and company "rape the public." Another source familiar with the conservative direct-mail industry wondered to Crawford, "How anyone of any sensitivity can bear to read those letters scrawled by little old women

MARK DANCEY

on Social Security who are giving up a dollar they cannot afford to part with ... without feeling bad is unbelievable."

Such qualms clearly did not carry the day—and now the practice is apparently too true to the heart of conservatism to die. In 2007 the *Washington Post* reported on the lucrative fundraising sideline worked up by syndicated columnist Linda Chavez. George W. Bush had nominated Chavez to be his first secretary of labor, but then backpedaled after reports that she had lied about an undocumented worker living in her house. Among the prime red-meat entries on her résumé is a book called *Betrayal: How Union Bosses Shake Down Their Members and Corrupt American Politics.* And while Chavez probably wouldn't have brought much reliable wisdom to the task of regulating organized labor, it's quite clear from the *Post* report that she had mastered the art of the shakedown. In her direct-mail career, she had

> used phone banks and direct-mail solicitations to raise tens of millions of dollars, founding several political action committees with bankable names: the Republican Issues Committee, the Latino Alliance, Stop Union Political Abuse and the Pro-Life Campaign Committee. Their solicitations promise direct action in the "fight to save unborn lives," a vigorous struggle against "big labor bosses" and a crippling of "liberal politics in the country."

But true to the Viguerie model, less than 1 percent of the money that Chavez's groups raised went to actual political activity. The rest went either back into further fundraising pitches or into salaries and perks for Chavez and her relatives. "I guess you could call it the family business," Chavez told the *Post.* I guess you could.

Waging Culture War for Fun and Profit

But the New Right's business model was dishonest in more than its revenue structure. Its very message—the alarmist vision of White Protestant Civilization Besieged that propelled fundraising pitch after fundraising pitch—was confabulatory too. The typical ploy ran a little something like this, from Heritage Foundation founder Paul Weyrich's Free Congress Research and Education Foundation:

> Dear Friend:
> Do you believe that children should have the right to sue their parents for being "forced" to attend church?
> Should children be eligible for minimum wage if they are being asked to do household chores?
> Do you believe that children should have the right to choose their own family?
> As incredible as they might sound, these are just a few of the new "children's rights laws" that could become a reality under a new United Nations program if fully implemented by the Carter administration.
> If radical anti-family forces have their way, this UN sponsored program is likely to become an all-out assault on our traditional family structure.

Following the standard scaremongering playbook of the fundraising right, Weyrich launched his appeal with some horrifying eventuality that sounded both entirely specific and hair-raisingly imminent ("all-out assault on our traditional family structure"—or, in the case of a 1976 pitch signed by senator Jesse Helms, taxpayer-supported "grade school courses that teach our children that cannibalism, wife swapping, and the murder of infants and the elderly are acceptable behavior"; or, to take one from not too long ago, the white-slavery style claim that "babies are being harvested and sold on the black market by Planned Parenthood"). Closer inspection reveals the looming horror to be built on a nonfalsifiable foundation ("could become"; "is likely to become"). This conditional prospect, which might prove discouraging to a skeptically minded mark, is all the more useful to reach those inclined to divide the moral universe in two—between the realm of the wicked, populated by secretive, conspiratorial elites, and the realm of the normal, orderly, safe, and sane.

Weyrich's letter concludes by proposing an entirely specific, real-world remedy: slaying the wicked can easily be hastened for the low, low price of a $5, $10, or $25 contribution from you, the humble citizen-warrior.

These are bedtime stories, meant for childlike minds. Or, more to the point, they are in the business of *producing* childlike minds. Conjuring up the most garishly insatiable monsters precisely in order to banish them from underneath the bed, they aim to put the target to sleep.

Dishonesty is demanded by the alarmist fundraising appeal because the real world doesn't work anything like this. The distance from observable reality is rhetorically *required*; indeed, that you haven't *quite* seen anything resembling any of this in your everyday life is a kind of evidence all by itself. It just goes to show how diabolical the enemy has become. He is unseen; but the redeemer, the hero who tells you the tale, can see the innermost details of the most baleful conspiracies. Trust him. Send him your money. Surrender your will—and the monster shall be banished for good.

Scaling Up

This method highlights the fundamental workings of all grassroots conservative political appeals, be they spurious claims of Barack Obama's Islamic devotion, the supposed explosion of taxpayer-supported welfare fraud, or the proliferation of weapons of mass destruction in Iraq.

And, in an intersection that is utterly crucial, this same theology of fear is how a certain sort of commercial appeal—a snake-oil-selling one—works as well. This is where the retail political lying practiced by Romney links up with the universe in which 23-cent miracle cures exist (absent the hero's intervention) *just* out of reach, thanks to the conspiracy of some powerful cabal—a cabal that, wouldn't you know it in these late-model hustles, perfectly resembles the ur-villain of the conservative mind: *liberals*.

In this respect, it's not really useful, or possible, to specify a break point where the money game ends and the ideological one begins. They are two facets of the same coin—where the con selling 23-cent miracle cures for heart disease inches inexorably into the one selling minuscule marginal tax rates as the miracle cure for the nation itself. The proof is in the pitches—the come-ons in which the ideological and the transactional share the exact same vocabulary, moral claims, and cast of heroes and villains.

> Dear Fellow Conservative,
> Do you know which special interest has given more money to the Obama and Clinton campaigns than any other?
>
> If you guessed "trial lawyers"—well, okay, that's too easy. But can you guess which special interest came in second?
>
> Labor unions? Nope. The Green Lobby? Nope. AARP? Wrong, again. NEA? Nyet.
>
> Give up? Okay, here's the answer: Wall Street.
>
> That's right. According to CNNMoney.com, Wall Street securities and investment firms have given over $35 million to Democratic candidates this election cycle.... If you've been wondering why the financial industry has been in meltdown—and taking your 401(k) or investment portfolio down with it—now you know.
>
> Let's face it: The former frat boys who populate Wall Street today understand economics about as well as the pinko professors whose courses they snored through.... Trusting them with your money is like trusting Bill Clinton to babysit your underage niece.
>
> But I know someone you can trust to manage your investments.... His name is Dr. Mark Skousen—that's "Dr." as in "Ph.D. in Economics and Monetary History," something you don't get by playing Beer Pong with your frat buddies. For the past 28 years, subscribers to his investment newsletter, *Forecasts & Strategies*, have profited enormously from his uncanny ability to predict major market trends before they happen.... For instance: In the early '80s, Dr. Skousen predicted that "Reaganomics will work" and said "a long decade of profits is coming."...
>
> The "bottom line," as they say? Don't let the Democrats run the country. And don't let Wall Street frat boys manage your investments. Do it yourself, with the genuinely expert guidance of free-

dom-loving economist Mark Skousen in *Forecasts & Strategies.*

Click here to learn more.

That letter is signed by Ann Coulter—and, truth be told, it reads like she wrote it. It is a perfect portrait of the nether region of the right-wing con, figure (politics) trading places with ground (commerce) a dizzying dozen times over in the space of just these several paragraphs. There is the bizarre linguistic operation that turns "liberal" (or, in Coulterese, "pinko") into a merely opportunistic synonym for "stuff you don't like." There's the sloganeering alchemy that conflates political and economic magical thinking ("freedom"!). There's shorthand invocation of Reagan hagiography. And then, presto: the suggestible readers on the receiving end of Coulter's come-on are meant to realize that they are holding the abracadabra solution to every human dilemma (vote out the Democrats—oh, and also, subscribe to Mark Skousen's newsletter for investors, while you're at it).

There's a kind of mystic wingnut great-circle-of-life aura to this stuff. Mark Skousen, a Mormon, is the nephew of W. Cleon Skousen, author of the legendarily bizarre Birchite tract *The Naked Communist*, which claimed to have exposed the secret forty-five-point plan by which the Soviet Union hoped to take over the United States government. (Among the sinister aims laid out in the document: gain control of all student newspapers; "eliminate all good sculpture from parks and buildings, substitute shapeless, awkward and meaningless forms.") Upon its publication in 1958 (it was republished in 2007 as an ebook), the president of the Church of Latter-day Saints, David O. McKay, recommended that all members read it. Mark Skousen is also author of a book called *Investing in One Lesson*, which cribs its title from the libertarian tract *Economics in One Lesson*, distributed free by conservative organizations in the millions in the fifties, sixties, and seventies (Reagan was a fan). He founded an annual Las Vegas convention called "FreedomFest"—2012 keynoters: Steve Forbes, Grover Norquist, Charles Murray, Whole Foods CEO John Mackey—which advertises itself as "the world's largest gathering of right-wing minds." This event points to another signal facet of the conservative movement's long con: convincing its acolytes that they are the *true* intellectuals, that anyone to their left is the merest cognitive pretender. ("Will this 3 Minute Video Change Your Life?" you can read on FreedomFest's website. Because three-minute videos are how intellectuals roll. Click here to learn more.)

The oilfield in the placenta is another perfect mélange of right-wing ideology and a right-wing money con. It begins with a signal ideological lie: that stem-cell research represents an outrage against the right to life (but the cultivation of embryos for in vitro fertilization does not). It then pulls the mark along with the right-wing fantasy that energy independence is only one miraculous technological breakthrough away (but the development of already existing alternative energy sources doesn't count as one of those breakthroughs). It all makes its own sort of internally coherent sense when you consider the salesman: James Dale Davidson is a founder of the National Taxpayers Union, a Richard Mellon Scaife–funded enterprise that gave Grover Norquist his start as a professional conservative. Davidson himself is a producer of *Unanswered: The Death of Vincent Foster*. "There is overwhelming evidence that Foster was murdered," he told the *Washington Post*. "They obviously have reasons they don't want this to come out … obviously there's something big they're trying to protect."

Of course, the childlike appeals won't work their full magic without the invocation of the conservative movement's childlike heroes. The Gipper appears in another splendid specimen received by *Human Events* readers—which is appropriate, because *Human Events* is where Reagan himself got a lot of the made-up stuff he spouted across his entire political career. "When President Ronald Reagan got cancer during his presidency," this one begins, "the great German doctor Hans Nieper, M.D., treated him. It would have been front-page news if it hadn't been hushed up at the time." ("*German doctors 'cook' cancer out of your body while you nap!*") "Many American cancer patients lose their hair and their vitality. But Reagan kept his famous pompadour hairstyle. He also kept his warm smile and vigorous style." ("*CLICK HERE to request German Cancer Breakthrough: A Guide to Top German Alternative Clinics.*") "Reagan lived for another 19 years. He died at age 93, and not from cancer." (*"Fortunately, as a journalist I'm protected by the First Amendment. I can tell you the truth without having to risk persecution from the authorities."*)

Miracle cures, get-rich-quick schemes, murderous liberals, the mystic magic mirage of a world without taxes, those weapons of mass destruction that Saddam Hussein had hidden somewhere in the Syrian desert—only connect.

Untruth and Consequences

And what of Willard M. Romney's part in the game? There's a lot going on with Romney's lying, not all of it related to his conservative identity; he was making things up as a habit, after all, back when he was a Massachusetts moderate. To a certain extent, Romney's lies are explicable in just the way a lot of pundits are explaining them. When you've been all over the map ideologically, and you're selling yourself to a party now built on extremist ideological purity, it takes a lot of tale-telling to cover your back. But that doesn't explain one

MARK DANCEY

overlooked proviso: these lies are as transparent to his Republican colleagues as they are to any other sentient being. Nor does it account for a still more curious fact—for all the objections that conservatives have aired over Romney's suspect purity during his campaign, *not one prominent conservative has made Romney's dishonesty part of the brief against him.*

It's time, in other words, to consider whether Romney's fluidity with the truth is, in fact, a feature and not a bug: a constituent part of his appeal to conservatives. The point here is not just that he lies when he says conservative things, even if he believes something different in his heart of hearts—but that lying is what makes you sound the way a conservative is supposed to sound, in pretty much the same way that curlicuing all around the note makes you sound like a contestant on *American Idol* is supposed to sound.

In part the *New York Times* had it right, for as much as it's worth: Romney's prevarications are evidence of simple political hucksterism—"short, utterly false sound bites," repeated "so often that millions of Americans believe them to be the truth." But the *Times* misses the bigger picture. Each constituent lie is an instance pointing to a larger, elaborately constructed "truth," the one central to the right-wing appeal for generations: that liberalism is a species of madness—an esoteric cult of out-of-touch, Europe-besotted ivory tower elites—and conservatism is the creed of regular Americans and vouchsafes the eternal prosperity, security, and moral excellence of God's chosen nation, which was doing just fine before Bolsheviks started gumming up the works.

A Romney lie in this vein is a pure Ronald Reagan imitation—as in this utterance from 2007: "In France," Romney announced on the campaign trail, "I'm told that marriage is now frequently contracted in seven-year terms where either party may move on when their term is up." And just as Reagan was found to be reciting film dialogue and jump-cutting anecdotes from his on-screen career into his pseudobiographical reminiscences on the stump, so it turns out that Romney picked up the marriage canard from the Homecoming Saga, a science fiction series written by Mormon author Orson Scott

Card. (Another reason for students of Romney's intellectual development to queasily recall that he told interviewers during that same 2008 presidential run that his favorite work of fiction was *Battlefield Earth*, the sci-fi opus by Scientology founder L. Ron Hubbard, a consummate shakedown artist in his own right.)

Either deliberately or through some Reaganesque slip of the unconscious, Romney's stump confabulations worked the same way that those legendary Viguerie direct-mail appeals did: since reality is never Manichean enough, fables have to do the requisite ideological heavy lifting—to frighten the target audience to do the fabulists' will. That's the logic of the pitch for the quivering conservative masses.

Once, I gave a speech to a marquee assemblage of true members of the conservative elite, from William Bennett to Midge Decter to Alf Regnery, at the James Madison Program in American Ideals and Institutions, a conservative think tank that rich donors convinced Princeton University to house under its auspices. (Karl Rove made a cameo appearance, during which he bragged about making a Republican congressman cry.) In my remarks, I laid out what I took to be a disturbing moral pattern, what I naively thought would stir these folks into something like shame. Why was it, I asked, that whenever Richard Nixon needed someone to brazen out some patently immoral, illegal, or dishonest act, he frequently and explicitly sought out a veteran of the conservative movement—the same conservatives whose ideology in policy contexts he usually derided? Because, I said, "Nixon knew that if you had a dirty job to get done, you got people who answered the description he made of E. Howard Hunt and G. Gordon Liddy: 'good, healthy, right-wing exuberants.'"

I gave half a dozen examples of latter-day conservative exuberance, in my own admitted exuberance to rain down the shame: the phony "middle-of-the-road caucus" formed to secretly take over a National Student Association meeting from the right; the fliers the RNC put out during the 2004 election announcing that a president John Kerry would institute a plan to ban the Bible; the time Jerry Falwell lied that he'd never argued for the elimination of the public school system—"lying for the Lord," as Mormons call it. Then, as the question-and-answer period approached, I trembled, anticipating the conservative elite's chastened response. Yes, reader: *I was once just that naive.*

M. Stanton Evans, a legendary movement godfather, stood up. He said my invocation of Richard Nixon was inappropriate because Richard Nixon had never been a conservative. He proceeded, though, to make a striking admission: "I didn't like Nixon until Watergate"—at which point, apparently, Nixon finally convinced conservatives he could be one of them.

And that, at last, may be the explanation for Mitt Romney's apparently bottomless penchant for lying in public. If the 2012 GOP nominee lied louder than most—and even more astoundingly than during his prior campaigns—it's just because he felt like he had more to prove to his core following. Lying is an initiation into the conservative elite. In this respect, as in so many others, it's like multilayer marketing: the ones at the top reap the reward—and then they preen, pleased with themselves for mastering the game. Closing the sale, after all, is mainly a question of riding out the lie: showing that you have the skill and the stones to just brazen it out, and the savvy to ratchet up the stakes higher and higher. Sneering at, or ignoring, your earnest high-minded mandarin gatekeepers—"we're not going to let our campaign be dictated by fact-checkers," as one Romney aide put it—is another part of closing the deal. For years now, the story in the mainstream political press has been Romney's difficulty in convincing conservatives, finally, that he is truly one of them. For these elites, his lying—so dismaying to the opinion-makers at the *New York Times*, who act like this is something new—is how he has pulled it off once and for all. And at the grassroots, his fluidity with their preferred fables helps them forget why they never trusted the guy in the first place.

The People's Republic of Zuckerstan

JOHN SUMMERS

Ever since Mark Zuckerberg reappeared in Cambridge, Massachusetts, in 2011 and announced that this old city had growth potential after all, the region's public officials have been eagerly positioning themselves to ride a wave of digital startup commerce.

The state's Democratic governor, Deval Patrick, has been ardently lobbying corporate players in biotech to fall in with the Facebook titan and exploit the region's educated workforce. Massachusetts House Speaker Robert A. DeLeo sent an open letter to Zuckerberg begging him to follow through on his comment and locate an office here. "A lot has changed in Massachusetts in the eight years since Facebook moved out," DeLeo wrote. In 2012 legislators OK'd a $1 million "Talent Pipeline" to be run through the Massachusetts Technology Collaborative and allotted $50 million to a tech-and-science research matching fund, gilding an investment climate already rich with grant managers, laboratories, liberals, venture capitalists, and university degrees.

New York still has Wall Street, Phoenix has housing again, and for Shreveport, Louisiana, it's all the way with shale gas. And what do Cambridge and Greater Boston have to offer? They call it the "Innovation Economy."

It's a neat utopia: an entire economy rigged to a framework of intellectual capital, from PhD to patent, with a startup model of rapid development taking hold of cities like Austin, Berkeley, Boulder, Las Vegas, Raleigh, and Seattle. Still, it was a Boston-area small business that successfully peti-

From *The Baffler*, no. 24

tioned the White House to declare the first-ever "National Entrepreneurs' Day" in 2010. The president proclaimed a whole "National Entrepreneurship Month" the following year (November, in case you are thinking of starting a company) and created the White House "Startup America" initiative, devoted to "cutting red tape and accelerating innovation from the lab to the marketplace."

And it's Cambridge where you can take a stroll on the "Entrepreneur Walk of Fame," complete with stars for Steve Jobs and Bill Gates. Kendall Square, in MIT's neighborhood, has seen Amazon, Biogen, Google, Microsoft, Novartis, Pfizer, and Johnson & Johnson all move in or expand their office parks, research facilities, or life science laboratories since 2012, joining companies with longstanding ties to the MIT meritocracy, such as Sanofi, Millennium Pharmaceuticals, and Draper Laboratory. The list goes on. So does the networking—or, as this scrum for a new, world-defining synergy of big data, big pharma, and startups is elegantly known, the "clustering." The method is meant to wrest "competitive market advantage" (in the White House's words) out of physical proximity.

"Clustering" has spun out a miniature knowledge economy of its own around here, with brands like General Catalyst, Koa Labs, Atlas Venture, Spark Capital, Intrepid Labs, Dogpatch Labs, and Sandbox. You can't turn a corner without encountering some fair, summit, accelerator, catalyst, meetup, incubator, or kaffeeklatsch. News of the latest triumph at the hottest innovation center is hard to miss even for a moderate consumer of media gossip. (A tidbit: Someone at the MIT Media Lab founded Bluefin Labs, a social TV analytics startup that won the jackpot in 2013 when it was purchased by Twitter for $67.3 million!)

And so the question everywhere is: Where will the next Mark Zuckerberg turn up? The Harvard Innovation Lab? StartupLab Allston? Could it be MassChallenge or Startup Institute? Maybe the New Man (and, yes, the Innovation Economy is led almost exclusively by men) launching the next millennial app or social-media doodad will be found squatting in one of the "Innovation Districts" that have been demarcated by cities like Boston and Holyoke.

MICHAEL DUFFY

The Cambridge Innovation Center (CIC) is everyone's best bet. Based in Kendall Square, it's a retail office space for hundreds of startups, a movable brainstorm that smartly takes a piece of the action, a percentage of the New America. Or as Gov. Patrick put it during a visit to CIC's offices, it is

> a real incubator of wonderful ideas and economic growth for not just this neighborhood but frankly the whole of the Commonwealth and much of the country. We have been taking counsel . . . about ways that we can support this kind of economic growth, because we believe that innovation is our edge, it's where our future lies.

On November 8, 2013, reacting to Mark Zuckerberg's announcement that Facebook was expanding into Cambridge, CIC chief executive Tim Rowe nearly cried. "It's very emotional for Cambridge and Greater Boston to have Facebook come back," Rowe said. "It's the one that got away."

Feed Them

Who knows what innovations will crawl from between the interlocked toes of the technology corporations, venture capitalists, physicists, chemists, engineers, and biologists now incubating in the nation's creative class redoubts. *Collaboration* is the buzzword that sits tremulously like a fig leaf over the privatizing clusters in which America's future is restarted.

But if you think about the Innovation Economy as a model for urban development, you might find yourself wondering, *How new is this future, really?* The concept feels recycled because, in truth, it's just a semantic merger of the "New Economy" mantra of the 1990s with the "Knowledge Economy" that's ever popular in postindustrial management theory.

A mix of big corporations and investor-backed startup enterprises gathers around the shared strategic value of innovation, operating in an environment rich with public resources. The triumphant arc is chronicled in the rapid development of some new product and said to be personified by a Zuckerberg or a Gates, a captain of coding brimming with cowboy grit, pressing onward into the computerized frontier and all. The hero is the one who creates something from nothing, thus resolving the eternal pundit riddles of American life like *Can we keep our edge?* and *Are we still number one?*

Considering the slack in today's economy, you can see why the consensus is encouraging the inner entrepreneur in the new generation of scientists and technologists. If innovation really is the tonic for this disease, however, and if startup entrepreneurs and their corporate uncles really do transcend partisan ideologies, then some sign of health should be visible in the communities where they cluster.

And here's one clue worth pondering: In early summer 2013, Governor Patrick signed a "tech tax" on computer services that was supposed to raise the money badly needed to save the region's aging bridges, buses, roads, and subways from falling into disrepair from the additional density of Innovation Economy development. In early fall 2013, the same Governor Patrick signed a repeal of the same "tech tax."

The tech tax reversal neatly illustrates the law of economic development concealed within the Innovation Economy's magic wand. Call it the innovator's dogma: in response to the siren call of the future, the whole community must conform.

The innovator's dogma explains why, two months after reversing himself on the "tech tax," Governor Patrick decided to extend the operation of the aging subways and buses until 3 a.m. on weekends, a policy generations of the region's college students had failed to achieve. "Is this cool or what?" the Governor cooed.

Others warned that maintenance workers will bear the additional pressure and that the transportation system will decrease in safety. But the governor's special pleading knew no bounds: "This is about how we make the system modern for the kind of economic growth we have been experiencing and will be experiencing. The folks who work in the innovation sector—they live differently." He then left on a ten-day trade mission to tell business leaders in Japan, Singapore, and Hong Kong the good news.

The innovator's dogma means making *all* your city's peoples and institutions attractive to corporate professionals-in-training. That's why the first-ever "Police Innovation Conference" convened, and why it did so inside Microsoft's Cambridge headquarters. The conference was the dream of a former detective and public information officer who quit the force to join the startup community. The enterprising detective developed MyPD, an app that 125 police departments are using around the country.

It's why the superintendent of the Cambridge Public Schools has unfurled a reform program labeled "The Innovation Agenda: Educating Students for Their Future Not Our Past," as though understanding our past were not essential to creating their future. It's why the Cambridge Historical Society made "Innovation: How Cambridge Changed America" the theme of its benefit in 2012. And it's why the Cambridge Science Festival is held annually, with events in the field house of the high school.

The innovator's dogma can explain why state officials have redefined art and culture to accord with the White's House's desire to accelerate ideas "from the lab to the marketplace." A "Creative Industries Economy" is said by officials at the Massachusetts Department of Housing and Economic Development to be growing alongside the Innovation Economy. So they're holding "CreativeNext Resource Meetings."

These sound laboratory-like, all right, but sort of disturbing too, when you realize that the "Creative Economy" acknowledges only "the enterprises and people involved in the production and distribution of goods and services in which the aesthetic, intellectual, and emotional engagement of the consumer gives the product value in the marketplace."

Here's a definition broad enough to admit every form of "content" from web marketing to film, yet so narrow as to rule out the social conditions of sympathy, cooperation, and security in which creativity thrives—and never mind classic works of the twentieth century that were born in opposition to the market for consumer taste.

But the innovator's dogma deals in the world of commodities.

And Cambridge is teeming with products for solving problems we didn't know were problems. Hence Sqrrl Data Inc., started up by a group of former National Security Agency employees. Following the entrepreneur's playbook, the NSA technicians redeployed their government-funded spymastering to develop a commercial product that offers innovative expert protection against … spying. Edward Snowden's revelations did make these privacy entrepreneurs a bit nervous. Would public anger at the NSA taint their launch? Nyet! They discovered that what the people fear the market will then exploit. So these savvy NSA veterans scored a big infusion of venture capital and a larger office in Cambridge *as a result* of the revelations.

This, you see, is how innovation works. Mask political choices in the universalist rhetoric of the market. Purge the surrounding environment of social intelligence. Surge into the space with vested interests masquerading as public ones, and then call in the future for cover.

Cambridge, so understood, will be little different from any other city where entrepreneurs come to model their dreams. According to Brad Feld's *Startup Communities: Building an Entrepreneurial Ecosystem in Your City* (2012), cities where innovation happens are divisible by two: "Leaders of startup communities have to be entrepreneurs. Everyone else is a feeder into the startup community."

In the "feeders" category are colleges and universities ("a source of fresh blood") and governors, whose only job is to help companies grow by shaping society to suit their needs. The reason is obvious to Brad Feld. "Startups are at the core of everything we do," he writes. "An individual's life is a startup that begins at birth. Every city was once a startup, as was every company, every institution, and every project. As humans, we are wired to start things."

In the long run, however, nothing we "feeders" do can ever truly satisfy the innovator's dogma. As Feld observes, "entrepreneurs are going to do what they do, which is create new things (products, companies, jobs, and industries) out of nothing."

Brad Feld's comically narcissistic portrayal of the entrepreneur's prerogative hardly reflects the whole lot of them, and his version of the Innovation Economy model never quite works with its intended focus on plunder and exploitation. Still, Feld is a graduate of MIT, a successful venture capitalist, a cofounder of the prestigious accelerator fund TechStars, and a founding adviser to President Obama's Startup America Partnership. He's a "leader."

The Innovation Economy's futurist model of urban development is, in other words, propaganda for the present system of power—it's class interest presenting itself in the guise of prosperity, and it appears to be the best that these most liberal of liberal Democrats have to offer to the nation.

Where this fraternity of entrepreneurs and their municipal handlers travel to remodel society in the image of a private company, inequality is synchronized to follow, and liberalism, which once robustly opposed privileges and monopolies, provides cover for ushering out those who haven't been given the password.

So come along, while there's still time, and let's tour the People's Republic of Zuckerstan. Observe the residents fleeing, the acres being enclosed in office parks and laboratories, the moguls smiling, and the thought leaders humming tidings of the future. Be sure to notice all the ways in which the composite picture doesn't add up to progress.

See the View, Don't Be the View

Cambridge is actually a more interesting city than all this boosterism would lead you to expect, with a great many pockets of autonomous activities and attractions. The parks are open and clean; the grocery stores, pubs, cafes, schools, hospitals, fire stations, and churches are plentiful. We have a beautiful new library. Well-established amenities such as pedestrians' right of way and Fresh Pond (our own dedicated supply of fresh water!) make it some sort of idyll. The city's nickname, "The People's Republic of Cambridge," has more than a little merit behind it.

Now and then my family and I even catch sight of a rainbow flashing in the sky outside our kitchen window. At such gossamer moments, we don't envy the knowledge workers slaving away on artificial intelligence in their labs up the street. Compared to them, we feel like the Little Prince, who needs only to move his chair a few feet to watch the sunset whenever he wants to. It's not everything, but it's enough.

The groundwork for innovating this idyll was stirred by Question 9, a referendum that repealed rent control in Massachusetts in 1995 and began the unsettling of nearly everyone unable to compete in the housing market. Developers had tried for years to repeal the regulation in the only three cities in the state where it had remained in place—Boston, Brookline, and Cambridge. Oddly enough, business flaks could never persuade residents of those cities to voluntarily pay higher rents. So, in a fit of class pique, the Small Property Owners Association and the Massachusetts Homeowners Coalition put the question to a statewide referendum, and then sat back and watched voters in Western Massachusetts teach Eastern liberals a thing or two about economic fairness.

The market has been driving the poor and the working class out of these cities ever since, and the Innovation Economy is finishing them off, cleaning house for the new guests. The cost of housing in Cambridge and Greater Boston has zoomed, with rising rents taking a growing share of dwindling low- and middle-incomes. Partly by design, partly by accident, the corporate consolidation of the housing stock will wind up leaching diversity from neighborhoods by pricing residents out and installing corporate professionals in their place. Innovation means the price of existing goes up.

Not only is there no master plan from government officials to address the housing emergency, but it was their master plan that caused it. Between 2010 and 2013, while the state's leading Democratic politicians went around the country selling off the region's neighborhoods to corporate partners in the Innovation Economy, the number of homeless people in Massachusetts rose by 14 percent. (The national number went in the opposite direction.) Significant gains in jobs outside commercial science and biotech have not materialized; indeed, the jobless rate for those who don't have a college credential is twice that of degree-holders. So we can expect the Innovation Economy to send more of the region's poorest and most vulnerable residents scrambling with their children into temporary shelters and motels. Housing is the hinge of class formation.

Nearly all the Innovation Economy construction has simply added to the region's phalanx of luxury homes, condominiums, towers, laboratories, auditoriums, and office parks. The capital investment in the machinery of invention (filtered through the region's tax-exempt colleges, hospitals, and institutes) is staggering. The University of Massachusetts, Boston, is opening a science complex to the tune of $182 million and 220,000 square feet. Boston University is adding two buildings to its science and engineering complex, one of them seven stories tall and 150,000 square feet and the other eleven stories and 165,000 square feet. (Big, in other words.) Add another $225 million for Northeastern University's science and research center. "We think of Boston as one large campus," Northeastern president Joseph E. Aoun told the *Boston Globe*.

Two months before President Aoun boasted of the industry's imperial ambitions, Harvard won approval to carry out a long-delayed plan for developing 359 acres of unused land it owns in the Boston neighborhood of Allston. In addition to fortifying its Innovation Lab, Harvard will build a sixty-thousand-square-foot, three-thousand-seat basketball arena; a two-hundred-room hotel and conference center; and three new buildings for the business school.

Commercial developers once considered Cambridge a tough community to crack, due to all the smarty-pants intellectuals and community groups bleating for affordable housing and air to breathe. And it's still true that the city is full of pesky intellectuals. According to Amazon, Cambridge was the fourth "most well-read city" in America in 2013. But residents haven't exactly been buying up pamphlets on utopian socialism. Cambridge, in fact, ranked as Amazon's number-one market in the "Business & Investing" category. Evidently, this city of nonprofits lies awake reading business books with visions of cashing in.

And this is, no doubt, one reason that neighborhood associations haven't been able to do much more than slow the bulldozers and cranes that rip, bend, and scrape along Massachusetts Avenue, the main thoroughfare that connects MIT with the city's Central Square. Millennium Pharmaceuticals, having overcome several years of community opposition, is now expanding into a 250,000-square-foot office and lab complex. The move enlarges a twenty-seven-acre complex (on MIT-owned land) called University Park, which comprises nine research and office buildings, a parking garage, a supermarket, and a hotel, along with restaurants and luxury apartment towers intended for "wealthy individuals and couples who want to see the view, rather than be the view," according to the developer, Forest City Boston.

Across the street, also on MIT-owned land, the life sciences corporation Novartis is constructing office buildings and laboratory space—a 550,000-square-foot, $600 million campus designed by the architect Maya Lin. "This campus," the company assures us, "will be a life sciences gateway and will provide an important connection between Kendall and Central Squares. It will bring vibrancy to the area with ample green space, pedestrian connection and street level retail space."

Novartis, the city's fourth largest employer, is a central player in the Innovation Economy sweepstakes. So it's better not to mention that it's also a global leader in not-curing cancer, with an all-too-recent history of toxic dumping, safety violations, price-gouging, bribery, and sex discrimination. In a case it finally lost in 2013, Novartis sued the government of India for rejecting a patent application for its cancer drug Gleevec. To prevent companies like Novartis from blocking the availability of low-cost generic drugs, Indian patent law requires applicants to show they have "significantly" improved upon previous drugs. Novartis took the case all the way to the Indian Supreme Court. In 2010 it lost a class action sexual discrimination suit brought by women sales reps and managers over pregnancy, promotion, and pay. That suit cost the company $3.3 million in compensatory damages to twelve women and $250 million in punitive damages to the larger class.

The year before, Novartis made headlines by refusing to donate vaccines during the swine flu pandemic. But the company's world headquarters in Basel is currently being redesigned after the fashion of Cambridge's Kendall Square, complete with a Frank Gehry building. The adverse legal verdicts pile up. The innovation juggernaut rumbles on.

When platoons of large rats are displaced from underground and come skulking into homes and basements, it makes for well-attended community meetings. But opposition to Innovation Economy–style development has no sure voice in the political class and only a marginal position in the city's social structure. Property owners, who benefit from the booming real estate market, have seen their taxes remain relatively low. Out-of-state campaign donations from developers have grown to unprecedented levels in municipal elections.

Those who would argue for a diversity of economic models are largely the voices of the dispossessed, shouting curses from the back of the moving van. The November 5, 2013, election for Cambridge City Council saw an unusually lively field of candidates and four new councilors put into office, bearing many indications of discombobulation. Only 24 percent of the city's eligible voters went to the polls, though—among the lowest turnouts ever recorded in the People's Republic.

Smell the Funk

For what does a neighborhood's history count against the demands of the future? It's not a question pundits dwell on when they urge concessions on behalf of stagnation-killing knowledge economies. But the fate of Central Square, the neighborhood in which Millennium and Novartis are building, is sort of important to those who live and work there, especially considering the dead-zone look of nearby Kendall Square.

Confounding years of efforts to make Kendall into a neighborhood, Innovation Economy development cannot support a civic culture there. The office parks and laboratories are set back off the street. Long, barren blocks surround them. The lab workers log late hours in these zipped-up complexes, darting in and out of the neighborhood for food and drink, and not much else.

All this new commercial building in Central isn't expected to be finished until 2015. What will the neighborhood look like by then? A bedroom community for thousands of corporate professionals? The rents are already inflated, thanks to the legions of MIT and Harvard graduate students and postdoctoral fellows doubling- and tripling-up in local apartments—the region's vast academic proletariat that tends to higher education's other function (the teaching).

Central Square has been Cambridge's downtown, its seat of government, and a bellwether of financial speculation since roughly the 1850s. It started attracting moneyed interest even earlier, when Boston investors realized that Cambridge was their most direct territorial route to points west and northwest. The first bridges over the Charles River dramatically reduced the distance the gentleman rulers of yore had to travel between Harvard Square and the Boston State House.

By the turn of the twentieth century, thousands of first- or second-generation Irish were living in Central Square alongside rural New Englanders, Swedes, Portuguese, Poles, Russians, Jews, Greeks, and Canadians. Most worked in manufacturing and joined churches and labor organizations. In the 1960s Sgt. Brown's Memorial Necktie Coffeehouse organized antiwar protests and counseled draft resisters there. The political activity was made possible by the low cost of office space.

To the outside world, including many students, Cambridge has seemed an academic town, monopolized by Harvard and MIT. That impression never used to be true, however; to see the diversity of community in the city, one needed only to venture beyond the campuses and walk through Central Square, which lies right in between them without belonging to either one.

Over the last few years, the Mayor's Red Ribbon Commission on the Delights and Concerns of Central Square has gathered politicos, urban planners, and small business leaders to discuss the implications of MIT's Innovation Economy construction as it crawls past the perimeter of Kendall Square and disrupts the settled social facts of Central. The commission presents a street-by-street view of the likely effects on the neighborhood's parking spaces, transportation depots, plazas and parks, signage, storm-water retention, street lighting, and so on.

Everyone agrees Central Square is the civic center of Cambridge, the heart of the city's collective identity. Everyone agrees it's funky. Everyone is sure they want more creativity there, as opposed to less; they love creativity so much. And everyone wants Central Square to encourage the innovation-friendly habits of celebrating, enriching, increasing, connecting, and diversifying.

This admirable consensus has an air of make-believe about it, however. Small business owners have leverage only through the Central Square Business Association, and the Cambridge City Council has leverage over the developers mainly by virtue of its mogul-licensing capacities: handing out permits for parking lots and exemptions for height and density. Such powers are not nothing, but they're pretty small-caliber ammunition, useful more for a negotiated surrender than a fighting vision.

"Central Square needs a brand," a report issued by the Red Ribbon Commission insists, chasing its own tail:

> A brand for Central Square is about establishing a connection, then a relationship, with those most important to your success. A brand is just the first step.... A brand will integrate and analyze all of the branding/perception information collected over the past few years. It will also develop consistent, compelling core brand messaging that provides the framework for brand assets and communications tools (advertising, web site, social media, public relations, etc.)...
>
> We are not starting from scratch: this is not an exercise in creating an entirely new brand for Central Square. Rather, it's about capturing the essence of Central Square in a compelling, consistent message architecture. After all... Central Square is nothing if not authentic. Its brand must be authentic, as well.

There, there, one wants to say. But the panic is real. As Novartis and Millennium maneuver corporate professionals cheek by jowl with Rodney's Book Store and Cheapo Records, increasing everyone's cost of existing, Central Square's avant-garde faces the usual tragic choice of growing, compromising, or leaving.

"They're soulless, there's no life there." That's what Catherine

Carr Kelly, executive director of the Central Square Theater, told me when I asked her about the biotech laboratories and offices coming next door. The theater dedicates a part of each season's program to something called the Catalyst Collaborative. Its purpose is to produce an emotional identification with science and to host discussions of ethical issues typically ignored in the normal run of innovation. The idea grew out of a salon at the home of a professor at MIT, which owns the theater's building.

The owners of the Middle East nightclub, the neighborhood's largest and most popular creative drinking spot, decided on a less artful compromise. In October 2013 they announced a plan to build four or five floors of residential housing *on top of* their iconic club—but not for their employees or entertainers. The owners said they would have preferred to build spaces suitable for musicians and artists, but it's not in the cards.

Such stories could make you skeptical about the most celebrated achievement of city planners thus far: a successful request for the state to designate Central Square as an official "Cultural District." The designation doesn't bring any funding to offset the spike in rents, and the boundaries are arbitrary, but hey, "Cultural District" has been conveyed on official government stationery, so the neighborhood's "brand" has been determined: it's culture—only, a culture that has no meaningful power to arrest the flight of the funky.

Tea and Sympathy

Once, I was pushing my daughter in her stroller along Massachusetts Avenue in Central Square when a man with his back against the wall and a cup in his hand began trying to wave us over. We didn't stop. He stuck his foot out in front of the stroller's wheel. My daughter nearly went flying, and would have landed hard on the sidewalk were it not for her restraints. Neither of us was hurt—only scared and angry, respectively.

I remembered this encounter when I read comments by the owner of a local real estate company complaining that while the Innovation Economy has sent the market booming, the human streetscape is still something of a loss leader:

> Not long ago I was walking through Central Square with my kids after their dance class. We see this guy just lying there, completely bloodied on the sidewalk. The cops showed up and took him away. The thing is, that's something I see consistently: three or four times a year.

Yeah, I thought to myself, ask not why the man is "just lying there"; ask why your daughter has to step over such ghastly sights "three or four times a year."

The realtor's interview appeared in a glossy minimagazine called *Scout Cambridge*, which describes itself as "Direct—Vibrant—Local" for independent business interests. An issue showed up in my mailbox in September 2013, proclaiming itself a "direct-mailed bimonthly to every home and business in Cambridge, reaching more than 47,600 postal addresses." Infospam for the Innovation Economy, in other words.

And the cover story in which the broker's tactless interview appeared, "At a Crossroads," contained a noticeably frank display of opinion regarding the last remaining obstacles to Cambridge's gilded future as a playground for startup professionals.

"At a Crossroads," written by reporter Scott Kearnan, celebrates the Innovation Economy's stimulus to "higher-end residences and mixed-use buildings" cropping up in Central Square alongside the "upscale establishments" that are now jockeying for position in the nightlife and entertainment spectrum. There was that "hipster music lounge" that closed, but thankfully it reopened as "a higher-end hipster cocktail bar." Any local knowledge worker can join a ready-made scene at the nearby Middlesex Lounge, with its "hipster-y alt vibe." The owners of the restaurant Pu Pu Hot Pot are reopening as Patty Chen's Dumpling Room, "with slicker sheens and higher price tags."

But then the quest for expensive dumplings takes a disturbing turn. The numbers are down in most of what the city planners call "creative experience establishments" in Central. *Scout Cambridge* asks the owner of the "sleek Asian spot" Moksa for his thoughts. "Our dining room clientele is mostly in the daytime. At night there's not a lot of activity," he replies. "When I was young, the square was vibrant. There was so much stuff going on."

What happened to the vibrancy? Homeless, drug-addicted, poor people began hanging around the benches and plazas, creeping around our creative peripheries, jawboning, congregating outside convenience store windows waiting for the lottery numbers, smelling bad, tripping strollers: the jerks.

Central Square may now be R&D headquarters for a global cartel of life-science and tech corporations, but it's also home to many of the city's poor. They hobble down the same sidewalks that front Patty Chen's Dumpling Room in order to partake of a buffet of government and social programs, from WIC (Women, Infants, and Children) to Loaves and Fishes at the First Korean Church.

Like the innovation meetups dotting the neighborhood, mentors and support personnel gather around these social services, but the conversations are more about the present-tense struggle to survive than the brave new world—more tea and sympathy than beer and bullshit. Nor will the religious poor be easy to send packing. The Salvation Army owns a building in Central Square. So do the YWCA and YMCA.

Leave it to *Scout Cambridge* and longtime small business owner Suzan Phelps—the proprietor of a sex-toy emporium called Hubba Hubba—to lay it on the line. "There are still too many bums around," Phelps told *Scout*. "There are people on drugs, people who don't work, and they roam around the square begging or sleeping on benches. And that keeps people away. It keeps money away from Central Square."

The person behind *Scout Cambridge*, Holli Banks, is a creative-class entrepreneur transplanted from New York to Somerville, a city adjacent to Cambridge, in 2008. When she couldn't land a job, she didn't hang out on the street like a vagrant, for goodness' sake: "I thought, I better come up with something to do." She decided to give a glossy magazine a whirl, winning over independent advertisers with obnoxious cover stories like "At a Crossroads" by following the formula crystallized by city monthlies in the 1990s boom: sell transient and dislocated professionals their new metropolis as a lifestyle accessory.

Somerville's squares and enclaves now host outdoor arts and music festivals and offer delicious ethnic fare—and, yes, cupcakes. The town—whose previous claim to renown (or notoriety) was spawning the entrepreneurial, if distinctly unvibrant, career of recently convicted gangland murderer James "Whitey" Bulger—is now the sort of place where creative people can live. The new residents are doctors, lawyers, businessmen, scientists, immigrant professionals, and university department heads—you know, the kind of persons who know nothing about conniving.

As the yuppies came and domesticated the place—well, maybe you can guess what happened next. In 1997 Somerville's Davis Square made *Utne Reader*'s list of fifteen "hippest places to live" in the United States or Canada. And that was the beginning of the end. In 2012 local pol Frank Bakey provided NPR with an admirably clear statement of this civic renewal policy and then thoughtfully illustrated the ground-level prerequisite for innovation: "We don't have the crime rate that we probably had years ago ... because the troublemakers can't afford to live here anymore." What can you do?

If you are Suzy Phelps, you pick up your bag of tricks and skedaddle. In October 2013, soon after her photograph appeared in *Scout Cambridge* and arrived in everyone's mailboxes, Hubba Hubba was washed away in a tide of Innovation Economy payola. The store's landlord, the Dance Complex, suddenly decided to upsell the space long stacked with whips, chains, and other delectables. And so, like the opening act of a countercultural war of all against all, the Dance Complex gave Hubba Hubba until Halloween to wind up its affairs. The Dance Complex explained the eviction notice with a logic that might have served as Hubba Hubba's motto: "We saw a demand and wanted to fill it."

Museum of Activism

Cambridge is still made up of progressives and liberals, as opposed to, say, conservatives. The city is liberal in the sense that it has restaurants with names like Patty Chen's Dumpling Room and the cosmopolitanism contrived for them tastes bold and exotic on the tongue. It is liberal in allowing life-science capitalism to run biomedical laboratories that would be illegal in some countries and unseemly in some U.S. states. And Cambridge, alas, is liberal enough to listen to a dildo retailer slagging the poor in a fake magazine that's not so obliquely campaigning to purge them. Both the retailer and the magazine are *independent*. They can be assumed to be *progressive*.

Whether Cambridge will remain liberal or progressive enough to protect its pantries, shelters, needle exchanges, and mental health programs from the housing emergency remains to be seen. I'm hopeful. Mercy for the poor won't easily be defeated in a city with a tradition of it. But with a civic vacuum opening up between their remnants and the transient professionals, what will liberalism be good for, other than making development deals?

The suppression of public discussion is more effective than you might think possible in a city where 44 percent of adult residents have a graduate or professional degree. In fact, there's barely any journalism to help us figure out the basic details of what's happening in the entrepreneur's republic, much less what it portends. The liberal consensus believes in the higher education industry. Higher education wants innovation, not complaints.

And what does journalism want? Well, the wild ride of innovation is covered by the region's only remaining large newspaper, the *Boston Globe*, with hugs for the industry's miraculous discoveries and supercool events. Here's one entirely representative headline from the Metro section: "Flat Out, Totally Wired: Computer Hackers Match Wits at MIT, Yielding Ingenious—and Wacky—Creations." Meanwhile, the paper's *Innovation Economy* and *The Hive* blogs serve up "some advice for entrepreneurs, Google style," to pick a typical example from the relentless torrent of boosterism. One winter day in 2013, a story about how the city's digital entrepreneurs use printed business cards made the front page. ("Many people find it more efficient to slip a card to someone's hand. Sure, the data have to be input to a device later, but some consider that extra step a plus.")

There is still a lot of good and necessary reporting in the *Globe*, some of it reflected in parts of this story. Yet this reader doesn't exactly get the sense that skepticism is high on the editorial agenda, especially as new owner John W. Henry's why-I-bought-a-newspaper essay in October 2013 dutifully trotted out the Innovation Economy's talking points. Henry, who is also a principal owner of the Boston Red Sox, promised to "make the *Globe* a laboratory for major newspapers across the country," and to "capture the vibrancy of a region on the move," and, of course, to "seek to be at the cutting edge of solutions, cures, accountability, and results."

The kind of activist journalism that wants to grasp the root of conflict came to life in Boston around Columbus Day 2011, after the first Occupy Boston protesters in Dewey Square were arrested and dragged off to jail. Inspired by this show of force, and by the example of the *Occupied Wall Street Journal*, the group called its publication the *Occupy Boston Globe*. That morphed into the *Boston Occupier*, which printed and distributed twenty-five thousand broadsheet copies on November 18, 2011.

The *Boston Occupier* financed these early issues with a fundraising campaign that netted all of $9,355, and then fell victim to attrition among its all-volunteer collective, halting publication in April 2013 after printing fifteen issues. It was a significant achievement, given the panic of the Innovation Economy's major institutions. (Harvard didn't exactly use OWS as a teachable moment. After the first tents went up in Harvard Yard, the school massed police officers at every gate and established security checkpoints that turned back everyone not carrying some form of Harvard-issued identification.)

The *Occupier* met its fate one month after the Boston *Phoenix*, by then the region's oldest alt-weekly, ceased publishing after forty-seven years, citing financial losses too big to sustain. WFNX, the *Phoenix*'s radio station, also closed.

Those media enterprises failed because they were organized around coverage of social problems. *BostInno*, a startup media website whose story is their polar opposite, has succeeded because it offers little to anybody who is not part of the Innovation Economy.

It's a fast-moving mouthpiece that publishes trend-spotting nuggets about venture capital and tech investment and duly recites the crazy doings of the region's totally awesome entrepreneurs as if economic affairs were a football game and journalism were a matter of jazzing up press releases.

The site's founders started out in approved Zuckerstan fashion, in an expensive college dorm room, and then scored an investment from one of their wealthy parents. *BostInno* was advised by *BuzzFeed*'s founder, himself a graduate of the MIT Media Lab, and rather quickly realized the dream of every startup by getting itself acquired by a big corporation. The franchise is now moving into the high-end events business with "*BostInno*'s Boston Fest"—and expanding to a city near you.

What does the new digital media want? Office space, for starters.

BostInno accepted office space from MassChallenge, a Boston-based startup accelerator ("we help entrepreneurs win") even while covering events held by MassChallenge. The *Boston Globe*'s "Innovation Economy" columnist is among the *organizers* of "Unpitch Boston," a free conference for venture capitalists and entrepreneurs.

Conflicts of interest are a way of life in the new media future. The *Innovation Hub* radio show at WGBH, the region's largest public radio and television broadcaster, is underwritten by the Harvard Innovation Lab. The show's chirpy sycophancy trails entrepreneurs as they romp through public education, opine on the "competitiveness" of American workers, ponder their own nervy creativity, envision "America in 2050," and establish hot spots like, well, the Harvard Innovation Lab, which is conveniently located in Allston, just down the street from WGBH's studios.

Innovation Hub was on hand to celebrate its underwriter's opening day in 2011 and to interview the dean of the Harvard Business School as he recited the officially approved lessons from Mark Zuckerberg's return to the campus earlier that same year. "When [Zuckerberg] came here and he visited," the dean said, "I think he reimagined in his mind, he wondered, at least it made me wonder whether, if this space existed, and if he'd met the right kind of people here, could he have started Facebook across the street or could he have started it in Kendall Square?"

All well and amusing, this incantation, but the Innovation Economy's monopoly of opinion means unresolved contradictions stay unresolved. Consider the city's vote to approve Harvard's new Allston campus. Here's Harvard president Drew Gilpin Faust after the unanimous vote:

> Our plans came together drawing on the contributions of many people, over many meetings, over months and years. The Harvard Allston Task Force deserves special recognition and thanks for their guidance, input, and critical questions along the way.

Now here's a member of that Harvard Allston Task Force, speaking on the same day:

> Harvard handles development with an exclusive focus on what Harvard thinks is best for Harvard. There's never any public discussion on what does the neighborhood need.

This discrepancy could explain why Harvard doesn't teach journalism to its undergraduates. Why should it? It's not as if the students demand a robust independent perspective (as a glance at the *Harvard Crimson* can attest) or the Innovation Economy requires one. The most frequently awarded grade at Harvard is A, and Introduction to Computer Science has become one of the most popular undergraduate courses. "I think everyone is interested in how you make large amounts of money," the class's teaching assistant said on the magical day Zuckerberg dropped by to chat with the students, a comment that also explains the collective swoon of the city's liberal newspaper, blogs, TV, and radio programs.

Or as Alex Jones, director of Harvard's Shorenstein Center on Media, Politics and Public Policy told a reporter in 2009 after being asked about the steep decline in interest among Harvard students in journalism as a profession, "It's purely [a] matter of economics, because they're not stupid." Jones neatly points up how the innovator's dogma has eclipsed the culture of principled activism. No, really, *follow the money*.

The One-Hundred-Million-Dollar Question

The People's Republic of Zuckerstan might have less and less room for poor or middle-income families and no interest in alternative models of development, but innovation economies are fine places to park overaccumulating capital. The city, indeed, could hardly be more hospitable to titans of business. That the billionaire investor Carl Icahn exerts such a heavy influence over Cambridge biotechs Biogen Idec and Genzyme is some kind of strange for sure. Once upon a time, the liberal city could join the nation in reviling Icahn's brand of speculation as noxious corporate raiding. Now, as innovation whittles away the social basis of activism, Carl Icahn is celebrated as an "activist investor."

Or consider the fossil fuel billionaire David H. Koch, enemy number one in the minds of progressives across the country for, among other things, funding organizations that deny global warming. Koch sits on the board of public television broadcaster WGBH and underwrites NOVA, its science program—and that's the least of this entrepreneur's involvement with the Innovation Economy.

Over at MIT, the David H. Koch Institute for Integrative Cancer Research is an especially high-minded startup that owes its existence to a $100 million donation from, yes, David H. Koch. The March 4, 2011, dedication ceremony was headlined by MIT's then-president Susan Hockfield, who locked eyes with the robber baron and said the following: "David, as you know well, I rarely am at a loss for words, but I simply cannot express sufficiently my gratitude for your vision, your generosity, and your enthusiasm. Thank you so much." The audience gave him a standing ovation.

Meanwhile, down in Washington, D.C., Koch Industries was lobbying the U.S. Department of Health and Human Services not to add formaldehyde to the government's list of "known carcinogens." One of the country's top producers of formaldehyde is Georgia-Pacific, which is a subsidiary of Koch Industries. Koch Industries ranks high among the country's worst belchers of dangerous chemicals. David Koch's battle for his company's right to pump a cancer-causing agent into our homes had been years in the making, and isn't exactly over.

How gratifying for him to attend the dedication of an institute that bears his name and to bathe in all that gratitude from the first woman president of his alma mater. Just six months before the dedication, Koch had had to quietly discontinue service on a cancer board of the National Institutes of Health after *The New Yorker* called adverse attention to the conflict of interest involved in his participation. Koch betook himself to MIT, which emblazoned his name on a building.

"I read stuff about me and I say, 'God, I'm a terrible guy,'" the baron told the *New York Times* about his prestige in Cambridge. "And then I come here and everybody treats me like I'm a wonderful fellow, and I say, 'Well, maybe I'm not so bad after all.'"

Some sort of pragmatic calculation is the only attitude the city's liberalism permits in the presence of philanthropy as high finance. Choke down the paradox of cancer-causing Koch Industries donating a wad of money to a maybe cancer-curing Koch Institute. Weigh the costs and benefits. On one side, there's the man's tax-deductible donations. On the other, there's the company's profits as one of the largest toxic polluters in the country. Do the math, and see who comes out ahead.

Only, if you are one of those poor unfortunates of contemporary history who was frankly never very good at math, or someone for whom corruption kindles a sense of indignation—rather than quiet, agreeable resignation—or maybe a person whose head hurts when encountering acts of staggering cynicism, well, then, *you have a problem*: If David Koch wants to cure cancer so badly, then why don't his companies stop mass producing the chemicals that are known to cause it?

Since this question is typically considered out of bounds in the Innovation Economy scheme of things, and since so many of its advocates are wealthy, educated, liberal do-gooders, you have to wonder if we aren't a bit gauche even to think of it. Maybe the question is silly, a relic from pre-innovation days. Maybe commodified science and technology do, in fact, contain the ethical resources for self-correction in the matter of global warming, and the entrepreneur's moral isolation isn't as desolate as we've made it out to be. Maybe we are too quick to find fault with the angels and barons of the age, too harsh in our suspicions. Wonder, not skepticism, is the preapproved response to striking displays of innovation, after all.

Then there's the memory of Aaron Swartz to remind us what can happen when skepticism takes a wrong turn down an alleyway in Zuckerstan.

Swartz, you might recall from the storm of grief that followed his untimely death in January 2013, was a young computer programmer, entrepreneur, and activist on fellowship at Harvard back in 2010. He might have chosen to become a model citizen of Zuckerstan, had he not gotten himself interested in such supposedly obsolete issues as the corrupting influence of money on scientific research. "We need to download scientific journals and upload them to file sharing networks," he once wrote. "We need to fight for Guerilla Open Access."

Swartz's alleged crime, which allegedly took place at MIT in 2010, was evading its network security for the purpose of downloading about 4.8 million journal articles from an academic database. Swartz, that is, had a distinctly Zuckerstanian flair for accessing unauthorized data sets. But unlike our hero Zuckerberg, he was not let off with an administrative warning from confused but tolerant elders, and he did not then start up a social networking company or see his hacking made into a celebrated movie.

Instead, two MIT police officers and one U.S. Secret Service agent chased Aaron Swartz into a parking lot near Central Square, cornered him, and arrested him on January 6, 2011. Swartz was arraigned in Cambridge District Court and charged with two felonies of breaking and entering MIT's campus. The Superior Court for Middlesex County indicted him on six more felony counts, including "accessing a computer without authorization" and larceny.

Then the U.S. Attorney's Office in Boston, getting in on this action, brought a more terrible federal indictment down on the head of the twenty-four-year-old. Swartz was rearrested, held in lockup, fingerprinted by the U.S. Marshals Service, and rereleased.

In September 2012 he was reindicted, and now there were thirteen felony counts, including wire fraud. The negotiations that proceeded were complex. But the charges, which at one point carried a maximum penalty of ninety-five years in prison and $3 million in fines, were clearly meant to terrorize him.

Swartz committed suicide in his New York apartment. And though the U.S. Attorney's Office went off to assail other bogus threats to the sanctity of scientific data on behalf of the business class, MIT was forced by public opinion to investigate what, if any, responsibility it had for his death.

Their answer, as you might expect by now, turned out to be none. The internal investigation concluded that the institute's leadership had adopted a clear and consistent policy of "neutrality" as Swartz's case dragged on, that it had preferred to see itself as a bystander rather than as victim or advocate. MIT, the investigation concluded, had cooperated fully with the federal prosecution, turning over evidence even before receiving subpoenas. But the school's administration formed "no opinion" on the merits of the case.

Swartz's longstanding ties to MIT were well known to the administration. The internal investigation mentioned his frequent presence at the MIT Free Culture Group, his participation in the MIT Mystery Hunt puzzle competition, and his speech before an audience of the MIT Computer Science and Artificial Intelligence Laboratory. His father was a consultant at the MIT Media Lab. When he was eighteen he was "accelerated" by the entrepreneurians at the "Y Combinator" boot camp, which took place on the campus. Arriving in Cambridge from California in June 2005, he described his first impression of the campus on his personal blog:

> In one of the meeting rooms I found a large box someone had built out of wood, the inside covered in foam padding. Inside was a strange-looking device, a switch, and a bunch of wires. Outside was a light (currently off) that said "DIRECT FROM THE FUTURE".

> I tried figuring out what the box was, with little success. The whole thing felt like a puzzle out of Myst or something.

A puzzle this future would remain. Swartz's family repeatedly requested that MIT say something on his behalf during the long prosecution. But MIT refused even to announce that it had adopted neutrality. The internal investigation candidly explained why the tight-lipped doctrine held through the tumult that followed the shocking end:

> There were very few direct contacts made with the MIT administration to encourage a change on the part of MIT from neutrality to advocacy. MIT's student newspaper, *The Tech*, reported regularly on the progress of the case, but this did not prompt any editorials or opinion pieces before Aaron Swartz's suicide. Nor did people who later criticized MIT for not advocating for Aaron Swartz approach the MIT administration making the case for MIT to advocate for him before his suicide.

In evaluating this passage, it may help to remember that Swartz's two-year prosecution took place at a time when hundreds of millions of dollars were filtering into Innovation Economy institutions. His downloading of academic articles may have seemed innocuous to outsiders, but the lords of these networks knew better. In a climate of imperial expansion, his infraction was too trivial to let go.

Every institution that intersected with Swartz's case in Cambridge, in fact, was a member of the Innovation Economy, but nobody had more to lose over those few years than MIT, which proceeded to overtake Harvard as the number-one-ranked university in the world. That MIT climbed to the tippity top of the influential "QS World University Rankings" from 2011 to 2013 is a testament to the strategic value of science and technology deployed in startup cities around the world, as well as the institute's ability to recruit major donors like David H. Koch to the cause.

And it's why, confronted by a tragedy that unfolded right under its nose, the number-one university in the world can complain that nobody lobbied it hard enough to make it do something. Taking a stand for Swartz would have dragged MIT down from its rising position in the Innovation Economy's fable of classless utopia. Advocating leniency for this particular rule-breaking entrepreneur would have mired the school in the murky world of conflicting interests. How much safer to do nothing.

What does the Innovation Economy require of MIT? To be a global pacesetter in entrepreneurship? Check. A local real estate kingpin? Check. An institution that's prepared to discuss what philanthropy is really for, how cultural power masquerades as "economic development," or why Aaron Swartz was prosecuted? No, not really.

The school's leadership has long served patrons in the U.S. military and corporate boardrooms. During the Cold War, MIT virtually turned itself into a Pentagon division, providing the basic research and personnel for strategic radar systems, guided missiles, and the Apollo space program, spinning off companies and excelling at the strategic disciplines of electronics, aeronautics, materials science, and physics. In the 1950s the school became a byproduct of defense spending, and very much available for infiltration. The Center for International Studies (now part of the political science department) did who-knows-what for the Central Intelligence Agency, its primary sponsor.

But science is now migrating, like every other field of marketable intellectual endeavor, to the donor class. And to this shakeout MIT's leadership brings a noticeably fine track record of adaptation, one that guarantees large parts of Cambridge will be the intellectual property of the 1 percent, the progressive city sponsored by Pentagon spending. The military and intelligence establishment, the tech industry, and MIT have been hand-in-glove for ages, and you can bet they are watching us from Kendall Square, neutrally.

You can almost admire the technical consistency of the respective applications of institutional "neutrality" to the cases of David H. Koch and Aaron Swartz, the celebrated polluter and the despised democracy activist—the walking, talking conflict of interest and the scholar of conflicts of interest. That one went away smiling and the other wound up dead has nothing to do with MIT's core business, which is to innovate.

The Soul of Startup City

And so we arrive at the ultimate contradiction of the Innovation Economy's mode of development. As we have observed, this new republic depends on reengineering the cultural environment. For the market's winnings, a frame of acceptance must be created to justify the community's losses. Irony must erode, so that corporate entrepreneurs can be presented as nonconformists; nonprofits must absorb surplus profit, so that hundreds of millions of dollars in government payments, grants, and contracts, along with tax incentives, subsidies, and exemptions, can be banked for subsequent transfer to the market; even the old method of "clustering" must sound futuristic, so that its actual origins in socialist redoubts like New York's Greenwich Village (today an innovation hub, naturally) can be forgotten.

The Innovation Economy necessitates such cultural changes, but it offers no independent argument for freely choosing them. Instead, the manifest destiny of business touts *innovation* as if it were synonymous with *progress*, rather than one among its many necessary qualities, and leaves it at that.

So you can be sure the next time a wealthy college dropout like Mark Zuckerberg filches a banal idea from a couple of wealthier classmates and wants to beat them to midmarket, he need not ride the golden carpet to Silicon Valley and let Stanford or Cal Tech garner all the credit and cash. In Cambridge, teams of elites will regulate the general production from startup to corporate behemoth and make it easy for him to optimize the same thing today that he optimized yesterday. The new man of the Innovation Ideology will be free to code in the morning, head to the laboratory in the afternoon, and brag after dinner, without ever having to read books.

Innovation for what else? Not for art, literature, music, history, dance, sculpture, painting, philosophy, religion, poetry, or drama, the traditional means by which a diverse community grows conscious and formulates its standards of value. The governor of Massachusetts won't be stopping by your office to encourage you in your efforts at moral reasoning about philanthropy, the state legislature won't be allocating millions of dollars in matching grants for your next novel about how the homeless live, and the websites that have replaced the newspapers won't report on your subway concert.

Nor should you expect a place to live where you can pursue such pointless *passions* after you've passed through the Innovation Agenda in the public schools, gawked at the robot zoo in the field house, and suffered through your youthful set-tos with tech-toting police. In the system of rewards and incentives surrounding the Innovation Economy, talent in the fine arts has no place, and criticism is a special order of dubious. It's not creativity unless it employs cutting-edge technology, recruits a big donor, or rewards investors.

Actual progress would make community benefit the objective of urban policy, rather than the unreliable byproduct of commercial competition, and remedy the dangerous cultural imbalance by universalizing the principle of subsidy.

Something like Bertrand Russell's "vagabond's wage" proposal might perform this trick. Under Russell's proposal, every person would be entitled to a wage "sufficient for existence but not for luxury," in an amount large enough to remove the possibility of being distracted by hunger yet small enough not to encourage excessive idleness. "It is true that poverty is a great evil, but it is not true that material prosperity is in itself a great good," Russell wrote. Those who understand why this is so are those from whom our most lasting discoveries and large ideas may come. Meanwhile, some form of basic income guarantee could reduce homelessness and lessen the unnatural stress of salesmanship (fewer people would feel pressured to prematurely test their talents in silly competitions). And there would be time to insist on our collective right to the city.

The mechanism for funding a basic income guarantee could further entrench the very form of exchange that the Innovation Economy model is rigged to win, if the money means limitless commercial development. A lovely garden here for a crappy park there. A lotta condominiums here for a percentage of affordable units there. Millions of square feet of public space permanently enclosed in security-patrolled office parks, in exchange for a periodic festival.

And what if Russell's proposal or something like it were to succeed by spinning out a Cambridge cultural renaissance in music, art, film, literature, painting, and poetry? Then what? Another countercultural bohemia could serve as the avant-garde of consumerism, developing all the new forms of expression and pleasure to be simulated by the next generation of corporate technologists and monetized by the next generation of investors. But at the very least, a campaign would highlight the entrepreneur's utter dependence on unpaid labor and public goods and give us time to come up with alternative forms of social change that do not continue to deplete the diversity of the human environment.

Every city changes in multiple ways at once, of course, and, if you hang on long enough to see entrepreneurs blow in and out, you can find surprises lying between the feeders and the leaders. This much we discovered during a routine conversation with our landlord several years ago.

For a long time we had assumed he charges us abnormally low rent because he is one of those bleeding-heart liberals for which the city is famous. Not exactly, as it turns out.

We learned his father and mother had immigrated to Cambridge from Portugal half a century ago, back when a robust working class called the city home. Eventually his parents realized their portion of the American Dream, even saving enough money to purchase a small residential building in which generations of families, including ours, went on to live happily on the lower end of the scale. All along, they kept the rent affordable.

Now they're gone, and their kind of Cambridge is also going; still, their son—our landlord—upholds family tradition and refuses to give in to greed.

You know, that sort of thing may save this city yet.

Of Flying Cars and the Declining Rate of Profit

DAVID GRAEBER

A secret question hovers over us, a sense of disappointment, a broken promise we were given as children about what our adult world was supposed to be like. I am referring not to the standard false promises that children are always given (about how the world is fair, or how those who work hard shall be rewarded), but to a particular generational promise—given to those who were children in the fifties, sixties, seventies, or eighties—one that was never quite articulated as a promise but rather as a set of assumptions about what our adult world would be like. And since it was never quite promised, now that it has failed to come true, we're left confused: indignant, but at the same time embarrassed at our own indignation, ashamed we were ever so silly to believe our elders to begin with.

Where, in short, are the flying cars? Where are the force fields, tractor beams, teleportation pods, antigravity sleds, tricorders, immortality drugs, colonies on Mars, and all the other technological wonders any child growing up in the mid-to-late twentieth century assumed would exist by now? Even those inventions that seemed ready to emerge—like cloning or cryogenics—ended up betraying their lofty promises. What happened to them?

We are well informed of the wonders of computers, as if this is some sort of unanticipated compensation, but, in fact, we haven't moved even computing to the

From *The Baffler*, no. 19

point of progress that people in the fifties expected we'd have reached by now. We don't have computers we can have an interesting conversation with, or robots that can walk our dogs or take our clothes to the Laundromat.

As someone who was eight years old at the time of the Apollo moon landing, I remember calculating that I would be thirty-nine in the magic year 2000 and wondering what the world would be like. Did I expect I would be living in such a world of wonders? Of course. Everyone did. Do I feel cheated now? It seemed unlikely that I'd live to see *all* the things I was reading about in science fiction, but it never occurred to me that I wouldn't see *any* of them.

At the turn of the millennium, I was expecting an outpouring of reflections on why we had gotten the future of technology so wrong. Instead, just about all the authoritative voices—both left and right—began their reflections from the assumption that we do live in an unprecedented new technological utopia of one sort or another.

The common way of dealing with the uneasy sense that this might not be so is to brush it aside, to insist all the progress that could have happened has happened and to treat anything more as silly. "Oh, you mean all that *Jetsons* stuff?" I'm asked—as if to say, but that was just for children! Surely, as grown-ups, we understand *The Jetsons* offered as accurate a view of the future as *The Flintstones* offered of the Stone Age.

Even in the seventies and eighties, in fact, sober sources such as *National Geographic* and the Smithsonian were informing children of imminent space stations and expeditions to Mars. Creators of science fiction movies used to come up with concrete dates, often no more than a generation in the future, in which to place their futuristic fantasies. In 1968 Stanley Kubrick felt that a moviegoing audience would find it perfectly natural to assume that only thirty-three years later, in 2001, we would have commercial moon flights, city-like space stations, and computers with human personalities maintaining astronauts in suspended animation while traveling to Jupiter. Video telephony is just about the only new technology from that particular movie that has appeared—and it was technically possible when the movie was showing. *2001* can be seen as a curio, but what about *Star Trek*? The *Star Trek* mythos was set in the sixties, too, but the show kept getting revived, leaving audiences for *Star Trek Voyager* in, say, 2005 to try to figure out what to make of the fact that according to the logic of the program, the world was supposed to be recovering from fighting off the rule of genetically engineered supermen in the Eugenics Wars of the nineties.

By 1989, when the creators of *Back to the Future II* were dutifully placing flying cars and antigravity hoverboards in the hands of ordinary teenagers in the year 2015, it wasn't clear if this was meant as a prediction or a joke.

The usual move in science fiction is to remain vague about the dates, so as to render "the future" a zone of pure fantasy, no different than Middle Earth or Narnia or, like *Star Wars*, "a long time ago in a galaxy far, far away." As a result, our science fiction future is, most often, not a future at all, but more like an alternative dimension, a dream-time, a technological Elsewhere, existing in days to come in the same sense that elves and dragon-slayers existed in the past—another screen for the displacement of moral dramas and mythic fantasies into the dead ends of consumer pleasure.

Might the cultural sensibility that came to be referred to as postmodernism best be seen as a prolonged meditation on all the technological changes that never happened? The question struck me as I watched one of the recent *Star Wars* movies. The movie was terrible, but I couldn't help but feel impressed by the quality of the special effects. Recalling the clumsy special effects typical of fifties sci-fi films, I kept thinking how impressed a fifties audience would have been if they'd known what we could do by now—only to realize, "Actually, no. They wouldn't be impressed at all, would they? They thought we'd be *doing* this kind of thing by now. Not just figuring out more sophisticated ways to simulate it."

That last word—*simulate*—is key. The technologies that have advanced since the seventies are mainly either medical technologies or information technologies—largely, technologies of simulation. They are technologies of what Jean Baudrillard and Umberto Eco called the "hyperreal," the ability to make imitations that are more realistic than originals. The postmodern sensibility, the feeling that we had somehow broken into an unprecedented new historical period in which we understood that there is nothing new; that grand historical narratives of progress and liberation were meaningless; that everything now was simulation, ironic repetition, fragmentation, and pastiche—all this makes sense in a technological environment in which the only breakthroughs were those that made it easier to create, transfer, and rearrange virtual projections of things that either already existed, or, we came to realize, never would. Surely, if we were vacationing in geodesic domes on Mars or toting about pocket-size nuclear fusion plants or telekinetic mind-reading devices no one would ever have been talking like this. The postmodern moment was a desperate way to take what could otherwise only be felt as a bitter disappointment and to dress it up as something epochal, exciting, and new.

In the earliest formulations, which largely came out of the Marxist tradition, a lot of this technological background was acknowledged. Fredric Jameson's "Postmodernism, or the Cultural Logic of Late Capitalism" proposed the term "postmodernism" to refer to the cultural logic appropriate to a new, technological phase of capitalism, one that had been heralded by Marxist economist Ernest Mandel as early as 1972. Mandel had argued that humanity stood at the verge of a "third technological revolution," as profound as the Agricultural or Industrial Revolution, in which computers, robots, new energy sources, and new information technologies would replace industrial labor—the "end of work" as it soon came to be called—reducing us all to designers and computer technicians coming up with crazy visions that cybernetic factories would produce.

End-of-work arguments were popular in the late seventies and early eighties as social thinkers pondered what would happen to the traditional working-class-led popular struggle once the working class no longer existed. (The answer: it would turn into identity politics.)

Jameson thought of himself as exploring the forms of consciousness and historical sensibilities likely to emerge from this new age.

What happened, instead, is that the spread of information technologies and new ways of organizing transport—the containerization of shipping, for example—allowed those same industrial jobs to be outsourced to East Asia, Latin America, and other countries where the availability of cheap labor allowed manufacturers to employ much *less* technologically sophisticated production-line techniques than they would have been obliged to employ at home.

From the perspective of those living in Europe, North America, and Japan, the results did seem to be much as predicted. Smokestack industries did disappear; jobs came to be divided between a lower stratum of service workers and an upper stratum sitting in antiseptic bubbles playing with computers. But below it all lay an uneasy awareness that the postwork civilization was a giant fraud. Our carefully engineered high-tech sneakers were not being produced by intelligent cyborgs or self-replicating molecular nanotechnology; they were being made on the equivalent of old-fashioned Singer sewing machines, by the daughters of Mexican and Indonesian farmers who, as the result of WTO- or NAFTA-sponsored trade deals, had been ousted from their ancestral lands. It was a guilty awareness that lay beneath the postmodern sensibility and its celebration of the endless play of images and surfaces.

Why did the projected explosion of technological growth everyone was expecting—the moon bases, the robot factories—fail to happen? There are two possibilities. Either our expectations about the pace of technological change were unrealistic (in which case, we need to know why so many intelligent people believed they were not) or our expectations were not unrealistic (in which case, we need to know what happened to derail so many credible ideas and prospects).

Most social analysts choose the first explanation and trace the problem to the Cold War space race. Why, these analysts wonder, did both the United States and the Soviet Union become so obsessed with the idea of manned space travel? It was never an efficient way to engage in scientific research. And it encouraged unrealistic ideas of what the human future would be like.

Could the answer be that both the United States and the Soviet Union had been, in the century before, societies of pioneers, one expanding across the Western frontier, the other across Siberia? Didn't they share a commitment to the myth of a limitless, expansive future, of human colonization of vast empty spaces, that helped convince the leaders of both superpowers they had entered into a "space age" in which they were battling over control of the future itself? All sorts of myths were at play here, no doubt, but that proves nothing about the feasibility of the project.

Some of those science fiction fantasies (at this point we can't know which ones) could have been brought into being. For earlier generations, many science fiction fantasies *had* been brought into being. Those who grew up at the turn of the century reading Jules Verne or H. G. Wells imagined the world of, say, 1960 with flying machines, rocket ships, submarines, radio, and television—and that was pretty much what they got. If it wasn't unrealistic in 1900 to dream of men traveling to the moon, then why was it unrealistic in the sixties to dream of jet packs and robot laundry-maids?

In fact, even as those dreams were being outlined, the material base for their achievement was beginning to be whittled away. There is reason to believe that even by the fifties and sixties, technological innovation was slowing down from the heady pace of the first half of the century. There was a last spate in the fifties when microwave ovens (1954), the Pill (1957), and lasers (1958) all appeared in rapid succession. But since then, technological advances have taken the form of clever new ways of combining existing technologies (as in the space race) and new ways of putting existing technologies to consumer use (the most famous example is television, invented in 1926, but mass produced only after the war). Yet, in part because the space race gave everyone the impression that remarkable advances were happening, the popular impression during the sixties was that

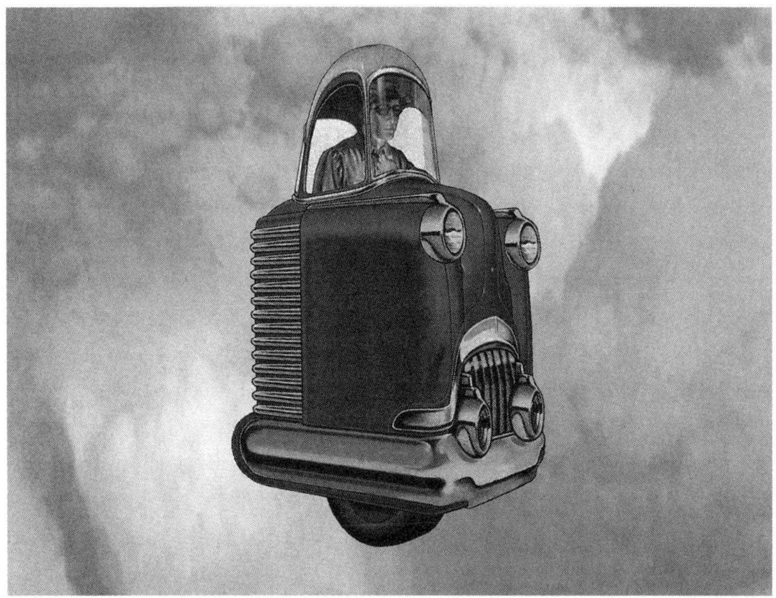

MARK S. FISHER

the pace of technological change was speeding up in terrifying, uncontrollable ways.

Alvin Toffler's 1970 bestseller *Future Shock* argued that almost all the social problems of the sixties could be traced back to the increasing pace of technological change. The endless outpouring of scientific breakthroughs transformed the grounds of daily existence and left Americans without any clear idea of what normal life was. Just consider the family, where not just the Pill, but also the prospect of in vitro fertilization, test tube babies, and sperm and egg donation were about to make the idea of motherhood obsolete.

Humans were not psychologically prepared for the pace of change, Toffler wrote. He coined a term for the phenomenon: "accelerative thrust." It had begun with the Industrial Revolution, but by roughly 1850, the effect had become unmistakable. Not only was everything around us changing, but most of it—human knowledge, the size of the population, industrial growth, energy use—was changing exponentially. The only solution, Toffler argued, was to begin some kind of control over the process, to create institutions that would assess emerging technologies and their likely effects, to ban technologies likely to be too socially disruptive, and to guide development in the direction of social harmony.

While many of the historical trends Toffler describes are accurate, the book appeared when most of these exponential trends halted. It was right around 1970 when the increase in the number of scientific papers published in the world—a figure that had doubled every fifteen years since, roughly, 1685—began leveling off. The same was true of books and patents.

Toffler's use of *acceleration* was particularly unfortunate. For most of human history, the top speed at which human beings could travel had been around twenty-five miles per hour. By 1900 it had increased to one hundred miles per hour, and for the next seventy years it did seem to be increasing exponentially. By the time Toffler was writing, in 1970, the record for the fastest speed at which any human had traveled stood at roughly 25,000 mph, achieved by the crew of Apollo 10 in 1969, just one year before. At such an exponential rate, it must have seemed reasonable to assume that within a matter of decades, humanity would be exploring other solar systems.

Since 1970, no further increase has occurred. The record for the fastest a human has ever traveled remains with the crew of Apollo 10. True, the commercial airliner Concorde, launched in 1969, reached a maximum speed of 1,400 mph. And the Soviet Tupolev Tu-144, which flew first, reached an even faster speed of 1,553 mph. But those speeds not only have failed to increase; they have decreased since the Tupolev Tu-144 was canceled and the Concorde was abandoned.

None of this stopped Toffler's own career. He kept retooling his analysis to come up with new spectacular pronouncements. In 1980 he produced *The Third Wave*, its argument lifted from Ernest Mandel's "third technological revolution"—except that while Mandel thought these changes would spell the end of capitalism, Toffler assumed capitalism was eternal. By 1990 Toffler was the personal intellectual guru to Republican congressman Newt Gingrich, who claimed that his 1994 "Contract With America" was inspired, in part, by the understanding that the United States needed to move from an antiquated, materialist, industrial mind-set to a new, free-market, Information Age, Third Wave civilization.

There are all sorts of ironies in this connection. One of Toffler's greatest achievements was inspiring the government to create an Office of Technology Assessment (OTA). One of Gingrich's first acts on winning control of the House of Representatives in 1995 was defunding the OTA as an example of useless government extravagance. Still, there's no contradiction here. By this time, Toffler had long since given up on influencing policy by appealing to the general public; he was making a living largely by giving seminars to CEOs and corporate think tanks. His insights had been privatized.

Gingrich liked to call himself a "conservative futurologist." This, too, might seem oxymoronic; but in fact, Toffler's own conception of futurology was never progressive. Progress was always presented as a problem that needed to be solved.

Toffler might best be seen as a lightweight version of the nineteenth century social theorist Auguste Comte, who believed that he was standing on the brink of a new age—in his case, the Industrial Age—driven by the inexorable progress of technology, and that the social cataclysms of his times were caused by the social system not adjusting. The older feudal order had developed Catholic theology, a way of thinking about man's place in the cosmos perfectly suited to the social system of the time, as well as an institutional structure, the Church, that conveyed and enforced such ideas in a way that could give everyone a sense of meaning and belonging. The Industrial Age had developed its own system of ideas—science—but scientists had not succeeded in creating anything like the Catholic Church. Comte concluded that we needed to develop a new science, which he dubbed "sociology," and said that sociologists should play the role of priests in a new Religion of Society that would inspire everyone with a love of order, community, work discipline, and family values. Toffler was less ambitious; his futurologists were not supposed to play the role of priests.

Gingrich had a second guru, a libertarian theologian named George Gilder, and Gilder, like Toffler, was obsessed with technology and social change. In an odd way, Gilder was more optimistic.

Embracing a radical version of Mandel's Third Wave argument, he insisted that what we were seeing with the rise of computers was an "overthrow of matter." The old materialist Industrial Society, in which value came from physical labor, was giving way to an Information Age where value emerges directly from the minds of entrepreneurs, just as the world had originally appeared ex nihilo from the mind of God, just as money, in a proper supply-side economy, emerged ex nihilo from the Federal Reserve and into the hands of value-creating capitalists. Supply-side economic policies, Gilder concluded, would ensure that investment would continue to steer away from old government boondoggles like the space program and toward more productive information and medical technologies.

But if there was a conscious, or semi-conscious, move away from investment in research that might lead to better rockets and robots, and toward research that would lead to such things as laser printers and CAT scans, it had begun well before Toffler's *Future Shock* (1970) and Gilder's *Wealth and Poverty* (1981). What their success shows is that the issues they raised—that existing patterns of technological development would lead to social upheaval and that we needed to guide technological development in directions that did not challenge existing structures of authority—echoed in the corridors of power. Statesmen and captains of industry had been thinking about such questions for some time.

Industrial capitalism has fostered an extremely rapid rate of scientific advance and technological innovation—one with no parallel in previous human history. Even capitalism's greatest detractors, Karl Marx and Friedrich Engels, celebrated its unleashing of the "productive forces." Marx and Engels also believed that capitalism's continual need to revolutionize the means of industrial production would be its undoing. Marx argued that, for certain technical reasons, value—and therefore profits—can be extracted only from human labor. Competition forces factory owners to mechanize production, to reduce labor costs, but while this is to the short-term advantage of the firm, mechanization's effect is to drive down the general rate of profit.

For 150 years, economists have debated whether all this is true. But if it is true, then the decision by industrialists not to pour research funds into the invention of the robot factories that everyone was anticipating in the sixties, and instead to relocate their factories to labor-intensive, low-tech facilities in China or the Global South, makes a great deal of sense.

As I've noted, there's reason to believe the pace of technological innovation in productive processes—the factories themselves—began to slow in the fifties and sixties, but the side effects of America's rivalry with the Soviet Union made innovation appear to accelerate. There was the awesome space race, alongside frenetic efforts by U.S. industrial planners to apply existing technologies to consumer purposes, to create an optimistic sense of burgeoning prosperity and guaranteed progress that would undercut the appeal of working-class politics.

These moves were reactions to initiatives from the Soviet Union. But this part of the history is difficult for Americans to remember, because at the end of the Cold War, the popular image of the Soviet Union switched from terrifyingly bold rival to pathetic basket case—the exemplar of a society that could not work. Back in the fifties, in fact, many United States planners suspected the Soviet system worked better. Certainly, they recalled the fact that in the thirties, while the United States had been mired in depression, the Soviet Union had maintained almost unprecedented economic growth rates of 10 percent to 12 percent a year—an achievement quickly followed by the production of tank armies that defeated Nazi Germany, then by the launching of Sputnik in 1957, then by the first manned spacecraft, the Vostok, in 1961.

It's often said the Apollo moon landing was the greatest historical achievement of Soviet communism. Surely the United States would never have contemplated such a feat had it not been for the cosmic ambitions of the Soviet Politburo. We are used to thinking of the Politburo as a group of unimaginative gray bureaucrats, but they were bureaucrats who dared to dream astounding dreams. The dream of

MARK S. FISHER

world revolution was only the first. It's also true that most of them—changing the course of mighty rivers, this sort of thing—either turned out to be ecologically and socially disastrous, or, like Joseph Stalin's one-hundred-story Palace of the Soviets or a twenty-story statue of Vladimir Lenin, never got off the ground.

After the initial successes of the Soviet space program, few of these schemes were realized, but the leadership never ceased coming up with new ones. Even in the eighties, when the United States was attempting its own last grandiose scheme, Star Wars, the Soviets were planning to transform the world through creative uses of technology. Few outside of Russia remember most of these projects, but great resources were devoted to them. It's also worth noting that unlike the Star Wars project, which was designed to sink the Soviet Union, most were not military in nature: as, for instance, the attempt to solve the world hunger problem by seeding lakes and oceans with an edible bacteria called spirulina, or to solve the world energy problem by launching hundreds of gigantic solar-power platforms into orbit and beaming the electricity back to earth.

The American victory in the space race meant that, after 1968, U.S. planners no longer took the competition seriously. As a result, the mythology of the final frontier was maintained, even as the direction of research and development shifted away from anything that might lead to the creation of Mars bases and robot factories.

The standard line is that all this was a result of the triumph of the market. The Apollo program was a Big Government project, Soviet-inspired in the sense that it required a national effort coordinated by government bureaucracies. As soon as the Soviet threat drew safely out of the picture, though, capitalism was free to revert to lines of technological development more in accord with its normal, decentralized, free-market imperatives—such as privately funded research into marketable products like personal computers. This is the line that men like Toffler and Gilder took in the late seventies and early eighties.

In fact, the United States never did abandon gigantic, government-controlled schemes of technological development. Mainly they just shifted to military research—and not just to Soviet-scale schemes like Star Wars, but to weapons projects, research in communications and surveillance technologies, and similar security-related concerns. To some degree this had always been true: the billions poured into missile research had always dwarfed the sums allocated to the space program. Yet by the seventies, even basic research came to be conducted following military priorities. One reason we don't have robot factories is because roughly 95 percent of robotics research funding has been channeled through the Pentagon, which is more interested in developing unmanned drones than in automating paper mills.

A case could be made that even the shift to research and development on information technologies and medicine was not so much a reorientation toward market-driven consumer imperatives, but part of an all-out effort to follow the technological humbling of the Soviet Union with total victory in the global class war—seen simultaneously as the imposition of absolute U.S. military dominance overseas, and, at home, the utter rout of social movements.

The technologies that did emerge proved most conducive to surveillance, work discipline, and social control. Computers have opened up certain spaces of freedom, as we're constantly reminded, but instead of leading to the workless utopia Abbie Hoffman imagined, they have been employed in such a way as to produce the opposite effect. They have enabled a financialization of capital that has driven workers desperately into debt, and, at the same time, provided the means by which employers have created "flexible" work regimes that have both destroyed traditional job security and increased working hours for almost everyone. Along with the export of factory jobs, the new work regime has routed the union movement and destroyed any possibility of effective working-class politics.

Meanwhile, despite unprecedented investment in research on medicine and life sciences, we await cures for cancer and the common cold, and the most dramatic medical breakthroughs we have seen have taken the form of drugs such as Prozac, Zoloft, or Ritalin—tailor-made to ensure that the new work demands don't drive us completely, dysfunctionally crazy.

With results like these, what will the epitaph for neoliberalism look like? I think historians will conclude it was a form of capitalism that systematically prioritized political imperatives over economic ones. Given a choice between a course of action that would make capitalism seem the only possible economic system and a course of action that would transform capitalism into a viable, long-term economic system, neoliberalism chooses the former every time. There is every reason to believe that destroying job security while increasing working hours does not create a more productive (let alone more innovative or loyal) workforce. Probably, in economic terms, the result is negative—an impression confirmed by lower growth rates in just about all parts of the world in the eighties and nineties.

But the neoliberal choice has been effective in depoliticizing labor and overdetermining the future. Economically, the growth of armies, police, and private security services amounts to dead weight. It's possible, in fact, that the very dead weight of the apparatus created to ensure the ideological victory of capitalism will sink it. But it's also easy to see how choking off any sense of an inevitable, redemptive future that could be different from our world is a crucial part of the neoliberal project.

At this point all the pieces would seem to be falling neatly into place. By the sixties, conservative political forces were growing skittish about the socially disruptive effects of technological progress, and employers were beginning to worry about the economic impact of mechanization. The fading Soviet threat allowed for a reallocation of resources in directions seen as less challenging to social and economic arrangements, or indeed directions that could support a campaign of reversing the gains of progressive social movements and achieving a decisive victory in what U.S. elites saw as a global class war. The change of priorities was introduced as a withdrawal of big-government projects and a return to the market, but in fact the change shifted government-directed research away from programs like NASA or alternative energy sources and toward military, information, and medical technologies.

Of course this doesn't explain everything. Above all, it does not explain why, even in those areas that have become the focus of well-funded research projects, we have not seen anything like the kind of advances anticipated fifty years ago. If 95 percent of robotics research has been funded by the military, then where are the Klaatu-style killer robots shooting death rays from their eyes?

Obviously, there have been advances in military technology in recent decades. One of the reasons we all survived the Cold War is that while nuclear bombs might have worked as advertised, their delivery systems did not; intercontinental ballistic missiles weren't capable of striking cities, let alone specific targets inside cities, and this fact meant there was little point in launching a nuclear first strike unless you intended to destroy the world.

Contemporary cruise missiles are accurate by comparison. Still, precision weapons never do seem capable of assassinating specific individuals (Saddam, Osama, Qaddafi), even when hundreds are dropped. And ray guns have not materialized—surely not for lack of trying. We can assume the Pentagon has spent billions on death ray research, but the closest they've come so far are lasers that might, if aimed correctly, blind an enemy gunner looking directly at the beam. Aside from being unsporting, this is pathetic: lasers are a fifties technology. Phasers that can be set to stun do not appear to be on the drawing boards; and when it comes to infantry combat, the preferred weapon almost everywhere remains the AK-47, a Soviet design named for the year it was introduced: 1947.

The Internet is a remarkable innovation, but all we are talking about is a super-fast and globally accessible combination of library, post office, and mail-order catalogue. Had the Internet been described to a science fiction aficionado in the fifties and sixties and touted as the most dramatic technological achievement since his time, his reaction would have been disappointment. *Fifty years and this is the best our scientists managed to come up with? We expected computers that would think!*

Overall, levels of research funding have increased dramatically since the seventies. Admittedly, the proportion of that funding that comes from the corporate sector has increased most dramatically, to the point that private enterprise is now funding twice as much research as the government, but the increase is so large that the total amount of government research funding, in real-dollar terms, is much higher than it was in the sixties. "Basic," "curiosity-driven," or "blue-skies" research—the kind that is not driven by the prospect of any immediate practical application, and that is most likely to lead to unexpected breakthroughs—occupies an ever smaller proportion of the total, though so much money is being thrown around nowadays that overall levels of basic research funding have increased.

Yet most observers agree that the results have been paltry. Certainly we no longer see anything like the continual stream of conceptual revolutions—genetic inheritance, relativity, psychoanalysis, quantum mechanics—that people had grown used to, and even expected, a hundred years before. Why?

Part of the answer has to do with the concentration of resources on a handful of gigantic projects: "big science," as it has come to be called. The Human Genome Project is often held out as an example. After spending almost $3 billion and employing thousands of scientists and staff in five different countries, it has mainly served to establish that there isn't very much to be learned from sequencing genes that's of much use to anyone else. Even more, the hype and political investment surrounding such projects demonstrate the degree to which even basic research now seems to be driven by political, administrative, and marketing imperatives that make it unlikely anything revolutionary will happen.

Here, our fascination with the mythic origins of Silicon Valley and the Internet has blinded us to what's really going on. It has allowed us to imagine that research and development is now driven, primarily, by small teams of plucky entrepreneurs, or the sort of decentralized cooperation that creates open source software. This is not so, even though such research teams are most likely to produce results. Research and development is still driven by giant bureaucratic projects.

What has changed is the bureaucratic culture. The increasing interpenetration of government, university, and private firms has led everyone to adopt the language, sensibilities, and organizational forms that originated in the corporate world. Although this might have helped in creating marketable products, since that is what corporate bureaucracies are designed to do, in terms of fostering original research, the results have been catastrophic.

My own knowledge comes from universities, both in the United States and Britain. In both countries, the last thirty years have seen a veritable explosion of the proportion of working hours spent on administrative tasks at the expense of pretty much everything else. In my own university, for instance, we have more administrators than faculty members, and the faculty members, too, are expected to spend at least as much time on administration as on teaching and research combined. The same is true, more or less, at universities worldwide.

The growth of administrative work has directly resulted from introducing corporate management techniques. Invariably, these are justified as ways of increasing efficiency and introducing competition at every level. What they end up meaning in practice is that everyone winds up spending most of their time trying to sell things: grant proposals; book proposals; assessments of students' job and grant applications; assessments of our colleagues; prospectuses for new interdisciplinary majors; institutes; conference workshops; universities themselves (which have now become brands to be marketed to prospective students or contributors); and so on.

As marketing overwhelms university life, it generates documents about fostering imagination and creativity that might just as well have been designed to strangle imagination and creativity in the cradle. No major new works of social theory have emerged in the United States in the last thirty years. We have been reduced to the equivalent of medieval scholastics, writing endless annotations of French theory from the seventies, despite the guilty awareness that if new incarnations of Gilles Deleuze, Michel Foucault, or Pierre Bourdieu were to appear in the academy today, we would deny them tenure.

There was a time when academia was society's refuge for the eccentric, brilliant, and impractical. No longer. It is now the domain of professional self-marketers. As a result, in one of the most bizarre fits of social self-destructiveness in history, we seem to have decided we have no place for our eccentric, brilliant, and impractical citizens. Most languish in their mothers' basements, at best making the occasional acute intervention on the Internet.

If all this is true in the social sciences, where research is still carried out with minimal overhead largely by individuals, one can imagine how much worse it is for astrophysicists. And, indeed, one astrophysicist, Jonathan Katz, has recently warned students pondering a career in the sciences. Even if you do emerge from the usual decade-long period languishing as someone else's flunky, he says, you can expect your best ideas to be stymied at every point:

> You will spend your time writing proposals rather than doing research. Worse, because your proposals are judged by your competitors, you cannot follow your curiosity, but must spend your effort and talents on anticipating and deflecting criticism rather than on solving the important scientific problems. . . . It is proverbial that original ideas are the kiss of death for a proposal, because they have not yet been proved to work.

MARK S. FISHER

That pretty much answers the question of why we don't have teleportation devices or antigravity shoes. Common sense suggests that if you want to maximize scientific creativity, you find some bright people, give them the resources they need to pursue whatever idea comes into their heads, and then leave them alone. Most will turn up nothing, but one or two may well discover something. But if you want to minimize the possibility of unexpected breakthroughs, tell those same people they will receive no resources at all unless they spend the bulk of their time competing against each other to convince you they know in advance what they are going to discover.

In the natural sciences, to the tyranny of managerialism we can add the privatization of research results. As the British economist David Harvie has reminded us, "open source" research is not new. Scholarly research has always been open source, in the sense that scholars share materials and results. There is competition, certainly, but it is "convivial." This is no longer true of scientists working in the corporate sector, where findings are jealously guarded, but the spread of the corporate ethos within the academy and research institutes themselves has caused even publicly funded scholars to treat their findings as personal property. Academic publishers ensure that findings that are published are increasingly difficult to access, further enclosing the intellectual commons. As a result, convivial, open-source competition turns into something much more like classic market competition.

There are many forms of privatization, up to and including the simple buying up and suppression of inconvenient discoveries by large corporations fearful of their economic effects. (We cannot know how many synthetic fuel formulae have been bought up and placed in the vaults of oil companies, but it's hard to imagine nothing like this happens.) More subtle is the way the managerial ethos discourages everything adventurous or quirky, especially if there is no prospect of immediate results. Oddly, the Internet can be part of the problem here. As Neal Stephenson put it:

> Most people who work in corporations or academia have witnessed something like the following: A number of engineers are sitting together in a room, bouncing ideas off each other. Out of the discussion emerges a new concept that seems promising. Then some laptop-wielding person in the corner, having performed a quick Google search, announces that this "new" idea is, in fact, an old one; it—or at least something vaguely similar—has already been tried. Either it failed, or it succeeded. If it failed, then no manager who wants to keep his or her job will approve spending money trying to revive it. If it succeeded, then it's patented and entry to the market is presumed to be unattainable, since the first people who thought of it will have "first-mover advantage" and will have created "barriers to entry." The number of seemingly promising ideas that have been crushed in this way must number in the millions.

And so a timid, bureaucratic spirit suffuses every aspect of cultural life. It comes festooned in a language of creativity, initiative, and entrepreneurialism. But the language is meaningless. Those thinkers most likely to make a conceptual breakthrough are the least likely to receive funding, and, if breakthroughs occur, they are not likely to find anyone willing to follow up on their most daring implications.

Giovanni Arrighi has noted that after the South Sea Bubble, British capitalism largely abandoned the corporate form. By the time of the Industrial Revolution, Britain had instead come to rely on a combination of high finance and small family firms—a pattern that held throughout the next century, the period of maximum scientific and technological innovation. (Britain at that time was also notorious for being just as generous to its oddballs and eccentrics as contemporary America is intolerant. A common expedient was to allow them to become rural vicars, who, predictably, became one of the main sources for amateur scientific discoveries.)

Contemporary, bureaucratic corporate capitalism was a creation not of Britain, but of the United States and Germany, the two rival powers that spent the first half of the twentieth century fighting two bloody wars over who would replace Britain as a dominant world power—wars that culminated, appropriately enough, in government-sponsored scientific programs to see who would be the first to discover the atom bomb. It is significant, then, that our current technological stagnation seems to have begun after 1945, when the United States replaced Britain as organizer of the world economy.

Americans do not like to think of themselves as a nation of bureaucrats—quite the opposite—but the moment we stop imagining bureaucracy as a phenomenon limited to government offices, it becomes obvious that this is precisely what we have become. The final victory over the Soviet Union did not lead to the domination of the market, but in fact cemented the dominance of conservative managerial elites, corporate bureaucrats who use the pretext of short-term, competitive, bottom-line thinking to squelch anything likely to have revolutionary implications of any kind.

If we do not notice that we live in a bureaucratic society, that is because bureaucratic norms and practices have become so all-pervasive that we cannot see them or, worse, cannot imagine doing things any other way.

Computers have played a crucial role in this narrowing of our social imaginations. Just as the invention of new forms of industrial automation in the eighteenth and nineteenth centuries had the paradoxical effect of turning more and more of the world's population into full-time industrial workers, so has all the software designed to save us from administrative responsibilities turned us into part- or full-time administrators. In the same way that university professors seem to feel it is inevitable they will spend more of their time managing grants, so affluent housewives simply accept that they will spend weeks every year filling out forty-page online forms to get their children into grade schools. We all spend increasing amounts of time punching passwords into our phones to manage bank and credit accounts and learning how to perform jobs once performed by travel agents, brokers, and accountants.

Someone once figured out that the average American will spend a cumulative six months of life waiting for traffic lights to change. I don't know if similar figures are available for how long it takes to fill out forms, but it must be at least as long. No population in the history of the world has spent nearly so much time engaged in paperwork.

In this final, stultifying stage of capitalism, we are moving from poetic technologies to bureaucratic technologies. By poetic technologies I refer to the use of rational and technical means to bring wild fantasies to reality. Poetic technologies, so understood, are as old as civilization. Lewis Mumford noted that the first complex machines were made of people. Egyptian pharaohs were able to build the pyramids only because of their mastery of administrative procedures, which allowed them to develop production-line techniques, dividing up complex tasks into dozens of simple operations and assigning each to one team of workmen—even though they lacked mechanical technology more complex than the inclined plane and lever. Administrative oversight turned armies of peasant farmers into the cogs of a vast machine. Much later, after cogs had been invented, the design of complex machinery elaborated principles originally developed to organize people.

Yet we have seen those machines—whether their moving parts are arms and torsos or pistons, wheels, and springs—being put to work to realize impossible fantasies: cathedrals, moon shots, transcontinental railways. Certainly, poetic technologies had something terrible about them; the poetry is likely to be as much of dark satanic mills as of grace or liberation. But the rational, administrative techniques were always in service to some fantastic end.

From this perspective, all those mad Soviet plans—even if never realized—marked the climax of poetic technologies. What we have now is the reverse. It's not that vision, creativity, and mad fantasies are no longer encouraged, but that most remain free-floating; there's no longer even the pretense that they could ever take form or flesh. The greatest and most powerful nation that has ever existed has spent the last decades telling its citizens they can no longer contemplate fantastic collective enterprises, even if—as the environmental crisis demands—the fate of the earth depends on it.

What are the political implications of all this? First of all, we need to rethink some of our most basic assumptions about the nature of capitalism. One is that capitalism is identical with the market, and that both therefore are inimical to bureaucracy, which is supposed to be a creature of the state.

The second assumption is that capitalism is in its nature technologically progressive. It would seem that Marx and Engels, in their giddy enthusiasm for the industrial revolutions of their day, were wrong about this. Or, to be more precise: they were right to insist that the mechanization of industrial production would destroy capitalism; they were wrong to predict that market competition would compel factory owners to mechanize anyway. If it didn't happen, that is because market competition is not, in fact, as essential to the nature of capitalism as they had assumed. If nothing else, the current form of capitalism, where much of the competition seems to take the form of internal marketing within the bureaucratic structures of large semi-monopolistic enterprises, would come as a complete surprise to them.

Defenders of capitalism make three broad historical claims: first, that it has fostered rapid scientific and technological growth; second, that however much it may throw enormous wealth to a small minority, it does so in such a way as to increase overall prosperity; third, that in doing so, it creates a more secure and democratic world for everyone. It is clear that capitalism is not doing any of these things any longer. In fact, many of its defenders are retreating from claiming that it is a good system and instead falling back on the claim that it is the only possible system—or at least the only possible system for a complex, technologically sophisticated society such as our own.

But how could anyone argue that current economic arrangements are also the only ones that will ever be viable under any possible future technological society? The argument is absurd. How could anyone know?

Granted, there are people who take that position—on both ends of the political spectrum. As an anthropologist and anarchist, I encounter anticivilizational types who insist not only that current industrial technology leads only to capitalist-style oppression, but that this must necessarily be true of any future technology as well, and therefore that human liberation can be achieved only by returning to the Stone Age. Most of us are not technological determinists.

But claims for the inevitability of capitalism have to be based on a kind of technological determinism. And for that very reason, if the aim of neoliberal capitalism is to create a world in which no one believes any other economic system could work, then it needs to suppress not just any idea of an inevitable redemptive future, but any radically different technological future. Yet there's a contradiction. Defenders of capitalism cannot mean to convince us that technological change has ended—since that would mean capitalism is not progressive. No, they mean to convince us that technological progress is indeed continuing, that we do live in a world of wonders, but that those wonders take the form of modest improvements (the latest iPhone!), rumors of inventions about to happen ("I hear they are going to have flying cars pretty soon"), complex ways of juggling information and imagery, and still more complex platforms for filling out forms.

I do not mean to suggest that neoliberal capitalism—or any other system—can be successful in this regard. First, there's the problem of trying to convince the world you are leading the way in technological progress when you are holding it back. The United States, with its decaying infrastructure, paralysis in the face of global warming, and symbolically devastating abandonment of its manned space program just as China accelerates its own, is doing a particularly bad public relations job. Second, the pace of change can't be held back forever. Breakthroughs will happen; inconvenient discoveries cannot be permanently suppressed. Other, less bureaucratized parts of the world—or at least, parts of the world with bureaucracies that are not so hostile to creative thinking—will slowly but inevitably attain the resources required to pick up where the United States and its allies have left off. The Internet does provide opportunities for collaboration and dissemination that may help break us through the wall as well. Where will the breakthrough come? We can't know. Maybe 3-D printing will do what the robot factories were supposed to. Or maybe it will be something else. But it will happen.

About one conclusion we can feel especially confident: it will not happen within the framework of contemporary corporate capitalism—or any form of capitalism. To begin setting up domes on Mars, let alone to develop the means to figure out if there are alien civilizations to contact, we're going to have to figure out a different economic system. Must the new system take the form of some massive new bureaucracy? Why do we assume it must? Only by breaking up existing bureaucratic structures can we begin. And if we're going to invent robots that will do our laundry and tidy up the kitchen, then we're going to have to make sure that whatever replaces capitalism is based on a far more egalitarian distribution of wealth and power—one that no longer contains either the super-rich or the desperately poor willing to do their housework. Only then will technology begin to be marshaled toward human needs. And this is the best reason to break free of the dead hand of the hedge fund managers and the CEOs—to free our fantasies from the screens in which such men have imprisoned them, to let our imaginations once again become a material force in human history.

Feral Houses

JAMES GRIFFIOEN

I live in the city of Detroit among tens of thousands of vacant and abandoned homes. These houses—most of them burned and collapsing—are a constant reminder that this city, where two million people once lived, is now home to much less than one million. Some estimate that there are as many as seventy thousand vacant houses in Detroit, along with twenty-five thousand acres of prairie where homes and entire neighborhoods once stood.

As the city disappears, nature flourishes. I take my bird dog pheasant "hunting" on the empty street grid of an old Slovakian neighborhood. I've seen a pair of red foxes trot into our abandoned Beaux-Arts train station. I had a face-to-face encounter with a wild badger in the city's abandoned zoo, which is also home to a pack of feral dogs that once attacked my family at a nearby playground.

"Feral" means reversion to a wild state, as from domestication. It comes from the Latin root *fera*, for wild beast, but it also has a connection to another Latin word, *feralis*, literally, belonging to the dead. Though it is usually used to describe animals, "feral" could also be used to describe some of the abandoned homes in Detroit. For a few months every summer, some of them disappear behind ivy or untended shrubs and trees planted generations ago. They may belong only to the dead, and yet every year they teem with a new kind of life. ⚜

From *The Baffler*, no. 18

Feral House No. 17 (2009), Marcus Street, Detroit (demolished).

Feral House No. 7 (2008), Marlborough Street, Detroit (still standing).

Feral House No. 13 (2009), Ashland Street, Detroit (demolished).

Feral House No. 11 (2009), Walden Street, Detroit (currently occupied).

Feral House No. 26 (2009), Highland Park (status unknown).

PART TWO

THE ARTS OF REGRESSION

Dead End on Shakin' Street

THOMAS FRANK

My hometown is vibrant. Its status as such is certified, official, stamped on both sides.

There was a time, though, when it wasn't, when my friends and I would laugh at Kansas City's blandness: its harmless theater productions, its pretentious suburbs, its private country clubs, its eternal taste for classic rock. We called it "Cupcake Land," after a favorite Richard Rhodes essay from the eighties. The city knew nothing of the bold ideas of our robust generation, we thought: it had virtually no music subculture; it was deaf to irony; hell, it actually tried to drive out of business the last surviving club from its jazz-age glory days.

Maybe that was the sort of criticism everybody made of their Midwestern hometowns back then. Well, those hometowns have certainly turned the tables on us today. Our enthusiasm for music is a dead thing now in these post-alternative decades, a mere record collection that we occasionally cue up after one Scotch too many to help remember the time when art seemed to matter.

But Kansas City doesn't need any reminders. The place fairly quivers with vitality now. It is swarming with artists; its traffic islands are bedecked with the colorful products of their studios. It boasts a spectacular new performing arts center designed by one of those spectacular new celebrity architects. It even has an indie-rock festival to call its own. And while much of the city's flowering has been organic and spontaneous, other parts of its renaissance were engineered by the very class of

From *The Baffler*, no. 20

civic leaders we used to deride for their impotence and cluelessness. At that Kansas City indie-rock festival, for example, the mayor himself made a presentation, as did numerous local professionals and business leaders.

Besides, as everyone knows, cupcakes are cool nowadays, like yoga or something—the consummate expression of the baker's artisanal vibrancy.

Your hometown is probably vibrant, too. Every city is either vibrant these days or is working on a plan to attain vibrancy soon. The reason is simple: a city isn't successful—isn't even a city, really—unless it can lay claim to being "vibrant." Vibrancy is so universally desirable, so totemic in its powers, that even though we aren't sure what the word means, we know the quality it designates must be cultivated. The vibrant, we believe, is what makes certain cities flourish. The absence of vibrancy, by contrast, is what allows the diseases of depopulation and blight to set in.

This formulation sounded ridiculous to me when I first encountered it. Whatever the word meant, "vibrancy" was surely an outcome of civic prosperity, not its cause. Putting it the other way round was like reasoning that, since sidewalks get wet when it rains, we can encourage rainfall by wetting the sidewalks.

But to others, the vibrancy mantra is profoundly persuasive. The pursuit of the vibrant seems to be the universal job description of the nation's city planners nowadays. It is also part of the Obama administration's economic recovery strategy for the nation. In the fall of 2011, the National Endowment for the Arts launched "ArtPlace," a joint project with the nation's largest banks and foundations, and ArtPlace immediately began generating a cloud of glowing euphemisms around the central, hallowed cliché:

> ArtPlace is investing in art and culture at the heart of a portfolio of integrated strategies that can drive vibrancy and diversity so powerful that it transforms communities.

DAVID MCLIMANS

Specifically, vibrancy transforms communities by making them more prosperous. ArtPlace says its goal is not merely to promote the arts but to "transform economic development in America," a project that is straightforward and obvious if you accept the organization's slogan: "Art creates vibrancy and increases economic opportunity."

And that, presumably, is why everyone is so damn vibrant these days. Consider Akron, Ohio, which was recently the subject of a conference bearing the thrilling name "Greater Akron: This Is What Vibrant Looks Like." Or Boise, Idaho, whose citizens, according to the city's Department of Arts and History, are "fortunate to live in a vibrant community in which creativity flourishes in every season." Or Cincinnati, which is the home of a nonprofit called "Go Vibrant" as well as the Greater Cincinnati Foundation, which hands out "Cultural Vibrancy" grants, guided by the knowledge that "Cultural Vibrancy is vital to a thriving community."

Is Rockford, Illinois, vibrant? Oh my god yes: according to a local news outlet, the city's "Mayor's Arts Award nominees make Rockford vibrant." The Quad Cities? Check: As their tourism website explains, the four hamlets are "a vibrant community of cities sharing the Mississippi River in both Iowa and Illinois." Pittsburgh, Pennsylvania? Need you even ask? Pittsburgh is a sort of Athens of the vibrant; a city where dance parties and rock concerts enjoy the vigorous boosting of an outfit called "Vibrant Pittsburgh"; a place that draws young people from across the nation to frolic in its "numerous hip and vibrant neighborhoods," according to a blog maintained by a consortium of Pittsburgh business organizations.

The vibrations are just as stimulating in the component parts of this exciting new civilization. The people of creative-land use vibrant apps to check their bank accounts, chew on vegetarian "vibrancy bars," talk to one another on vibrant cellphones, and drive around in cars painted "vibrant white."

Then there are the unfortunate places from which the big V is said to have receded, like the "once-vibrant" Cincinnati/Northern Kentucky International Airport, where remediation efforts are thankfully under way. Detroit has for years provided the nation's thoughtful class with sobering lessons on what happens when the vibrant evaporates, and the fear that such a fate might befall other scenes and other communities still occasionally makes headlines. A looming "shortage of vibrancy" reportedly gave the Connecticut business community quite a scare in 2007, while the city fathers of Cleveland took a peep at all that was vibrating in Seattle back in 2002 and suspected that they were losing the race: "Without that vibrancy, Cleveland may decline."

The real Sahara of the vibrant, though, is that part of America where lonely Midwestern farmers live among "crumbling reminders of more vibrant days." This is a land from which vibrancy has withdrawn its blessings; the disastrous depopulation that has followed is, if we follow the guideposts of vibrancy theory, the unavoidable consequence. In small towns, bored teenagers turn their eyes longingly to the exciting doings in the big cities, pining for urban amenities like hipster bars and farmers' markets and indie-rock festivals. Like everyone else, they want the vibrant and they will not be denied.

As with other clichés, describing a city as "vibrant" was once a fairly innovative thing to do. Before 1950, the adjective was used mainly to describe colors and sound—the latter of which, after all, is transmitted through the air with vibrations. People's voices were often said to be "vibrant." As were, say, notes played on an oboe. To apply the adjective to a "community" or a "scene," on the other hand, was extremely unusual back then. In fact, the word "vibrant" does not seem to appear at all in the 1961 urban classic *The Death and Life of Great American Cities*, even though that book is often remembered as the very manifesto of vibrancy theory. How the expression made the leap from novelty to gold-plated bureaucratic buzzword is anyone's guess.

It is a cliché that I personally associate with NPR—not merely because announcers on that network tend to hymn the vibrant with complete indifference to the word's exhaustion, but because they always seem to believe they are saying something really fresh and profound about a place or a "scene" when they tag it thus. But the real force behind our mania for the vibrant is the nation's charitable foundations. For organized philanthropy, "vibrant" seems to have become the one-stop solution for all that ails the American polis. A decade ago there were other obsessions: multiculturalism, or public-private synergy, or leadership programs. But now it's, *Get southern Illinois some vibrancy, and its troubles are over.*

"A vibrant arts community strengthens our region," declares the website of the Seattle Foundation, describing art as a way of attracting and retaining awesome corporate employers. The New England Foundation for the Arts spends its substance "to nurture a vibrant ecology for dance." The Kresge Foundation "seek[s] to build strong, vibrant communities—enlivened by the presence of healthy cultural organizations and well-resourced artists." The S. D. Bechtel Jr. Foundation says it's "dedicated to advancing a productive, vibrant, and sustainable California." The Greater Tacoma Community Foundation hands out "Vibrant Community" grants to local nonprofits, while the "Vibrant Communities" program of Montreal's J. W. McConnell Family Foundation seems to be a sort of anti-poverty initiative.

But while everyone agrees that "vibrancy" is the ultimate desideratum of urban life, no one seems to be exactly sure what vibrancy is. In fact, the Municipal Art Society of New York recently held a panel discussion—excuse me, a "convening"—of foundation people to talk about "Measuring Vibrancy" (it seems "the impact of arts and cultural investments on neighborhoods . . . is hard to quantify"). In retrospect, it would have been far better to convene such a gathering *before* all those foundation people persuaded the cities of the nation to blow millions setting up gallery districts and street fairs.

Even ArtPlace, the big vibrancy project of the NEA, the banks, and the foundations, is not entirely sure that vibrancy can be observed or quantified. That's why the group is developing what it calls "Vibrancy Indicators": "While we are not able to measure vibrancy directly," the group's website admits, "we believe that the measures we are assembling, taken together, will provide useful insights into the nature and location of especially vibrant places within cities."

What are those measures? Unfortunately, at the time of this

writing, they had not yet been announced. But a presentation of preliminary work on the "Vibrancy Indicators" did include this helpful directive: "Inform leaders of the connection between vibrancy and prosperity."

Got that? We aren't sure what vibrancy is or whether or not it works, but part of the project is nevertheless "informing" people that it does. The meaninglessness of the phrase, like the absence of proof, does not deter the committed friend of the vibrant: if you know it's the great good thing, you simply push ahead, moving all before you with your millions.

This is not the place to try to gauge the enormous, unaccountable power that foundations wield over American life—their agenda-setting clout in urban planning debates, for example, or the influence they hold over cash-strapped universities, or their symbiosis with public broadcasters NPR and PBS.

My target here is not their power, but their vacuity. Our leadership class looks out over the trashed and looted landscape of the American city, and they solemnly declare that salvation lies in an almost meaningless buzzword—that if we chant that buzzword loud enough and often enough, our troubles are over.

The Baffler has mocked, analyzed, and derided money's cultivation of the cool since our earliest days in print. Just think of all the permutations of urban hipness that have flickered by since we undertook that mission: Rollerblading near water. "Potemkin bohemias" like Chicago's Wicker Park. Richard Florida's "creative class." And while each in turn drew the cheers of the bystanders, utilities were privatized to disastrous effect, the New Economy came and went, the real estate bubble grew and burst, the banks got ever bigger, state governments declared war on public workers, and the economy went off a cliff.

It is time to acknowledge the truth: that our leaders have nothing to say, really, about any of this. They have nothing to suggest, really, to Cairo, Illinois, or St. Joseph, Missouri. They have no comment to make, really, about the depopulation of the countryside or the deindustrialization of the Midwest. They have nothing to offer, really, but the same suggestions as before, gussied up with a new set of clichés. They have no idea what to do for places or people that aren't already successful or that have no prospects of ever becoming cool.

And so the dull bureaucrat lusts passionately for the lifestyle of the creative artist, but beneath it all is the harsh fact that foundations have been selling the vibrant, under one label or another, for decades; all they've done this time is repackage it as a sort of prosperity gospel for Ivy League art students. As the name of a suburban St. Louis street festival puts it, without the smallest detectable trace of irony, "Let Them Eat Art."

In the face of this deafening silence, let us propose a working hypothesis of what makes up the vibrant. Putting aside such outliers as the foundation that thinks vibrancy equals poverty remediation and the car rental company that believes it means having lots of parks, it's easy to figure out what the foundations conceive the vibrant to be. Vibrant is a quality you find in cities or neighborhoods where there is an arts or music "scene," lots of restaurants and food markets of a certain highbrow type, trophy architecture to memorialize the scene's otherwise transient life, and an audience of prosperous people who are interested in all these things.

Indeed, art production is supposed to be linked, through the black box of "vibrancy," to prosperity itself. This is something so simple that one proponent has illustrated it with a flowchart; it is something so obvious that just about everyone concerned agrees on it.

"Corporations see a vibrant cultural landscape as a magnet for talent," goes the thinking behind Kansas City's vibrancy, according to one report; it's "almost as vital for drawing good workers as more-traditional benefits like retirement plans and health insurance." (Did you catch that, reader? Art is literally a substitute for compensating people properly. "Let them eat art," indeed.) And so when the Cincinnati foundation known as ArtsWave[I] informs the world that "the arts create vibrant neighborhoods and contribute to a thriving economy," they are voicing a sentiment so commonplace in foundation-land that it is almost not worth remarking on.

How does art do these amazing things? you might ask. Reasoning backwards from the ultimate object of all civic planning—attracting and retaining top talent, of course—the ArtPlace website pronounces thusly:

> The ability to attract and retain talent depends, in part, on quality of place. And the best proxy for quality of place is vibrancy.

Others have spelled out the formula in more detail. We build prosperity by mobilizing art-people as vibrancy shock troops and counting on them to . . . well . . . *gentrify* formerly bedraggled parts of town. Once that mission is accomplished, then other vibrancy multipliers kick in. The presence of hipsters is said to be inspirational to businesses; their doings make cities interesting and attractive to the class of professionals that everyone wants, their colorful japes help companies to hire quality employees, and so on. All a city really needs to prosper is a group of art-school grads, some lofts for them to live in, and a couple of thrift stores to supply them with the ironic clothes they crave. Then we just step back and watch them work their magic.

This, then, is how far it's gone. The vibrant is the public art of today. It is Official. Our leaders think it will solve the problems of the cities large and small. Our leaders believe it will help to pull us out of our persistent economic slump.

In this respect, we are counting on our artists for considerably more than we did during the country's last experience with economic breakdown, but also—in other respects—considerably less. In the thirties, the federal government launched a number of programs directly subsidizing artists. Painters got jobs making murals for the walls of post offices and public buildings; theater troupes staged plays; writers collected folklore; photographers combed the South documenting the lives of sharecroppers. But no one expected those artists to pull us out of the Depression by some occult process of entrepreneurship-kindling. Instead, government supported them mainly because they were unemployed. In other words, government then did precisely the opposite of what government does today: in the thirties, we protected artists from the market while today we expose them to it, imagining them as the stokers on the hurtling job-creation locomotive.

Both then and now we heard much about "scenes." The public art of the thirties was, famously, concerned with "the American scene," via the style known as "regionalism." Thomas Hart Benton painted Missouri scenes, John Steuart Curry painted Kansas scenes, and unemployed authors assembled tour guides to every state in the union. In today's more vibrant version, though, the artist himself is the spectacle, the subject of the tour guide. His primary job is not really to produce art but to participate in a "scene"—in an act that is put on for well-heeled spectators. Indeed, this act is essential to the vibrant: in order to bring the economic effects that "the arts" are being counted upon to bring—attracting and retaining top talent for a city's corporations, remember—the artist himself must be highly visible. He must run a gallery, patronize cool coffee shops and restaurants, or rehab run-down buildings.

The federal programs of the thirties produced "art for the millions" and aimed to improve both cities and rural settlements, to make them more livable for everyone. Today, however, we have a different audience in mind. Vibrancy is a sort of performance that artists or musicians are expected to put on, either directly or indirectly, for the corporate class. These are the ones we aim to reassure of our city's vibrancy, so that they never choose to move their millions (of dollars) to some more vibrant burg. An artist who keeps to herself, who works in her room all day, who wears unremarkable clothes and goes without tattoos—by definition she brings almost nothing to this project, adds little to the economic prospects of a given area. She inspires no one. She offers no lessons in creativity. She is not vibrant, not remunerative, not investment-grade.

Vibrancy theory reveres the artist, but it also insults those who would take artistic production seriously. Think of the purblind art that this philosophy would guarantee us, were we to take it to heart and follow its directions to the letter. The public art of the thirties was often heavy-handed, close to propaganda even, but it was also critical of capitalist institutions and intensely concerned with the lives of ordinary people. The vibrant, on the other hand, would separate the artist from such boring souls. The creative ones are to be ghettoized in a "scene" which it is their job to make "vibrant," thereby pumping up real estate prices and inspiring creative-class onlookers. But what of the people no one is interested in attracting and retaining? Millions of Americans go through their lives in places that aren't vibrant, in areas that don't have a "scene," in jobs that aren't rewarding, in industries that aren't creative; and their experiences are, almost by definition, off limits for artistic contemplation.

Instead of all that, the aesthetic of the vibrant proposes a kind of tail-chasing reverence for creativity itself, the awesome creativity that is supposed to inspire the businessman-spectator and lead him or her to conjure up bold and outside-the-box thoughts. Consider the trophy buildings that are, inevitably, the greatest expression of vibrancy theory—the assorted Frank Gehry and pseudo-Gehry buildings that every city council seems to believe it must build as a sort of welcome mat to the creative class. Regardless of the particular shape that each structure's fluttering and swooping exterior takes, the point of the buildings is, in a general sense, to flaunt their eccentricity, to conspicuously defy the straight lines and cheap construction materials of the conventional buildings that surround them.

And this would not be *The Baffler* if we didn't take this opportunity to swing the sledgehammer at the obvious contradiction here. On the one hand, vibrancy theory treats the artist as a sort of glorified social worker, whose role is to please children and stimulate businessmen and somehow support the community. But the means by which the community is to be supported is always some species of vanguardism or conspicuous creativity. The whole point of the vibrant is to build prosperous communities; and yet prosperous communities, with their Babbitt-like complacency and their straight lines and their conventional building materials, are precisely what we expect artists to flout and defy.

A second problem: the monuments to creativity that we are constructing all across America these days are supposed to be a reaction against the top-down city planning that once caused soulless public housing towers to be built all across the land. How different is it, though, to tear down entire city blocks in order to build, say, a vast performing arts center whose lines aren't strictly rectilinear?

For that matter, why is it any better to pander to the "creative class" than it is to pander to the traditional business class? Yes, one strategy uses "incentives" and tax cuts to get companies to move from one state to another, while the other advises us to emphasize music festivals and art galleries when we make our appeal to that exalted cohort. But neither approach imagines a future arising from something other than government abasing itself before the wealthy.

Let's say that the foundations successfully persuade Akron to enter into a vibrancy arms race with Indianapolis. Let's say both cities blow millions on building cool neighborhoods and encouraging private art galleries. But let's say Akron wins. Somehow its planned vibrancy catches on and, thanks to a particularly piquant theater group, it is able to steal away Indianapolis's businesses. Akron "attracts and retains"; it becomes a creative-class Paris. It leaves Indianapolis an empty hulk on the prairie.

What then? Is the nation better served now that those businesses are located in Akron rather than in Indianapolis? Or would it have been more productive to spend those millions on bridges, railroads, highways—hell, on lobbyists to demand better oversight for banks?

History is more than a conflict between square millionaires and cool millionaires, however, and once you grasp this, you realize that it doesn't take a whole lot of "creativity" to come up with real answers to the big problems. You just need to change the questions slightly. How about, instead of serving some targeted fraction of the master class, we chose to give an entirely different group of Americans what they wanted? Even if those Americans weren't cool? What would that look like?

A while ago I was talking about rural depopulation with an officer of a Kansas farmers' organization; as it happened, he had thought about the problem a great deal. Using arts festivals to make small towns appear "vibrant" was not one of his suggestions, however. Instead, he proposed universal health coverage, since independent farmers find it difficult to get insurance nowadays and are often driven to seek corporate employment by this brute fact of rural life.

Other solutions to the problem of rural depopulation are just as easy to come up with. Outlaw corporate agriculture, which would encourage not only small farms but food diversity as well. Use zoning rules to restrict big-box stores, thereby saving small-town merchants. Make college excellent and affordable, so that graduates aren't forced by the weight of student debt to seek corporate employment. Rewrite NAFTA and take other steps to stop the decline of manufacturing.

For any of this to happen, though, the vibrancy Ponzi scheme first has to bottom out. The bombed-out heartland must learn to resist the urgings of the foundation grandees and fix its gaze instead on the far less beguiling reverie of durable, productive enterprise.

Some places, however, have gone so far down the vibrant brick road that there appears to be nothing to do but patiently await the final Götterdämmerung of the creative class. So hop to it, Akron: convert your very last rubber factory to an artist's loft, bring on the indie-rock festivals and have Santiago Calatrava design you a sweeping new titanium City Hall. Go vibrant—and go for broke.

NOTES

1 This organization used to be some dreadful highbrow outfit called the Fine Arts Fund, until the day in 2010 that it turned on and got hip and figured out that its mission should be "to advance the vitality and vibrancy of Greater Cincinnati by mobilizing the creative energy of the entire community." Behold: ArtsWave was born.

Hoard d'Oeuvres

Art of the 1 percent

RHONDA LIEBERMAN

When you've got the big house, and you're driving a Jaguar, what differentiates you from every asshole dentist in the Valley? Art was a way for Eli to distinguish himself.

—SHELLEY DE ANGELUS, ELI BROAD'S FORMER CURATOR

Art collecting is the most esteemed form of shopping in our culture today.

Thorstein Veblen saw conspicuous consumers as throwbacks—creatures ruled by primitive drives of predation and emulation. Yet the fashion-victimized accumulators of pelf with the historical equivalents of a big house and a Jaguar have always been pillars of society. In the age of landed gentry and indentured servants, Veblen notes, "vulgarly productive occupations" were stigmatized with the "marks of poverty and subjection," while predatory exploits were considered "honorific," a sign of "pecuniary strength."

Our neo-Gilded Age, like Veblen's merely Gilded one, is marked by a predatory culture permitting the feral rich to ravage the productive economy—seizing all the wealth for themselves and creating the most severe levels of income inequality since the onset of the Great Depression. While predators of yore awed rival chieftains with booty, harems, and slaves, today's Masters of the Universe raid companies, fire workers, extract rents, divert huge amounts of capital out of the economy to uglify our world—and hoard the pelts of middle-class pensions, pay, and life pros-

From *The Baffler*, no. 24

pects in their mansions, private kunsthalles, and yachts in the form of blue-chip (and capital-A) Art.

These feats of "pecuniary strength," while socially worthless and detrimental to productivity, are merely "reputable," as Veblen would explain in his trademark academic deadpan. For maximum prestige, the true distinction-seeking Master of the Universe must outdo rival assholes in conspicuous consumption.

And in today's digital economy, you can monitor this primal battle of achieving egos as it unfolds in real time, on computer screens. At auction, you watch incomparable works of art vanish into exchange value: all that's solid truly melts into air. The spectacle of yen, dollars, and euros mounting on the screen climaxes in the money shot: the sale price. Juicy sums are applauded, with murmurs of approval for the really big ones. The cult of wealth cheers as art launders the antisocial spoils of exploitation into status symbols, entrée to classy social circles, and even the solemn mantle of philanthropy. Fabulous.

The handy *Forbes* list of "billionaires with a passion for art" abounds with finance types with hoards worth more than $500 million. There is, for example, Henry Kravis of the storied Kohlberg Kravis Roberts takeover firm that minted billions in worthless junk bond paper during the 1980s. These days, Kravis's honorific predations fund his passion for impressionist and contemporary art, and like many a robber baron from the last Gilded Age, he now has a wing of the Met named after him. Hedge fund manager Steven Cohen breaks spending records for splashy pieces: in 2004 he doled out $8 million for Damien Hirst's *The Physical Impossibility of Death in the Mind of Someone Living*—a thirteen-foot shark encased in formaldehyde. (The beast at the center of the installation reportedly later rotted and had to be replaced.)

As trophies of exploit, Hirst's sharks, carcasses, butterfly wings, and diamond-studded skulls pack the savage punch of carnage itself, while boasting the added values of conspicuous expense and elaborate maintenance requirements. Less than two weeks after Cohen's hedge fund agreed to pay the government $616 million to settle accu-

CHRIS MULLEN

sations of insider trading, this tireless exemplar of the Veblenesque meritorious consumer snagged Picasso's *Le Rêve* for \$155 million (from rival hoarder Steve Wynn). A dream come true, all around, for the apostles of honorific exploit.

Bernie Madoff's prized piece of office art was a four-foot sculpture of a screw that he frequently dusted off himself (he, like Donald Trump and scores of other plutocrats, is a notorious neat freak). A defense lawyer pleaded for the valued object to be photoshopped out of court documents, lest it be prejudicial to members of the jury. When Madoff's Ponzi scheme went bust, J. Ezra Merkin, whose feeder funds supplied Madoff with investors, was no longer Mastering the Universe quite so comfortably. So he sold his stunning batch of Rothkos for $310 million. Whenever I see a Rothko I think of Madoff, and how the afterlife of modern art is now yoked to the pissing matches performed by the big swinging dicks of Wall Street.

Public Offerings

Long practiced in the finer points of destroying companies—and individuals—to loot their assets, finance now plunders public institutions too. Recently bankrupt Detroit is appraising pieces in the Detroit Institute of Arts for possible sale to private creditors. Honorific-minded buzzards are circling the city's treasure. The art is mere booty, of course. The real prey are the peons "tainted," as Veblen would say, with the "unworthiness of productive work." These, after all, were the poor saps whose earnings were gobbled up by the predators' financial instruments.

The Detroit spectacle is clearly a portent of things to come. Strapped public museums can't hope to compete with the big-ticket private art hoarders who send auction prices soaring. Private collectors are now "bulk-buying so many contemporary works," the *Guardian* reports, "that their various mansions are inadequate to house them all. But rather than leave extensive surpluses unseen in storage, they are choosing to share their hoards with the public. As the ultimate status symbol for the super-rich, the private museums even have a new label—'ego-seums.'"

Two top hoarders in particular have provided a tidy snapshot of the taste-in-bulk ethos of our neo-Gilded Age. Education huckster Eli Broad's Los Angeles pile of aestheticized loot nicely showcases the taste-free hoarder's ethos in its fullest robber baron excess. But for now, let's begin at the phony populist end of the spectrum, with the grotesque museum founded by Walmart heiress Alice Walton to "celebrate the American spirit."

"There is no document of civilization which is not at the same time a document of barbarism," wrote Walter Benjamin. In precisely this vein, Walton's new Crystal Bridges museum offers American-made art to strategically cover up the ugly reality Walmart has created. Spanning the colonial era to the present, the exhibition space's fulsome celebration of the American spirit eulogizes the nation of shared confidence and abundance, sustainable mortgages, and worker dignity that Walmart has brutally demolished. The notion that Walton's supremely self-satisfied kunsthalle might serve as a balm, let alone a monument, to the market-battered American spirit is analogous to, say, Genghis Khan inviting survivors of his Mongol hordes to admire an installation of his plunder.

Rebecca Mead's ingenuous *New Yorker* profile of the Walmart heiress glosses over the nasty context of Walton's wealth—which is a bit like writing about the history of the Pyramids without ever mentioning the slaves. Walmart is synonymous with a race to the bottom on every level. The biggest corporation in the world is also corporate welfare royalty: its "refusal to pay a living wage and benefits forces most of its employees onto public benefits like food stamps and Medicaid," writes *ThinkProgress* reporter Aviva Shen. "Each store's workforce consumes as much as $1.75 million in public benefits each year."

Sidestepping Walmart's labor-soaking business model, Mead's profile dotes on the person of Alice Walton, the gentle art appreciator and horse breeder who bids at Christie's auctions by phone while on horseback (a conspicuous leisure multitasker!) and charms the scribe with her low-maintenance toilette, "not," we are assured, "the expensively curated look of a Park Avenue matron":

> When guests visit, she cooks dinner herself, though she has help to do the cleaning up. She speaks with a broad Arkansas accent—Bill Clinton at his most down home—and when she talks about her museum project she avoids loftiness. "One of the great responsibilities that I

> have is to manage my assets wisely, so that they create value," she told me. "I know the price of lettuce. You need to understand price and value. You buy the best lettuce you can at the best price you can."

Like Marie Antoinette playing dairymaid at her vanity farm at Versailles, Walton deploys a beguiling set of down-home gestures to downplay any whiff of plutocratic privilege—a performance that is itself, by most measures, the ultimate display of plutocratic privilege. But Mead is duly impressed, and takes Walton's words at face value. Walton's frugality, we are told, (whether buying lettuce or art) reflects a responsibility to "create value"—and certainly not the malignant greed with which Walmart notoriously squeezes every last cent from its workers and suppliers. Amy Cappellazzo, Christie's auction honcho, weighs in to rave about the billionaire's "incredible" "lemonade and homemade cookies."

Don Bacigalupi, Walton's unctuous chief curator, supplies a mission statement that comes straight out of a Ford truck commercial: "We invite all to celebrate the American spirit in a setting that unites the power of art and the beauty of landscape." He dismisses critics of his employer's museum—on behalf of all the unwashed people now "living without art" in Arkansas whom the great patroness's plan of uplift must inevitably help.

Smells Like Art Spirit

As Walmart uglifies the country with big box stores, beggars communities with outsourced products and low-wage jobs without prospect of advancement, and thrives on surplus misery, Arkansas's down-home Marie Antoinette says, in so many words, *Let them eat art*. Employing an altogether apt but strangely unselfconscious historical analogy—a journalistic cry for help, perhaps?—Mead compares Walton to robber baron Henry Clay Frick, who also founded a "jewel box" of a museum. But *The New Yorker* scribe tactfully neglects to note that Frick, too, was a notorious union-buster, one who choreographed the cold-blooded murder of strikers in labor trouble spots like Ludlow, Colorado, and Homestead, Pennsylvania. Frick, like his successors on today's art scene, was eager to cleanse his name of brutal associations, and the most efficacious such strategy was to pile up canvases depicting a bygone age of mystic communal harmony and reflexive social deference. And in Mead's gee-whiz telling, this core collecting stratagem has barely changed since Frick's late-nineteenth-century heyday—except that instead of bagging Vermeers and Constables depicting pastoral Old World calm, Walton favors landscape-heavy Americana:

> Walton's ambition to found a major museum of American art first came to public attention in the spring of 2005, when she paid the New York Public Library a reported thirty-five million dollars for "Kindred Spirits," a masterpiece of the Hudson River School, by Asher B. Durand. The library's decision to deaccession the work was controversial. Durand's painting commemorates the friendship between Thomas Cole, the landscape painter, and William Cullen Bryant, the nature poet, depicting them standing on a rocky promontory that overlooks an idealized Catskills vista.

The bagging of this piece from a public library is the ultimate neo-Gilded Age exploit: turning the commons into a private asset. The social bond between the poet and painter—along with their viewpoint—is poached by a predator who has amassed her fortune by despoiling the very sort of rural landscape portrayed in *Kindred Spirits*. By the strange alchemy of the cult of wealth, the honorific soul who displays these trophies expects to be identified with them. Yet the spirit of acquisition here is anything but kindred to the subject matter of the canvas: Alice Walton's prized picture idealizes everything Walmart is not.

Prompted by that tableau, Mead asks Walton for her own definition of the American spirit. The reply is a veritable rampage of cognitive dissonance: "It is the ability to be the best you can be, and to take the opportunity that we have in this country to grow and learn and be the very best we can, and to help other people," explains a woman whose family wealth is equivalent to the wealth of the bottom 40 percent of Americans combined.

"My parents were both very patriotic," the folksy billionaire relates to her *New Yorker* stenographer, "and I just would never have considered collecting anything but American art." (Here, too, an ugly irony lurks just outside of *The New Yorker*'s portrait frame: Walmart "has been the vanguard of outsourcing U.S. manufacturing to China—at times some 10 percent of the U.S. trade deficit with China comes from Walmart alone," notes global culture site *Blouin Artinfo*.)

The Corporate Muse

Crystal Bridges is a sleek "starchitect"-designed facility—two armadillo-like structures connected by galleries around a reflecting pool—where visitors can admire the apparently bottomless self-regard of a retail colossus made fat on a global low-wage, nonunion labor force.

The museum's collection often supplies an unwitting critique of the whole enterprise's animating, uh, spirit. For instance, Norman Rockwell's *Rosie the Riveter*, blurbed by Crystal Bridges as "a transcendent symbol" of the "capabilities, strength, and determination" of American women, celebrates the female workforce mobilized during the Second World War—another mind-bending exercise in historical revision on the part of a corporation that in 2010 paid out $11.7 million in back wages and damages to women in Kentucky. A set of subsequent, much larger class action lawsuits alleging systematic gender discrimination at the company was struck down by the U.S. Supreme Court on the grounds that 1.5 million Walmart women are too large and diverse a group to be considered a class.

George Bellows's *The Studio*, which shows Bellows surrounded by family, depicts the kind of meaningful work, fully integrated with domestic life, that Walmart has disrupted and dehumanized into drudgery. The jazzy abstraction of Stuart Davis—whose goal, according to some art historians, was to "reconcile abstract art with Marxism and modern industrial society"—gruesomely serves, in this Bentonville terminus of maldistributed industrial prosperity, as the death mask of the artist's hopes.

Crystal Bridges' grotesque recontextualization of these works perversely invites the art appreciator to thank Walmart for "celebrating" everything it has exploited and destroyed—as if by enjoying these works you condone the Waltons' greed. Fairfield Porter's lyrical interiors, and even Lynda Benglis's blobs, are unwitting fronts for the corporate ogre.

"So how do people associated with this museum rationalize the exploitation that built it?" asks *Bloomberg* columnist Jeffrey Goldberg. The answer:

> Incredibly, by denying a connection to Wal-Mart.
>
> The executive director of Crystal Bridges, Don Bacigalupi, argues that the museum has virtually nothing to do with the corporate behemoth just down the road. Apart from a $20 million gift from Wal-Mart that underwrites free admission, Bacigalupi said, the money that funds the museum comes from an entirely different entity, the Walton Family Foundation.
>
> "Conflating a private individual and a private foundation with a corporation is a little misleading," Bacigalupi told me.

Goldberg nails it: "Bacigalupi seems like a bright man, so he must know that this statement is itself a little misleading. The Waltons are rich because they own about half of Wal-Mart. Wal-Mart has made them rich in part because it pays its workers as little as possible."

The name Crystal Bridges, indeed, evokes a range of American associations, be they aspirational or sadly indicative of the way we live now: it conjures the joint qualities of clarity and nostalgia—a cheesy country singer's rehab retreat, or perhaps something closer to a Scientology center. In physical terms, the museum most closely resembles the latter, with a ground plan and facade that suggest a newly landed spaceship in the Arkansas hills. Like the fever dreams of a Plutocrat Pollyanna, Walton's raptures about the American spirit deny the mayhem that the corporate cult casually externalizes into the public sphere. Its hoard of Americana flaunts the scalps of a culture conquered by "pro-business" depravity. A celebration of the American spirit, indeed.

Teaching to the Test of Time

The true collector is in the grip not of what is collected but of collecting.

—SUSAN SONTAG, *THE VOLCANO LOVER*

Don your pith helmet and bullshit waders and follow me, gentle readers, into the jungle of the feral rich—a.k.a. downtown Los Angeles, where Eli Broad, the biggest art-accumulating billionaire, will soon open his own robber-baron-style museum. The eponymous facility—no Oz-like reveries of transparent suspension structures for this mogul—will house Eli and Edythe Broad's two-thousand-piece collection. It will also, of course, double as an agitprop advertisement for its namesake's philanthropic career as one of the nation's leading privatizers of public education.

The so-called school reform agenda of the Broad Foundation, like the Walton family fortune, exemplifies the race to the bottom for everyone except the "honorific exploiters." Eli Broad, one of the richest art philanthropists in America (worth $6.9 billion as estimated by the "*Forbes* wealth team"; go wealth!), has been described as a "venture philanthropist . . . who wants to see results." And the results he likes best are naturally of the quid pro quo variety. "Eli's middle name is 'Strings Attached,'" *Los Angeles Times* art critic Christopher Knight told Morley Safer in a *60 Minutes* profile of the accountant turned art accumulator.

The strings attached to Broad's own fortune, unsurprisingly, are deeply entwined with the worst elements of the 2008 meltdown; one of his companies, SunAmerica, was sold to AIG in 1999. As *Artnet* noted after the *60 Minutes* profile aired, Broad's $2 billion philanthropic empire sprang from the early-aughts feeding frenzy in "cheap housing and insurance . . . two vast industries that soak the lower and middle classes at their most vulnerable." Thus engorged, the Broad Foundation (with its allies the Gates Foundation and, yes, the Walton Family Foundation) dabbles in social engineering and transfers public resources into private coffers by replacing public schools with market-based charters. The Broad Foundation, in short, is underwriting an ever-spreading fiefdom of teach-to-the-test mills that squelch the creative potential of the non-rich and hollow out the teaching profession into micro-managed, low-paid dronehood.

But lo, the patrician hand of art washes all these contradictions away. The hard-hitting investigative producers of *60 Minutes*, who reverently focused on Broad's $1.6 billion art collection, declared: "There is no one quite so civic minded in America."

In one exchange during the segment, Morley Safer eyes a sculpture dubiously—a ramshackle man supported by the wall:

> BROAD: "Well, it's Tom Friedman—who's quite an accomplished artist, I'm told."
> SAFER: "I'm told?" *[His reporterly skepticism at last roused by the market for contemporary art, if not by the education reform racket.]*
> BROAD: "You know, some of these artists, I've gotta learn more about."

Wielding the purse-power to make or break careers, this guy is one of the most influential people in the art world. He knows as much about art as he does about education—but that hasn't stopped the billionaire from imposing his world-conquering "vision" on both spheres of influence. The experts and practitioners who seek his funds (curators, dealers, art advisers, artists—and even more alarmingly, his legion of school reform advocates) are inclined to coddle him, not to question him.

Hard and Fast

It wasn't art that initially drew the high-flying former accountant to collecting. He got hooked when he discovered art accumulation "brought entrée to a different kind of social life," Connie Bruck tells us in her fascinating and (for a change) aptly skeptical *New Yorker* profile "The Art of the Billionaire: How Eli Broad Took Over Los Angeles." "Initially, Broad found a lot of contemporary art ridiculous," Bruck writes, and then quotes Broad's former curator: "But Eli is a quick learner. . . . Eli would ask everybody who was informed what their opinion was and put together his world view based on that. That's what a good C.E.O. does."

His venture philanthropy in L.A. uses his vast hoard of art and money to exploit his influence over public institutions for his own private benefit. As Bruck lays out Broad's take-no-prisoners approach to the art market, it soon becomes apparent that Broad is pursuing much the same plan of business dominance that has propelled a Mark Zuckerberg or a Jeff Bezos to the front ranks of moguldom: putting his name on as much as possible, while he drives hard bargains with rivals and the public sector, hires star architects, and presses them to cut corners. ("When you've got one eight-hundred-pound gorilla in the room, you're scared to death . . . nobody wants to alienate him," Christopher Knight told Morley Safer.)

A museum trustee likened Broad's antics on the board of Los Angeles's Museum of Contemporary Art in 2008 to "an attempted hostile takeover." After drama with an alphabet soup of classy institutions, including LACMA, MCAM, MOCA, UCLA, and even the Geffen and the Hammer, the Broad Collection, the great man's ego-museum, will open in 2015 to anchor a development project that will transform the Grand Avenue area, Broad hopes, into downtown L.A.'s Champs-Elysées. Jeffrey Deitch, who worked with Broad as a dealer and later as the ill-fated director of MOCA, is politic: "Eli is very conscious of value—he does not overpay." One example of Broad's ingenuity: he paid $7.7. million for the land where his ego-seum is sited—and because of a deal he struck with a city agency, he will receive a rebate on his construction costs that may exceed $10 million. As Bruck sums up: "In art as in business Eli found ingenious ways to pay less."

"And, yes, he admits that it's easier for him to analyze the price-per-square-foot of a museum building than to interpret a painting inside," goes a *Los Angeles Times* puff piece on the collector at home. "My first career was in public accounting," Broad explains. "So if I look at a spreadsheet I understand it quickly. Numbers are hard and fast."

Hoarding art is not only a power move for the predatory philanthropist; it's a rewarding hobby. "Collecting for me isn't just about buying objects," Broad enthuses. "It's an educational process, and I think it's made me a better person. I'd be bored to death if I spent all my time with other businesspeople, bankers, and lawyers."

Broad's favorite artist is often trotted out in his profiles: the irrepressible maker of market-glorified kitsch Jeff Koons. Koons's deluxe banal objects—*Michael Jackson and Bubbles*, *Rabbit*, *Balloon Dog*—are go-to status badges for the biggest spenders. The Broads own thirty-three Koonses. Glorifying banality and conspicuous consumption, the pieces require an absurd level of maintenance, and a "commitment" from the collector, as Koons the master-marketer phrases it. "Free of the vulgar taint of productive activity," as Veblen would say, the artist, an ex-Wall Street broker himself, speaks Broad's language of CEO micromanagement, overseeing more than eighty in-house employees in a relentless quest for aesthetic efficiency. "My responsibility," Koons has said, "is to educate people on what I'm looking for—every moment of the day."

Koons's work and sensibility have become so infused with titan-pleasing shibboleths that the Koons brand is all but identical with the billionaire id. Whether he's free-associating about "accepting yourself" and other self-help platitudes, comparing his various luxe-kitsch pieces to Old Masters, or making vague remarks about the sexual aspects and anthropomorphism of appliances, Koons's unflappable, peculiar Tony-Robbins-meets-art-CEO shtick, all delivered in the soothing, condescending tones of a nurse in a mental ward, is clearly a formula that works on billionaires. Demarcating a comfort zone of guilt-free privilege for the artist's collector client base, the Koons oeuvre creates the overarching impression that all aesthetic value is vaguely farcical and ever contingent, and that ambitious and worthy social virtues can be ascribed to whatever you're peddling with just the right verbal formulation. These are all also defining traits of the fortunes on which Koons collections are founded: the work and the patron's worldview enjoy a perfect state of mutual self-regard. Here, in short, is a sentimental education that beguiles even the maniacal, test-based control freak Eli Broad.

Homo Ludens; or, the High-End Hoarder Shopping Club

Art collecting, like every form of shopping, is a sport that steeps our Masters of the Universe in the thrill of the hunt. Whether at auction or at art fairs, deep-pocketed collectors flock to the buzz of the purchase—a sacred destination "where you can spend enormous amounts of money quickly and people will know," as a veteran observer astutely notes.

Here is how that great Anglophone tip sheet of the investor class, *The Economist*, describes the moguls-at-play spirit of one of the best-known shows:

> Art Basel, a Swiss art fair that is a regular stop for many collectors in June, is certainly about having fun.... The sociability of the fair contributes to the aversion that collectors have to going home empty-handed. Jay Smith, an investment adviser ... and an important donor of art to museums, admits: "When I don't buy anything, the fair feels dull. Buying makes you feel connected to what is going on."

In dissecting the surplus spiritual value attached to the art-buying ritual, *The Economist* channels Veblen minus his irony:

> Buying art doesn't just offer a sense of community, it engenders feelings of victory, cultural superiority and social distinction. Some say that it even fills a spiritual void. The term most commonly used by collectors, however, is that buying art gives them a "high." ... Buying expensive art is very competitive, which for a successful purchaser adds to the sense of conquest at acquisition.

For the High-End Hoarder Shopping Club, art fairs are a way to best rival consumers in a prestigious public venue—to achieve, in Veblen's parlance, "invidious distinction." Unloosed before the legitimizing canons of art, the instinct of pecuniary emulation runs amok: "Some collectors always want what other collectors want," explains Andrew Kreps, a New York dealer. By cultivating an inflated star system of artists like luxury brands, the art market enables the herd mode—and in this fashion, acquisitive types not sufficiently moved by connoisseurship can easily learn to covet brand names. In the *New York Observer*, an art fair veteran clues in a novice thusly:

"The key is everybody wants what everyone else wants."
"Which is?"
"That's part of the game, figuring out what everyone else wants."

Competitive buyers needn't trust their own eye or taste; they can hire personal shoppers, a.k.a. art advisers, to run around the fairs to scout out art for them, snapping photos to document the investment's appeal. Like fashion consultants, they tell clients what's trending or hot, what will best suit their art-user needs and budget. If this all sounds disconnected from actually experiencing art, it's because all the excess wealth sucked into the global art markets has fatally blurred the line between collecting and luxury retail.

The art fair is thriving in recent years as a shopping spectacle where the meritorious consumers (collectors) are the VIPs, while mere artists are accorded the welcome that, say, truffle pigs would get in a four-star restaurant. A mid-career artist at a respectable gallery said his dealer could hardly bother to acknowledge him at Frieze London, the luxe art fair—the dealer only wanted to talk to the collectors. Another artist marveled at the dubious skill set of her own name-brand dealer: "I don't even think he understands art—he's just good at making rich people feel comfortable buying. He's not too intellectual or weird." At this point, she gestures toward her head, and adds, apropos of him, "There's nothing in there." Art fairs now teem with glitzy side events, and ooze luxury sponsors and celebrities. It's no wonder, then, that they are starting to eclipse galleries as major showcases for work.

Tom Wolfe, our great journalistic connoisseur of status anxiety, has giddily portrayed the frenzy that ensues at the opening of Art Basel Miami. In *Back to Blood*, entitled consumers anxious to make the scene first (when it's most prestigious to be seen inside) are motored by fear of missing out; the collectors strain toward the art like maggots swarming on a carcass.

The whole spectacle represents a delicate balancing act of social hierarchy: art fair hype now threatens the snob appeal the events possess for the collecting class. Prominent and relentlessly self-promoting collector Adam Lindemann complains that buzz has dinged the specialness that formerly enveloped art fairs as super-exclusive shopping clubs for the rich. A native informant of entitled consumer petulance, Lindemann published a hissy fit in the *New York Observer* in 2011 demanding that the fairs do more to distinguish real "meritorious consumers" from looky-loos. "First and foremost," he wrote, "art fairs should be for collectors only; if you're not coming to buy art, get the hell out." What's more, Lindemann threatened to boycott Miami Basel unless the riffraff were expelled:

> Occupy Art Basel Miami Beach is a new movement designed to correct the ills of global art fairdom once and for all, and to send the dealers, the artists and especially the art-fair companies our message of protest: hell no, we won't go! ... We don't want to see one gawker, two socialites and three wannabes for every collector in the room. ... Occupy Art Basel Miami starts now, so, this year, join me in boycotting the damn thing. Let's flex our muscles. It's our collecting dollars fueling this perverse tchotchke bazaar on steroids, and if these people don't fix their fair, next year we'll riot.

After all that, Lindemann showed up anyway. And he needn't have panicked. The art market, like the rest of society, has already made itself over to pamper the 1 percent. The big box-ification of art galleries, and a carefully constructed system of art stars (monitored and enabled by gallerists, auction houses, curators, and personal art shoppers) appeals to the fashion victim in the honorific predator who wants a recognizable luxury brand.

"In the big box model," William Powhida writes, "every show has to sell well to cover the staggering operating costs of these museum-like operations from staffing to producing publications that confirm the value of the artists' work. In this model we face a kind of homogenization of taste oriented toward the 1% who can afford the attendant high prices like a $100k Dan Colen gum painting. Whether or not you like what Gagosian or Zwirner show is almost irrelevant to the situation."

In other words, the excess wealth thrown around by the predators has hollowed out the middle of the market. Mid-range collectors and artists are marginalized, starved of resources and support, in a shift that tightly parallels the post-Keynesian American economy in general; in both cases, the existing social contract has been reconfigured to serve the hoarding instincts of the lords of the market as they compete with rival predators for big-ticket trophies and drive prices out of all proportion. Koons, Hirst, and Richter are marketed like Gucci, Prada, and Chanel. Signature styles "immediately identifiable" as a brand-name artist's creations make "them easy status symbols," as the *Wall Street Journal* reported in 2012: "San Francisco dealer Anthony Meier says, 'Collectors want an iconic work in a format that everyone recognizes. Monkey see, monkey do.'"

"The great dealers used to be small," James Mayor, the Mayor Gallery's namesake owner, told an audience at London's Institute of Contemporary Art in 2013. "Now all the big galleries don't have time for the artist unless they're making millions."

As the art world adapts to the neo-Gilded Age by recasting itself as luxury retail, the power of the purse has effectively vanquished the last vestiges of the old art world: criticism, and the aesthetic judgment that informs it.

Instead, deluxe bean counters coddled by their courtiers simply want what other honorific predators have always wanted—to distinguish themselves from the other assholes. As to what their gladiatorial shopping rivalries mean for the rest of our common world, well, the last word properly belongs to Veblen. "The elimination from our surroundings of the pecuniarily unfit," he observes, "results in a more or less thorough elimination of that considerable range of elements of beauty which do not happen to conform to the pecuniary requirement." Buyer, beware.

A Cottage for Sale

The high price of sentimentality

A. S. HAMRAH

Our little dream castle
With every dream gone . . .

The Christmas Cottage, a biopic about the artist Thomas Kinkade, famous for the quaint-scary-ugly paintings he sells in shopping malls, is a cinematic portrait of the multimillionaire artist as a young man. Kinkade coproduced the movie, which went straight to DVD when it came out in 2008. In a pivotal scene, the budding "Painter of Light," home from college, gathers with his mother and younger brother on Christmas morning.

It's the mid-seventies in Placerville, California, a small town in the foothills of the Sierra Nevada. The Kinkades are a poor family living in a rundown house. Kinkade's mother, divorced from his father, has lost her job, and because she is generous to other people in the town—"she loaned people money, she gave people things"—and because she refuses assistance from anyone else, the Kinkades are about to lose what they call "the cottage." The bank is foreclosing; they've got only a few days left to pay.

Young Thom—the grown-up artist spells the short version of his name that way—and his brother have been working hard to raise money for their mother's overdue mortgage payment, but they haven't put together enough cash. They can't save the house, so understandably they don't have store-bought Christmas gifts to exchange. Instead, Thom (Jared Padalecki, from *Gilmore Girls*) presents his mother (Marcia Gay

From *The Baffler*, no. 18

Harden) with a picture of their house he's drawn himself, so she'll always have something by which to remember what they're about to lose.

At that moment, in bursts the rest of the film's cast, made up of character actors from old TV shows—Charlotte Rae from *The Facts of Life*, the guy who played Bull on *Night Court*. Are they there to save the day and end the film the way *It's a Wonderful Life* ends? Not exactly. They don't come bearing money to make things right with the bank the way the townspeople do in Capra's film. They arrive carrying tools and cans of paint. If the Kinkade cottage can't be saved for the Kinkades, they figure they can at least fix it up so it can be sold for more money than it would have if it remained broken down and leaky. They arrive in the nick of time not to save Maryanne Kinkade but to help her flip her house, and possibly to make sure its appearance doesn't drive down their own property values. They quickly get to work, and in a jiffy the cottage looks brand new.

But Maryanne is still stuck in the same sinking boat—it just looks nicer. That afternoon, true economic salvation arrives in the form of Peter O'Toole, decrepit but still more powerful than a troupe of yesterday's sitcom stars. The former Lawrence of Arabia, playing an old, dying painter who inhabits the barn next door, drags himself across the snowy wastes of the Kinkades' yard carrying an unknown masterpiece. At Christmas dinner, the painter, a renowned artist who has retired to Placerville, unveils what will be his last work on canvas. "You will sell it!" he thunders. "It should bring you enough to keep this cottage *forever*!"

And it does. The Kinkades save their house. The painting, the film's narration tells us, "is now owned by a museum in New York." Never mind that that isn't true—on the DVD commentary track Kinkade says he doesn't know the whereabouts of the painting that saved his childhood home. What's important is that in Thomas Kinkade's originating myth, two things happen. First, he substitutes a picture he's drawn of a house for the thing itself, giving the representation to his mother to replace the real thing; second, it is not community that saves the house, but the sale of a painting, which is worth much more. Young Thom learns a lesson the film pretends it isn't teaching. Community only goes so far; art is money in the bank.

Whoever has no house now, will never build one.

—RAINER MARIA RILKE, "AUTUMN DAY"

The day before I saw *The Christmas Cottage*, I saw Charlie Kaufman's film *Synecdoche, New York*, which begins with that line of Rilke's heard over a radio. The two films have a lot in common. Both are about painting, theater, old age, and death; both are about real estate. In *The Christmas Cottage*, young Thom paints a mural of Placerville in the town square while his mother rehearses a Christmas pageant at her church; in *Synecdoche, New York*, a theater director rehearses a play after his wife, a painter of miniatures, deserts him. *The Christmas Cottage* is a meta-movie like *Synecdoche, New York*—its alternate title could be *Being Thomas Kinkade*—but it's a meta-movie for God-fearing grandparents. It ends with Kinkade himself daubing a fleck of yellow on a painting of the cottage whose story we have just seen, the kind of painting Kinkade sells to old people in his mall stores.

Of the themes the two films share, it's real estate that seals the Kinkade-Kaufman connection. In fact, real estate links *Synecdoche, New York* to Thomas Kinkade's work in general, not just to *The Christmas Cottage*. In Kaufman's film, one character buys and lives out her life in a house that is always on fire. It's even on fire the first time a real estate agent shows it to her. The fire isn't explained; it's just part of the package. We have to accept it, just as we have to accept that the violent orange glow that emanates from the interior of nearly every house in a Kinkade painting merely indicates that the house is warm and inviting, not burning to the ground.

The appearance Kinkade houses have of being on fire is something that glares from his paintings. It's unsettling, but it's something people who like Kinkade paintings don't notice or don't mind.

Others recoil. Joan Didion mentions Kinkade in *Where I Was*

From, her memoir of California. A Kinkade painting, she writes,

> was typically rendered in slightly surreal pastels. It typically featured a cottage or a house of such insistent coziness as to seem actually sinister, suggestive of a trap designed to attract Hansel and Gretel. Every window was lit, to lurid effect, as if the interior of the structure might be on fire.

It's a passage that has become permanently associated with Kinkade; it's included in his Wikipedia write-up. On *The Christmas Cottage*'s commentary track, the artist tells a story he'd probably rather have people recall when they look at his work. He says that as the son of a single mother who worked late, he often came home to a house that was dark and cold, especially in winter. The "Kinkade glow" represents what he wished was there instead. He tells the story more than once, which raises a question or two: Didn't he maybe just want to burn the place down? Is his art really a form of arson?

The way Kinkade sells his paintings certainly bespeaks a desire to make people pay. At a time when massive numbers of homes are going into foreclosure all over the country, Kinkade's sales method seems designed to drive buyers further into debt. A big sign in the Kinkade gallery in Placerville promises Wells Fargo financing—twelve months interest-free—$0 down—fifteen-minute approval.

Kinkade's sales system is confusing. It includes licensed gallery stores, their websites, his own website, and other venues as well. As I write this, Kinkade's main website is offering "Sizzling Summer Deals—Up to 70 Percent Off!" Does that indicate a new understanding of the plight of the people he calls "my collectors," or is it a Kinkadian fire sale intended to unload stock that isn't moving in a bad economy?

When I visit the Placerville showroom, exalted in the system because it's his "Hometown Gallery," I notice a painting called *Sunday Outing* selling for $150,000. Kinkade's cottage paintings don't usually have people in them, but this one does. The family in it looks like they're fleeing a burning house. The price is written on the wall-tag in ballpoint pen over another price that has been covered with Wite-

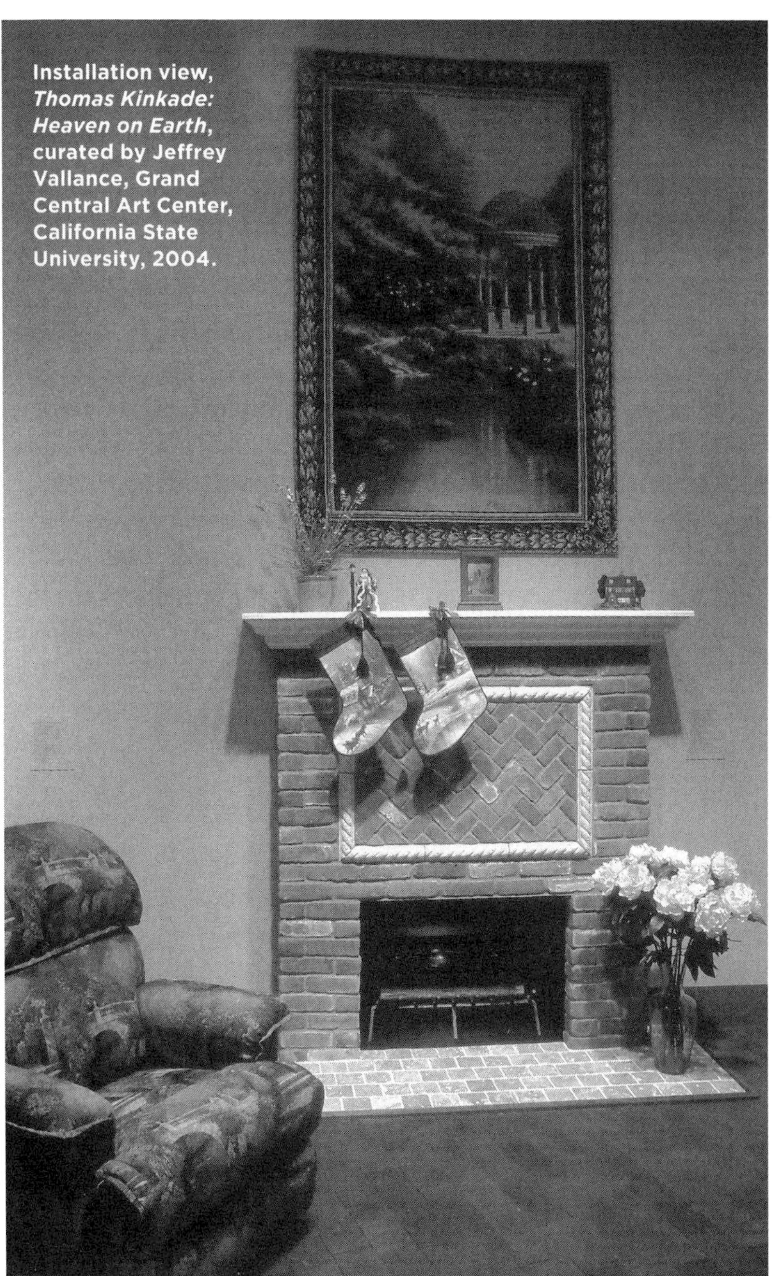

Installation view, *Thomas Kinkade: Heaven on Earth*, curated by Jeffrey Vallance, Grand Central Art Center, California State University, 2004.

M.O. QUINN

Out. I ask the saleslady working in the gallery if they've lowered the price of *Sunday Outing*, which is not one of the touched-up reproductions Kinkade is known for, but an original signed with "John 3:16" next to Kinkade's Norman-Rockwell-like signature. "Uh, no," she replies, with just a hint of the scorn you expect in an art gallery. "We actually raised it."

Why not? Kinkade can afford to dream. The one uncheckable factoid everything written on him can't fail to include is that supposedly one in twenty American homes has a Kinkade hanging in it. "What the heck, I'm a romantic," he says on the *Christmas Cottage* commentary track, explaining that he paints "an art that comforts your heart and reminds you of foundational things, a very sentimental kind of art." When Oscar Wilde wrote that "a sentimentalist is simply one who desires to have the luxury of an emotion without paying for it," he didn't know that someday an American painter would find a way to make sentimentalists pay for it in monthly installments.

The plate-glass display window of the Kinkade gallery on Main Street in Placerville features a big painting called *NASCAR Thunder*. The painting is detailed and complicated, featuring a termite-like mound of NASCAR fans filling stands that recede into the horizon. Jets and a blimp fly in formation overhead as fireworks explode in the sky. This painting is in Kinkade's lucrative-commission style, not in the gemütlich-unheimlich style of his cottage paintings. It's a vast fictional panorama that uses items from reality to gauze up a location of idealized American spectacle that never was and won't ever be. Kinkade moves further into the realm of Hansel and Gretel fantasy with his series of Disney commissions, one of which is called *Snow White Discovers the Cottage*.

What do these paintings mean in Placerville, a town that has seen better days as recently as 1852, the year the California Gold Rush ended? Outside the gallery, stores sell funny postcards of shacks reading "For Sale: California Home Bargain—Only $999,950.00." Postcards like that predate the mortgage crisis; out-of-whack real estate prices have long been a subject for humor at the funny-postcard level of American culture, and so have postcards of dilapidated shacks;

you can find them in every state. They keep disaster and unaffordability at arm's length. In Placerville these postcards remind me that the houses Kinkade paints were inspired by ones he saw in this town growing up, and that in a sixteen-point manifesto Kinkade wrote for the crew of *The Christmas Cottage* that was leaked to *Vanity Fair*, he advised the filmmakers to "favor shots that feature older buildings, ramshackle, careworn structures," to avoid filming "shopping centers and contemporary storefronts" like the kind in which his paintings are sold, and to "avoid anything that is shiny." In the windows of a nearby real estate agency, half the fliers note the houses for sale are "Bank Owned!!" Half the storefronts on Main Street are for rent. None of them is shiny.

The Christmas Cottage was not shot in Placerville (because of "logistics," says Kinkade on the DVD commentary track). According to the film's credits, it was shot in British Columbia, Canada, "in the Historical City of Fort Langley." A thorough search of Placerville's walls and hoardings turns up no mural of the town like the one young Kinkade paints in *The Christmas Cottage*. The woman who runs the Placerville Historical Museum tells me the mural does not exist and never existed. The closest thing, she says, is the painting he gave to the town's library. She hands me a xeroxed copy of a skeptical article about Kinkade from a 2002 issue of *Newsweek* she saves for tourists who inquire about the artist. "Given that art's value is predicated on scarcity, how can anyone create an appreciating market for mass-produced 'limited editions'?" the article asks, before letting readers know that Kinkade's factory "churns out 10,000 pieces a month, each signed by a 'DNA pen' containing drops of Kinkade's blood."

The closest things to outdoor murals in Placerville are the crude mountain-snow and duck-pond scenes painted on the boarded-up windows of a Main Street building that once housed a bar and a tae kwon do school. Both are out of business, and the building is falling down. Across the street, an Original Mel's Diner, filled with blown-up photos from *American Graffiti* printed with George Lucas's autograph, offers a competing, more specific nostalgia to the nebulous kind that informs Kinkade's cottage paintings. I have lunch there, wondering if I should order cottage cheese.

> *And the people lived in marvels of art—and ate and drank out of masterpieces—for there was nothing else to eat and to drink out of, and no bad building to live in; no article of daily life, of luxury, or of necessity, that had not been handed down from the design of the master, and made by his workmen.*
>
> —JAMES MCNEILL WHISTLER, "THE TEN O'CLOCK LECTURE"

The Thomas Kinkade Company has licensing agreements with more than fifty companies to produce various Kinkade-branded items. These include everything from books, clocks, night-lights, calendars, and candle holders to more elaborate-sounding artifacts: live flower arrangements, glow-in-the-dark puzzles, fuzzy posters, and "coasters made out of natural sandstone and/or dolomite/gypsum." You can get a Kinkade-branded checkbook cover and a book of Kinkade-branded personal bank checks and use them to pay for his paintings, or maybe for the mortgage on your house in the Kinkade-inspired Village at Hiddenbrooke, a gated community within a gated community in Vallejo, California.

When you look at Hiddenbrooke on a map, it hovers to the northeast of Vallejo like a stray kidney, an errant jellyfish, or a comic-strip thought bubble. The day I drove to the Kinkade village the gates were stuck open: the roads were being repaved, and the pavers had broken the gate. When the Village at Hiddenbrooke opened in 2001 and the houses there were selling for about $400,000, it got a lot of press, much of it sarcastic and disappointed because the development wasn't sufficiently Kinkadian and horrible.

While the houses superficially resemble those in Kinkade's paintings, they are not the fantasias you would expect. They are on small lots, each lot about a tenth of an acre. They stand close to each other, huddled under brown hills, not nestled alone in forests or by the seashore. The skies in Vallejo are blue and hot, not dramatic and variable like the skies in Kinkade's paintings. The houses feature details taken from Kinkade's work—turrets and dormers and exposed stonework—but they don't differ substantially from the other houses in Hiddenbrooke, except that many of those are bigger, built in a faux-Craftsman style on bigger lots, and set in the hills to give them a bird's-eye view of the development's golf course and the Kinkade village below.

In the early afternoon on the summer weekday I chose to visit, the Village at Hiddenbrooke has a deserted, eerie feel, like the set of a David Lynch film. It is quiet as I walk past the gate, save for the yapping of a small dog coming from inside one of the houses on one of the Village's seven little streets. I walk down the middle of these streets; no cars come by. None is parked by the curb or in a driveway, either. Being there is like being in a Children's Fairyland version of *The Omega Man*. The place is as depopulated as one of Kinkade's cottage paintings.

After wandering around for a while, I come to a cul-de-sac and meet a lone man standing in front of his house with a poodle. He identifies himself as Mr. Jensen. He moved to the Village at Hiddenbrooke with his wife when the development opened, he says, because she's a Kinkade fan. They have some Kinkades they've put on their walls. He tells me most of the people here decorate with Kinkades.

There were two foreclosures in the Village and two short sales that Mr. Jensen knew of. One Village short sale I investigated was for a four-bedroom, three-and-a-half-bath model the owners bought in 2005 for $675,000 and were selling at the insistence of the bank for $333,000. I ask Mr. Jensen about the school featured on the map of Hiddenbrooke that I hadn't been able to find as I drove around. The school was never built, he tells me, because the residents were afraid the city would force it to take local children from Vallejo. Hiddenbrooke residents do not want locals "coming over the hill," Mr. Jensen explains. "Ninety-five percent of the kids here go to private school, anyway," he says. "We don't need a school." What's wrong with locals coming over the hill? I ask. The explanation Mr. Jensen offers doesn't exactly answer the question, but he makes his meaning clear: "Vallejo is a dump."

Some sympathy was wasted on the house,
A good old-timer dating back along;
But a house isn't sentient; the house
Didn't feel anything. And if it did,
Why not regard it as a sacrifice,
And an old-fashioned sacrifice by fire,
Instead of a new-fashioned one at auction?

—ROBERT FROST, "THE STAR-SPLITTER"

Every weekday the city of Vallejo holds three auctions of foreclosed houses on the steps of the city hall. For as little as $40,000, investors and developers buy up houses that sold for as much as $400,000 four years ago. They often pay in cash. Whatever doesn't sell goes back to the bank. One morning while I watched the auctions, a twitchy, skinny teenager in denim boardshorts and a goatee tried to sell me "smoke."

The City of Vallejo is bankrupt. It went bankrupt in May 2008, the first city in California to declare bankruptcy since the economic downturn and only the second in the state's history. Inside city hall, an out-of-work contractor tells me "there's nothing. There's no new houses starting." He comes to the Planning Division once a week to check anyway. When he asks me what I'm doing there, another out-of-work contractor overhears me tell him I'm looking into foreclosed houses in the area. Without saying much he hands me the card of a loss-mitigation and loan-modification specialist named Vienna Train Bertolano.

I give her a call, and we meet the next day. We meet in a Mexican restaurant Bertolano co-owns. In addition to her work as a loan specialist and restaurateur, she also works as a legal assistant for a bankruptcy lawyer. Bertolano, who tells me to call her Vienna, is a petite Filipina in her mid-fifties with a slight accent. "Vallejo," she tells me, "was going to be the new Silicon Valley. It was a thriving market. People could buy investment homes here and see them go up 30 percent right away. When the bubble burst in late '06, middle- and lower-income buyers who could barely afford $1,500 a month in rent were stuck with $350,000 homes they'd bought with no money down. In 2005 there were never houses here for less than $300,000. Now there are over two thousand houses selling in Solano County for less than $100,000, many of them for around $35,000. The only people buying them are investors. And it's going to get a lot worse. It's going to be bleak."

I ask her about Hiddenbrooke. "Thirty to forty percent of homes in Hiddenbrooke have been foreclosed or short-sold," she says. "People were buying those places three or four years ago for around $750,000. Those people are out of those houses. Agents are trying to sell them for $350,000. Maybe they can get $250,000."

In Vienna's office we prepare to visit foreclosed properties in Hiddenbrooke by looking them up in a local real estate database. "Homes in Hiddenbrooke have lost 50 percent of their value or more!" Vienna exclaims in surprise as she scrolls through the listings. The first one we visited, a four-bedroom Kinkade house that had been on the market for six months, was going for $350,000.

The house has a short patch of grass out front that refers to a yard more than being one, like a display bed in a department store. A tiny patio out back overlooks the golf course parking lot. When we get inside, Bertolano looks around. "This is all standard stuff, no upgrades. This is a first-time homebuyer house. The previous owners didn't do anything. It doesn't look like anyone ever lived here. These are the cheap cabinets and countertops the place came with. There are a lot of houses in Hiddenbrooke better than this," she concludes.

We went to one, a giant pile right on the golf course with five bedrooms that sold for $1.3 million in 2007. It's now going for $500,000. There is a golfball-shaped hole in one of the garage windows, and I glimpse the white of stray balls through the shrubs out front. Although the house has been on the market for more than two years, inside it looks like whoever lived there left an hour ago, and in a hurry.

The house is filled with stuff. Dozens of kids' toys are strewn about. There are Spider-Man bedclothes balled up in a corner of the living room and a Superman standee lying flat in the family room. Each bedroom has a DVD player in it, with videogame boxes nearby. The case for a DVD called *Ghetto Brawls 2* sits on the kitchen counter. A bookshelf in the foyer holds only one item, a passenger safety card from Alaska Airlines. Dozens and dozens of real estate agents' cards are scattered on the kitchen counter and in the entranceway, each one with the smiling face of an agent printed on it.

The two-car garage is filled with dead houseplants, abandoned strollers, and baby seats. "Only a two-car garage?" asks Vienna. "These people lived lavishly," she points out. "You can tell they overextended themselves. I call them over-livers."

On the drive back to her restaurant, Vienna tells me a story about her neighborhood in Vallejo, which she describes as a nice place where mostly older people live. There was a bank-owned property across the street from her house, and a few weeks ago she'd noticed a white, middle-class family had moved in. "I was surprised to find out the house had sold or rented," she says. "But it hadn't." Her new neighbors were a family of squatters. "It takes two weeks to evict them," Vienna explains. "Last week they were fined for throwing beer cans into the street. Police came and gave them a ticket but couldn't tell them to leave."

Without this fatal spiritual flaw, he was capable
of becoming one of the greatest of our artists;
but instead he only became one of the strangest of our madmen.

—THÉOPHILE GAUTIER, "THE PAINTER"

In *The Christmas Cottage* we learned that Thomas Kinkade is no stranger to economic hardship. Nor is the Painter of Light a stranger to lawsuits. In 2001, when Kinkade's then publicly traded company, Media Arts Group, began liquidating Kinkade product at deep discount prices, owners of Kinkade gallery franchises began to wonder if they'd made wise investments. As the value of the company's stock plummeted, some speculated that the artist was deliberately driving down the price so he could buy back the company. In early 2004 he did just that, taking the business private for $32.7 million. Investors lost a lot of money, but now the business is owned solely by the Thomas Kinkade Company, an entity that has turned "light," according to its company profile, into an acronym for "Loyalty, Integrity, Growth, Honoring God, Trust." Like the acronym, it almost worked.

The FBI has reportedly been investigating Kinkade since 2006. According to news reports, the bureau's probe began after "at least" six former Kinkade Signature Gallery owners sued the Kinkade Company for fraud. They claimed the company persuaded them to invest in galleries and then undercut them by selling Kinkade reproductions direct to consumers for less than the galleries charged.

After years of appeals, Kinkade gallery owners have lately started to win their lawsuits. A gallery-owning couple from Virginia claims Kinkade executives rooked them by creating "a certain religious environment designed to instill a special relationship of trust" between them and the Kinkade Company; a judge recently awarded them $2.1 million. Another couple in Michigan was awarded $1.4 million.

It is hard to feel sorry for these people. After all, they put their life savings into the work of man whose best-known public utterance came when he got drunk at a Siegfried and Roy show in Las Vegas and repeatedly yelled the word "codpiece" at the magicians until he was calmed by his mother.

New owners of Kinkade galleries also have reason not to be thrilled. In March 2009, several months before a couple in Prescott, Arizona, bought a Kinkade gallery there, the Painter of Light himself made an appearance before five hundred fans to give a motivational talk and raise money for charity by drawing a sketch, maybe one not that different from the one he gave his mother that Christmas back in the seventies. The drawing was auctioned for $12,000. According to the *Prescott Daily Courier*, the audience believed the $12,000 would be split between two charities. They didn't know that Kinkade had arranged to keep 80 percent of the sales price himself, with the charities receiving only about $2,000.

Why was a wealthy painter like Kinkade using these charities' good names to collect a measly $10,000? The new gallery owners don't know. What they do know is that since the news of Kinkade's 80/20 split leaked out in late August, disgruntled Prescottians have been phoning their gallery and threatening to throw bricks through the window.

Obsessed by a fairy tale, we spend our lives searching for a magic door and a lost kingdom of peace from which we have been dispossessed by a greedy swindler.

—EUGENE O'NEILL, *MORE STATELY MANSIONS*

The house that was to be the playwright Eugene O'Neill's final harbor, the Tao House, sits in the hills above Danville, California, about 120 miles southwest of Placerville and 35 miles southeast of Vallejo. O'Neill and his wife purchased the Tao House and the ranchland around it in 1937, and the couple lived there until 1944, when O'Neill became too sick to write. While he was living there, he wrote many of his best plays, including *The Iceman Cometh* and *Long Day's Journey into Night*. The house is now a National Historic Site administered by the National Park Service.

Visitors can tour the Tao House Wednesdays through Saturdays. To get there, you wait for a bus in front of a supermarket, and then a park ranger drives you up the hill. In O'Neill's time the land was clear. Now there's a gated housing development there. After the housing development was built, the National Park Service had to ask permission to drive through it to get to the O'Neill site.

On the ride to see the study in which O'Neill wrote *More Stately Mansions*, the park ranger driving the bus points out some of the sights of the gated community. "Have you ever seen a house worth $1.85 million?" he asks. "That house on the left was valued at $1.85

million!" He doesn't say what it's worth now. We travel further into the gated community, and the driver points out another place. "You see that house on the right?" he asks. "That house has an infinity pool. Have you ever gone swimming in one of those? That's a pool that looks like it just falls off into space, like off the side of a cliff."

The tourists I'm with seem a little let down when we arrive at O'Neill's Tao House. It's just a two-story house. It's not even that big. Looking at O'Neill's Bessie Smith records and his book collection is a disappointment to them after almost seeing an infinity pool. Studying his tiny handwriting through a magnifying glass the Park Service provides doesn't excite them, either. Even the grave of O'Neill's dog, Blemie, doesn't move them very much, and they barely stop to look at themselves in the strange black mirror in the master bedroom.

Weep for what little things could make them glad.
Then for the house that is no more a house,
But only a belilaced cellar hole,
Now slowly closing like a dent in dough.

—ROBERT FROST, "DIRECTIVE"

O'Neill's contemporary Robert Frost is a counterbalance to Kinkade more than any other American artist. In poem after poem, Frost writes about abandoned houses, arson and fire, debt and loss. When he writes about a cottage, he writes about it because there's no one there anymore. His cottages are haunted by memories of the people who lived and died in them, or built them and lost them. They aren't glowy; they're cold, and they speak of a time in the life of this country when people earned their houses instead of getting them with no money down. The word "subprime" does not appear in his work.

Frost is associated with New England, but he was born out here, in San Francisco. As I write this, California's seasonal wildfires are turning the sky over Oakland black. "The best way is to come uphill with me," Frost wrote, "and have our fire and laugh and be afraid." While the fires rage in California this August, that strikes me as the best way to look at Kinkade too. Whatever his value as an artist, he has used his own experience to create a business that predicted, and in some ways replicates, the current mortgage crisis. His paintings of quaint houses with burning interiors substitute nostalgia for values and hope for community. The idea that these reproductions, gobbed with points of light, are a good investment isn't any different than the idea that flipping gated, golf-coursed mansions is the way to get rich. Kinkade is a living testament to how the triumph of kitsch values has repercussions in the marketplace, outside the world of taste.

Meanwhile, in a safer part of California, Kinkade is still sitting on his gold mine, at least until the FBI and the courts decide to take it away.

When I was getting ready to leave California, a news story broke in a town close to Placerville that made people forget about the fires. Phillip Garrido, who ran a printing and graphic design business out of his home, was arrested for abducting a girl in 1991, when she was eleven. He held her hostage for eighteen years in a makeshift compound in his backyard, and while she was his captive he fathered two children with her. Garrido, a religious fanatic, gave interviews after his arrest. "Wait till you hear the story of this house," he told a reporter. "You're going to find the most powerful story coming from the witness, the victim—you wait. If you take this a step at a time, you're going to fall over backwards, and in the end, you're going to find the most powerful heart-warming story."

There are a lot of houses in this country with Thomas Kinkade paintings in them, so when you tell people you're writing about Thomas Kinkade, you often find out their lives have been touched by his work; "highlighted" by it, you might say. I spoke with a young woman named Katie who works as a waitress at a California Pizza Kitchen in San Francisco. She told me her grandparents are Kinkade collectors who have left her and her siblings one Kinkade painting each from their collection. The paintings are reproductions they had highlighted at a Kinkade gallery, and they bought the proper gallery lighting equipment so they could display them the way Kinkade meant for them to be seen.

Katie says that if her grandmother were to die today (her grandfather has passed on), she wouldn't display her Kinkade where she lives, which is in a one-bedroom apartment in the Mission she shares with her girlfriend. The painting doesn't fit into her lifestyle right now, she tells me. It's too fancy and valuable. Maybe if she had a big house she would, but she doesn't, and she doesn't expect to anytime soon.

POSTSCRIPT

Thomas Kinkade died in bed on April 6, 2012. A lethal combination of alcohol and Valium killed him. He was fifty-four years old. His death was ruled accidental, but it has the feel of something closer to suicide. The artist had been drinking at home all night, said his girlfriend, Amy Pinto, with whom he'd been living. His wife, vacationing in Australia, claimed Kinkade died of natural causes. Pinto, who was there, explained that Kinkade "died in his sleep, very happy, in the house he built, with the paintings he loved and the woman he loved." It doesn't sound like he was all that happy.

Pinto produced two handwritten wills Kinkade scrawled in the months before his death. The wills, described as "squiggly notes" written in a hand made shaky by drink, left Pinto the house and $10 million. She was supposed to use the money to open a Kinkade museum, featuring paintings valued (by her lawyers) at $66 million. Nanette Kinkade posted a guard at the house after her estranged husband's death to make sure Pinto didn't steal anything.

The two women settled Kinkade's estate eight months later, "after months of name-calling and finger-pointing," according an article in the December 19, 2012, *San Jose Mercury News*. The settlement is secret. Pinto "accepted a deal in return for her silence."

Few details of Kinkade's last days have emerged. The *Mercury News* reported that the artist was a "fixture at local bars." His brother told the paper that "mean-spirited criticism of Kinkade's work and his estrangement from his wife and four daughters had taken its toll on the artist and factored into his alcoholism."

It was a dark ending for the Painter of Light, a Romantic ending in the nineteenth-century sense, something that could fit into the *Lives of the Artists*. It is sordid, tragic, and sodden, with women fighting over his possessions.

On the other hand, Kinkade overcame the disadvantages of his youth to scale the heights of American capitalism like no other artist of his time. A laughingstock in the big cities, he was the art hero of the hinterlands. He got there by eagerly resorting to questionable business practices that make the unregulated shenanigans of the legitimate art world look lazy and uncreative.

Because Kinkade is dead now, the quotation from Gautier's "Painter," printed above, means more than it did when I wrote "A Cottage for Sale" in 2009. Kinkade's "fatal spiritual flaw" seems like what killed him. His greed, which expressed itself in his desire to leave his mark on anything and everything, allowed him to spread his bad taste over every surface he could. His alcoholism may have been inherited; the spiritual malaise of his death speaks of something else. It indicts his relentless uglification of the world, the end result of his licensing deals, and the way he got people to pay for his crap with their nickels and dimes a little at a time, preferably with interest.

One gets the sense that Kinkade saw himself as a figure for the ages. Now the Internet offers endless parodies of his work. No obituary published after his death failed to mention how worthless the "highlighted" factory-made Kinkade paintings really were, and how they will not appreciate in value. Their value, it turns out, really was purely sentimental.

Kinkade's paintings are still produced and sold, although those squiggly wills make one wonder who painted some of the last ones to come off the line. His *Disney Dreams Collection*, for instance, one of his last commissioned sets, is still offered on his company's website. There's an anecdote I did not include in what I wrote in 2009. Once, while drunk at the Disneyland Hotel in Anaheim, California, Kinkade urinated on a statue of Winnie the Pooh while shouting, "This one's for you, Walt!"

A *Winnie the Pooh: So Much Better with Two* set of matched paintings, part of the Disney collection, was "published" in November 2013 by "we at the Thomas Kinkade Studios." The reproductions retail for $710 each, $1,020 for a foil-stamped limited edition. I wonder if Kinkade left something of himself behind in the paint that went into them? After all, we know that while he was alive his reproductions were auto-signed by a DNA pen containing drops of his own blood.

Fifty Shades of Late Capitalism

HEATHER HAVRILESKY

While we are still recovering from the trauma that finance capital has inflicted on our public world, a late-capitalist fairy tale manages the pain in the more private and intimate reaches of the sexual daydream. In one version of the story, a wide-eyed mermaid cleverly disguises her essential self in order to win the heart of a prince (*The Little Mermaid*). In another, a hooker with a heart of gold navigates her way to a happy ending by offering some happy endings of her own (*Pretty Woman*). Or there's the sassy secretary who shakes her moneymaker all the way to the corner office (*Working Girl*).

Fifty Shades of Grey follows this long history of class ascendancy via feminine wiles, but does so cleverly disguised as an edgy modern bodice-ripper. Forget that E. L. James's three-book series captures the intricacies of BDSM about as effectively as a "Whip Me!" Barbie doll decked out in a ball gag, dog collar, and assless leather chaps. Although admirers of the series sometimes credit it with liberating female desire by reimagining pornography for ordinary women (and introducing them to the unmatched thrills of leather riding crops and hard spankings), the story of Anastasia Steele and Christian Grey isn't really about dominance or bondage or even sex or love, despite all the Harlequin Romance–worthy character names. No, what *Fifty Shades of Grey* offers is an extreme vision of late-capitalist deliverance, the American (wet) dream on performance-enhancing drugs. Just as magazines such

From *The Baffler*, no. 22

as *Penthouse*, *Playboy*, *Chic*, and *Oui* (speaking of aspirational names) have effectively equated the moment of erotic indulgence with the ultimate consumer release, a totem of the final elevation into amoral privilege, James's trilogy represents the latest installment in the commodified sex genre. The money shot is just that: the moment when our heroine realizes she's been ushered into the hallowed realm of the 1 percent, once and for all.

So Brazen

The fantasy life of *Fifty Shades* certainly isn't focused on the sublime erotic encounter. The sex becomes hopelessly repetitive sometime around the third or fourth of the novels' countless, monotonously naughty encounters. Each dalliance begins with the same provocative come-on: the naive college graduate Anastasia and the dashing mogul Christian describe their desire to each other with all of the charmless unpredictability of servers mouthing their prescribed scripts at an Australian-themed steakhouse. Awkward openers ("I think we've done enough talking for now," "Now let's get you inside and naked") conjure the raw provocation of "How about a Bloomin' Onion to get you started?" Even tougher to take are the coy responses ("Oh, my!" "Why, Mrs. Grey, you have a dirty, dirty mouth!" "You're insatiable and so brazen"), repeated with gusto despite a total lack of shock value in evidence. Readerly expectations tick up ever so slightly as Grey issues some bossy commands—Stand here! Undress! Bend over! Spread your legs!—which seem at first blush to foretell a curve in the carnal road. But no such luck. Give or take a blindfold here or a butt plug there, the same hands explore the same places in the same ways with the same results. After the fifteenth or sixteenth time Anastasia and Christian "find [their] release together," they start to resemble tourists with no short-term memory, repeating the same docented visit to Graceland over and over again, drooling over the claustrophobic upholstered pool room and the mirrored wall and the fourteen-foot-long white leather couch afresh each time. By the third volume in the series, as every word out of Christian's mouth ("I

VICTOR KERLOW

see you're very wet, Anastasia") still triggers an overheated response from his paramour ("Holy shit!"), readers may find themselves hissing, "Mix it up a little, for fuck's sake!"

But let's not mistake sex for the main event. The endless manual jimmying and ripped foil packets and escalating rhythms and release-findings are just foreplay for the real climax, in which Anastasia recognizes that she's destined to abandon her ordinary, middle-class life in favor of the rarefied veal pen of the modern power elite. Until then, like a swooning female contestant on *The Bachelor*, Anastasia is offered breathtaking helicopter and glider rides, heady spins in luxury sports cars, and windswept passages on swift catamarans. She is made to gasp at Christian's plush office, with its sandstone desk and white leather chairs and its stunning vista, or his spacious, immaculate penthouse apartment, with its endless rooms filled with pricey furniture. She is treated to Bollinger pink champagne and grilled sea bass. She is offered a brand new wardrobe replete with stylish heels and gorgeous gowns and designer bras. She is lavished with diamond jewelry and flowers and a new luxury car of her own.

Soon the numbing parade of luxe brands—Cartier, Cristal, Omega, iPad, iPod, Audi, Gucci—takes on the same dulled impact as endlessly tweaked nipples and repeatedly bound wrists. Curiously (but perhaps not surprisingly), our heroine's responses to these artifacts of her ascendance are eerily similar to her sexual responses: "Oh, my!" "Yes." "Holy shit!" After that, the superior quality and enormous cost of each item are mulled over in excruciating detail. Just as traditional, male-centered pornography seems to feature a particularly clumsy, childish notion of sexiness, the concept of luxury on offer in *Fifty Shades* is remarkably callow. Like an update of the ostentatious, faux-tasteful wealth of *Dynasty*, Christian's penthouse, with its abstract art and dark wood and leather, represents the modern version of enormous flower arrangements and white marble and a house staff trussed up in cartoon-butler regalia. No detail of the environment feels organic or specific to Christian himself; instead, it reflects a prescribed corporate aesthetic of enormous wealth that for some reason James approaches with reverence rather than repulsion or dread. By the time this compulsive lifestyle voyeurism starts invading our narrator's routine visits to the bathroom ("The restrooms are the height of modern design—all dark wood, black granite, and pools of light from strategically placed halogens"), the author's veneration of arbitrary signifiers of class has begun to take on grotesque, faintly comedic proportions.

Against this backdrop of gleeful consumption, Anastasia's total life makeover takes shape. Having just graduated from college, she scales the corporate ladder from assistant to book editor in a matter of weeks, since Christian has thoughtfully purchased the publishing company where she works. When her boss bullies and sexually harasses her, Christian confronts him, has him fired, and installs Anastasia in his place. Her mild protests over this creepy, control-freak show of power—now *that's* some hard-core domination play—are just for show, of course. The underlying message is that Prince Charming swooped in and saved her from the indignities of the underclass. As if that's not enough, in the third book, *Fifty Shades Freed*, Christian announces that he's going to give the publishing company to his new wife, telling her, "This is my wedding present to you." Sounds just like a wildly successful, ultra-competitive entrepreneur, doesn't it, to give an entire business to his inexperienced inamorata, so that she can play make-believe at the office all day, while he adds a red mark in the "failures" column of his imperial spreadsheet?

Of Quasi-human Bondage

There's nothing that money can't buy in this world, whether it's respect, dignity, or imaginary political correctness. When Christian leads Anastasia to a palatial Mediterranean house with an expansive view of Puget Sound, then explains that he wants to demolish it so he can build a house for the two of them, Anastasia balks. "Why do you want to demolish it?" she asks. "I'd like to make a more sustainable home, using the latest ecological techniques," he replies. "Using the latest ecological techniques" is just another prescribed lifestyle choice, of course—a matter of image over substance, implying that, in the great march of progress, wrecking and discarding a massive old building is somehow more responsible than working with what's there.

When it comes to wasted resources, though, nothing is quite as indulgent as real live humans who are at your beck and call around the clock. Maybe this is why hundreds of pages in the *Fifty Shades* trilogy are dedicated to outlining even the most minor exchanges between this privileged couple and their army of handservants:

> "This is a Bolognese sauce. It can be eaten anytime. I'll freeze it." She [the cook Mrs. Jones] smiles warmly and turns the heat right down.
>
> Once we're airborne, Natalia serves us yet more champagne and prepares our wedding feast. And what a feast it is—smoked salmon, followed by roast partridge with a green bean salad and *dauphinoise* potatoes, all cooked and served by the ever-efficient Natalia.
>
> The waiter has returned with the champagne, which he proceeds to open with an understated flourish.
>
> Sawyer reenters, bearing a paper cup of hot water and a separate tea bag. He knows how I take my tea!
>
> Taylor opens the door and I slide out. He gives me a warm, avuncular smile that makes me feel safe. I smile back.

Like the most loyal and dedicated refugees from *Downton Abbey*, every one of the series' cooks and chauffeurs and security guards and assistants demonstrates polite restraint and obedient discretion in Christian and Anastasia's presence. Every careful movement and gesture, each bland remark and well-timed retreat into the background, evokes the ultimate service-economy fantasy. These interchangeable, faceless humans, whose ubiquity and professionalism we're meant to marvel over repeatedly, represent luxury possessions. They are warm but impassive, friendly but reserved, omnipresent but invisible. They register no disputes, no grudges, no rolled eyes, no missed days of work. Nothing seems to bring these strange, shadowy figures more satisfaction than serving Lord Grey and his Lady. Like the growing pile of high-end watches and cars and bracelets that the mildly transgressive power couple accumulates, these humans start to melt into an idealized mass of blindly loyal subservience, bestowing upon their masters an oversized sense of power. And in the midst of these deferential encounters, the long-suffering reader of the series finds some bitter and fugitive consolation in recalling that Anastasia's Russian royal namesake was exiled by the Bolsheviks.

Even though Anastasia is flanked by a cook who stands over her steaming pot like an adoring mother and a security guard who'd happily lay down his life to keep her safe, she soon develops a haughty attitude toward the help. By the second book, she's independently instructing Christian's staff on how to fulfill her wishes. By the third, she's fretting openly about her white-person problems. "I suppose it will be up to me to set the parameters by which Mrs. Jones and I will work together," she muses, wondering how she'll carry off the illusion of becoming the ultimate, dreamy wife fixing food for her man when there's a skilled cook in the kitchen at all times. Although we're meant to applaud Anastasia's down-to-earth urges (She still wants to cook! How adorable!), her inevitable devolution into an utterly useless, pampered aristocrat is naturally assumed—indeed, her growing incapacities are arguably the chief source of titillation and suspense in the whole series. Late in the third book, we find Anastasia upbraiding Gia, the female architect redesigning their brand-new house, for making eyes at Christian. Apparently Gia is blissfully unaware that she's just another faceless possession among many—but Anastasia is there to set her straight: "You're right to be nervous, Gia, because right now your work on this project hangs in the balance. But I'm sure we'll be fine as long as you keep your hands off my husband."

Yes, Ladies, He's Mine

Of course, Christian and Anastasia encounter each other as the most precious of high-end possessions. "You're mine," they tell each other over and over. Like a manicured update to Gollum from *The Lord of the Rings*, Anastasia imagines a world inhabited primarily by covetous rivals, from Gia ("Her isn't-he-dreamily-gorgeous-wish-he-were-mine flush does not go unnoticed"), to a friend of Christian's sister's, to Christian's "bitch troll" ex-girlfriend, to two random women in an elevator ("Yes, ladies, he's mine"). Likewise, Christian panics at Anastasia's smallest exchanges with her boss and male friends, even the coat-check guy at a club. ("Beside me Christian bristles and fixes Max with a back-off-now glare.") After punching out a guy who gets grabby with Anastasia on the dance floor, Christian tells Anastasia, "No one touches what's mine." In case we can't grasp that his woman is his most cherished commodity, jealously safeguarded with the mien of a bouncer, he spells it out for us: "You're so precious to me," he tells her in *Fifty Shades Freed*. "Like a priceless asset, like a child." To Christian, every man alive wants Anastasia. To Anastasia, every woman alive wants Christian. They navigate the world like matching, customized, his-and-her luxury sports cars, outfitted with matching (if, alas, faulty) emotional GPS systems.

In the real world, such severe possessiveness would create big problems for both parties. But in the fantasy world of *Fifty Shades*, pathology is recast as its own special kind of indulgence, a way of heightening the sensation of two superior humans looming over the mortal realm like demigods. The slow seduction that culminates in total possession and total power, which the first book sometimes depicts as a dark force to be escaped, is portrayed with accelerating breathlessness and adoration in the second and third volumes. Echoing the lawless privilege of girlie magazines, the so-called control freak within Christian (and subsequently, Anastasia) demonstrates not just that members of the moneyed class are above the law, but that they exist beyond ordinary ethical guidelines too. (This, by the way, is also the moral of the higher-brow forerunner of *Fifty Shades*: Bret Easton Ellis's *American Psycho*—which is a much more self-aware, if also somewhat numbing, excursus into the nexus between high consumer capitalism and soulless bondage sex, with the significant and oddly more realistic difference that Ellis's alpha-male protagonist is also a serial killer.)

Having complete and total control over every single aspect of your experience, including everyone around you, is the textbook definition of alienation—precisely how human beings are severed from each other and from their own humanity. Perversely, in *Fifty Shades*, this radical isolation is portrayed as a moment of transcendence rather than one of debasement. Armed with an apparently limitless will-to-commodification, our narrator recognizes that anything and everything in the world—objects, people, qualities one would like to appear to have—can be bought for a price. And the qualities of each owned thing reflect more glory back on the owner. "Six stallions, say, I can afford, / Is not their strength my property?" offers Mephistopheles in Goethe's *Faust*. "I tear along, a sporting lord, / As if their legs belonged to me."

Once you arrive at the tippity-top of the heap, you see, it's only natural that you should have complete freedom to do as you please. There's no need to apologize for bullying or throwing your weight around or expecting others to conform to your desires for them. You can wreck the house, or redesign it. You can shame the former submissive, or pay for her art school education and thereby keep her forever in your debt. And when there's trouble, it's your choice either to call the cops or take matters into your own hands. (Christian, predictably, likes to do the latter.) You are the master of all fates, including your own. You can run rampant over anything or anyone in your path.

Shakespeare captured this spirit of heedless oppression in *Julius Caesar*, when Brutus says of his friend and rival, "The abuse of greatness is when it disjoins remorse from power." Anastasia, who's been showered with priceless goods until she shares her paramour's reckless sense of entitlement, puts it a little differently: "Maybe I need to be restrained."

Adam Wheeler Went to Harvard

JIM NEWELL

On December 23, 2011, the dons of Harvard University finally got to see Adam Wheeler sentenced to a year in prison. Wheeler, a twenty-five-year-old whom they admitted in 2007 on the strength of an academic record he'd fabricated out of thin air, had been caught again—and this was not something a young gentleman does to America's most highly self-regarded institution of advanced credentialing.

A few months earlier, Wheeler had submitted a résumé to U.S. Green Data Inc., on which he said he had attended Harvard. Technically, this was true; he'd been one year short of graduating when someone at the school belatedly noticed that he had falsified the credentials that won him admission and that he had plagiarized the papers that won him scholarships and prestigious awards. But the ten-year probationary punishment that the Middlesex County Superior Court had meted out upon the discovery of his fabulism forbade him ever from claiming he had attended the school, and the new offending résumé landed on the desk of a Harvard alum, who forwarded it to a dean, who turned it over to the district attorney's office. And Adam Wheeler, who attended Harvard and who had been forced by the Court to lie about his having attended Harvard, was packed off to jail for lying about his having attending Harvard. The school of George W. Bush and Henry Kissinger (the war criminal who in 2012 was feted on campus as a conquering hero) took all appropriate measures to ensure that its name

From *The Baffler*, no. 20

would never be sullied by association with an immoral, egomaniacal charlatan, at least one who never held high office. And all the useful knowledge that Wheeler picked up in more than two years of classes was no longer something from which he could draw on to contribute to society.

College credential fraud may seem like a nitpicking offense for throwing a nonviolent offender into the overcrowded prison system for a tour of the seasons. But Wheeler embarrassed Harvard; his puncture of arbitrary power was so trifling that, paradoxically, it couldn't be ignored. Harvard officials had little choice but to make an example of him through an aggressive, custom-tailored prosecution whose real aim was to restore the correct order of things. Adam Wheeler, after all, is merely a mediocre public school graduate from Delaware. But Harvard—well, everyone knows that Harvard shines across the fair land as a beacon of meritocratic upward mobility universally accessible to a nationwide corps of upper-middle-class teenagers of arbitrary intellectual ability.

Take a look at the victim impact statement Harvard presented to the court in 2010, and notice how the country's mightiest and richest institution of enlightened learning asks for the maximum punishment to be inflicted upon a lying schoolboy. The victim wanted to send a message to the entire world that fraud on campus will not be tolerated, no ifs, ands, or buts about it:

> Wheeler's acts of deception and fraud not only harmed Harvard University directly, but also undermined the public perception of integrity in higher education nationally and around the world. We require honesty as well as excellence from our students, which is why, when we discovered Mr. Wheeler's fraudulent conduct, we brought it to the attention of the district attorney's office. In terms of sentencing, we believe restitution is appropriate, so that the financial aid and other funds that Mr. Wheeler stole from Harvard can be put to use to support deserving Harvard students. We also feel strongly that Mr. Wheeler should be prohibited from profiting from his fraudulent schemes for as long a period as the court has the

> power to impose. Were he permitted to profit from the notoriety he already has gained as a result of his flagrant dishonesty, all of higher education would continue to be negatively impacted.

It's not as though Harvard lacks for alums whom the institution should be ashamed to be associated with, or who have befouled "the public perception of integrity in higher education." Wheeler's final prosecution came just three years after a cabal of alumni known as the financial services sector destroyed the economy by playing computer games with the planet's accumulated wealth. There was former Harvard president, U.S. Treasury secretary, and deregulator extraordinaire Larry Summers; there was Summers's predecessor at Treasury and mentor in the intricate art of fucking up global economies of weaker nations for no good reason, Robert Rubin (AB '60 and member of the Corporation, Harvard's governing body); there was the CEO of America's most ruthless megabank ("the smart ones," in financial expert circles), Lloyd Blankfein (AB '75, JD '78); and then there were approximately 100 percent of the other key figures who engineered this wholly preventable near-reversion to the state of nature—all Crimson men with at least one tour of duty. The university offers no protest as these apocalypse machinists drop John Harvard's name in their pursuit of sinecures atop whatever remaining elite institutions and systems they have yet to destroy; instead, it covers them with laurels and showers them with money.

Take the case of Andrei Shleifer, a prominent Harvard economics professor and former head of the disgraced Russia Project at the Harvard Institute for International Development. In the nineties, Shleifer won a contract from the U.S. government to administer "shock therapy" to the Russian economy, to theorize and implement its transformation from failed socialism to a market economy dominated by private capital and guided by legal norms. The key to establishing a favorable investment climate was teaching the Russians respect for the rule of law—because every academic economist knows that underlying market economies lies a rational consensus, an agreement to play by the rules duly articulated and enforced. And out of this orthodoxy came not only a failed mission and a reaction inside Russian power circles that set a baleful course, but a tale of personal and institutional corruption as awesome as you are likely to find anywhere in scandal-plagued higher education, with sordid details of fabricated expense accounts, no-show jobs, and leisured junkets that make Adam Wheeler seem like a piker. The FBI and U.S. Attorney's Office investigations of Shleifer's activities turned up large quantities of credible evidence of money laundering, embezzlement, tax evasion, and fraud, evidence that directly implicated his wife, a hedge fund manager. In 2004 a Boston judge in the federal district court ruled Harvard liable for breach of contract in the Shleifer debauch and found the celebrated economist liable for conspiracy to defraud the U.S. government. Adam Wheeler's tangle of lies cost Harvard $45,000 and change, a pittance next to the $26.5 million they paid in the Shleifer settlement, the largest in the university's history.

The Russia Project, launched with all the overweening arrogance due the gilded dogmas of business, showed up the shock troops of the market's ideological vanguard as a pack of self-dealing crooks and swindlers who help themselves to giant heapings of public wealth when no one is looking. Yes, you already knew that. But how do you think Harvard responded as the evidence piled up and the investigation closed in on one of their own? Right again: Andrei Shleifer was promoted, given the coveted Whipple V. N. Jones chair in the department of economics after his pal and mentor Larry Summers intervened with the dean of the faculty. In other words, a closely conjoined pair of global market fraudsters successfully headed off accountability for their crimes by exploiting the elaborate masquerade that keeps Harvard's worship of power and money spinning. The undergraduate impostor is in jail. The economist, who has never presented the defense he said all along was forthcoming, is today what he has always been: a member in good—and indeed, ascendant—standing of the Harvard economics department, one of those superstar professors who travel abroad to give expert advice to

DAVID GOTHARD

backward peoples and then come back to campus to instruct drooling students in how the world works.

Nobody at Harvard, none of the admissions officials, deans, or professors who were too lazy or incompetent to notice Adam Wheeler's lies, appears to have been punished. At this most elite of elite institutions, it's standard operating procedure to shift the blame downward, so that Harvard can continue collecting donations from financial wizards and garlanding them with the occasional honorary degree. The journalism world, a collection pool for the few Harvard College graduates who rebelliously reject law or consulting careers but hardly have to make it the hard way (the *New York Times*, notably, reserves a junior reporter job or two each year for graduating staffers of the Harvard *Crimson*), has been thorough in its anti-journalistic investigations of the perps behind the '08 crash—low-income mortgage holders, minorities, recipients of unemployment benefits, congressman Barney Frank, and unionized public school teachers, to name only a few major players in this shadowy network—while the ever upward-falling meritocracy of high finance has been deemed too petulant to fail.

So there was a certain grim fitness to the high Victorian melodrama of Middlesex assistant district attorney John C. Verner seeking maximum punishment for the lying schoolboy. It's one thing to despoil retirement funds, lay waste to the mortgage sector, plunge countries to the brink of bankruptcy, and reduce the life expectancy of a whole people, but the American republic plainly will not stand for the trespass of writing "Harvard" on a job application—even if the young applicant in question needed that job in order to pay off some of the $45,000 and change in fines arising from the previous year's prosecution.

"Despite everything that has happened to Mr. Wheeler prior to being put on probation, he still continues to do what he has been doing: falsifying résumés, lying, and stealing," Verner pontificated, the winds of profound moral certitude puffing his every word. "Mr. Wheeler is not going to stop doing what he's doing"—saying he went to Harvard—"unless he's sentenced. He has to be punished."

Superior Court justice Diane M. Kottmyer obliged. Wheeler

was not mentally ill, she allowed, but "simply has a character flaw that makes him dishonest." Sending him to a mental facility would only feed "his sense of himself as a person who can do these things and get away with them without repercussions." And so Adam Wheeler was sentenced to one year in prison, for saying, truthfully, that he went to Harvard.

Wheeler came to Harvard to study English and left as a bit player in a twisted Dreiserian tragedy, exaggerated to hammy effect by a humiliated university covering its ass. He bought into Harvard's great enabling social myth at face value: the notion that twenty-first-century meritocratic advancement is available to all through the procurement of a college diploma. Like any rational economic actor, he sought to procure a diploma from the finest college, with maximum efficiency. Wheeler's crime, in the institution's eyes, was that he saw Harvard degrees for what they are—items for purchase that cloak the owner with a manufactured prestige that, in our pretend meritocracy, automatically raises one's market value upon the deal's closing. The only thing propping up that value is the admissions office's carefully maintained scarcity of supply—a luxury good ostensibly awarded to society's most able. So Wheeler once more called the bluff of the Harvard admissions crew: he gave them whatever song-and-dance they were looking for, and, shockingly, came close to completing the purchase.

It's quite apparent that Harvard administrators couldn't merely expel Wheeler and demand he return the money when they finally noticed the obvious lies on his academic résumé. There was an urgent example to be set here, after all: enterprising young minds watching the news coverage might have reasoned that the people who run Harvard are utter morons who caught Wheeler only after a final fabrication so flamboyant that he must have wanted to get caught. With the great meritocratic ruse at last exposed in the light of day, young strivers might well give it a go themselves. Even better, forget *going* to Harvard—why not simply throw "BA, Harvard" on the ol' résumé right now and start making tons of money playing financial computer games tomorrow? All Wheeler did, anyway, was spot major systemic inefficiencies and disingenuously exploit them for personal financial reward. And if Harvard is a place that would expel such a Capitalist of the Year, then it's everyone else's moral duty as Americans to pick up where he left off, and continue looting the place until it reaches a competitive market-clearing equilibrium: when looting a Harvard degree would no longer be worth the trouble—when Harvard, horror of horrors, becomes but one college of many!

To say that Harvard *caught* Wheeler in 2009 gives the school far too much credit. He'd almost certainly be selling crappy derivatives to some vain aristocrats in Eastern Europe right now if he'd just glided quietly through his senior year. Instead, he applied for Rhodes and Fulbright scholarships, for which he had to submit a résumé, a Harvard transcript, several letters of recommendation, and a project statement (on "cultural mobility"), all of which he must have known would be thoroughly vetted. Since these documents were nothing more than collections of absurd lies, anyone reviewing Wheeler's scholarship applications for a minute or two would certainly catch something. Plagiarists famously continue raising the stakes of their fabulations in the need to be caught, and to win some perverse admiration for their crooked genius. This seems to have been the case with Wheeler, who at this juncture in his fake career had come as close to turning himself in as possible without saying the words, "I'm guilty, you can take me away now." The moment of unraveling came when English professor James Simpson noticed that Wheeler had plagiarized the work of fellow professor Stephen Greenblatt.

That relatively recondite discovery led Harvard investigators to all of the much more obvious falsifications, ones that shouldn't have required the efforts of a professor reviewing Rhodes scholar applications with a fine-tooth comb to detect. As a junior, Wheeler had submitted a (plagiarized) research paper with the unassuming title "The Mapping of an Ideological Demesne: Space, Place, and Text from More to Marvell." The paper was nominated for Harvard's prestigious Thomas T. Hoopes prize—and it won. By the time he was a senior, Wheeler was peddling an even rosier view of his years at fairest Harvard. On his Rhodes application, he claimed to have a 4.0 average. He did not. His résumé said he had coauthored four books with a Harvard English professor. The professor he listed did not coauthor books with undergraduates, and college students, even at Harvard, typically do not have four advanced books in their oeuvre by senior year. Wheeler also wrote that he was fluent in Old Persian, Classical Armenian, and "Old English." Down here on planet Earth, the only reason you would select such a trifecta is to signal to your readers that you are fucking with them, and are not really fluent in any foreign languages. At Harvard, they loved it.

An investigation into Wheeler's initial application to Harvard proved, even more gobsmackingly, that the High Lords of America's most prestigious university couldn't smell bullshit if they were walking in a pasture half an hour past feeding time and felt a squish under their boots. Wheeler billed himself as a graduate of the Phillips Andover Academy who had scored a perfect 1,600 on his SATs. In reality, he had been an above-average student at Caesar Rodney High School in rural Delaware, where his parents, Richard (a former shop teacher) and Lee, now own an interior design firm. He scored a 1,160 and a 1,220 in his two stabs at the SATs.

Wheeler applied to Harvard as a transfer student, but—as you should be able to guess by now—he did not attend the school from which he told Harvard he was transferring. He alleged he was an MIT student who'd completed his first undergraduate year with straight A's—MIT doesn't grade first-years on the alphanumeric scale—and he submitted four fabricated letters of recommendation from actual professors. The real school Wheeler was transferring from was Bowdoin—a fine school, but one from which Wheeler had already been suspended for a semester during his sophomore year following accusations of, yes, plagiarism. The Harvard alumnus who interviewed the pretend MIT student during the transfer process should have been a wee bit concerned *when he went to interview Wheeler on Bowdo-*

in's campus. Wheeler, however, fed him some lie about enrolling in a course that was available only on Bowdoin's campus that semester.

Acting out the role of MIT transfer student delighted Wheeler well past his 2007 admission to Harvard. After the scandal broke, the *Crimson* published excerpts from emails he'd sent to fellow incoming transfer students. They're written in the cartoonish voice you'd expect of, say, a young con man clutching a pocket thesaurus as he impersonates a pretentious, overachieving MIT-to-Harvard student. "My own, brief, assessment of my character," he wrote, "is that I am sententious, crypto-tendentious, slightly pedantic with a streak of contrarianism, a fascination with any pedagogical approach to Shakespeare, and a decent sense of humor." Sports, of course, the striver dismissed as "a neighborhood faux-pas of epic proportions." And let's not even talk about his days and nights of isolation wandering through the deserts of MIT. "I was, to put it poorly, suckled upon the teat of disdain," Wheeler wrote, offering his new chums a spot of his "fluency" in Old English. "I was inspired therby [sic] to apply to Harvard, where the humanities, in short, are not, simpliciter, a source of opprobrium."

By the time Harvard set a date for Wheeler's disciplinary hearing in the fall of 2009, Wheeler had left campus, returned to Delaware, and asked the school to let him know whenever its disciplinarians reached the expulsion verdict that he knew was coming. He returned to Massachusetts in the spring of 2010 to spend some time in the clink following his indictment on twenty counts of larceny, identity fraud, falsifying an endorsement or approval, and the dazzlingly dystopian charge of "pretending to hold a degree"—all interchangeable criminal-ish terms emitted like a thick fog to conceal the one true bedrock offense, telling Harvard people a bunch of obvious lies that they pretended to believe because they were too lazy or vain to fact-check them for half a second, which made Harvard look incompetent.

Later that year, when the initial judge in the case convicted Wheeler and handed down his ten-year probation sentence, the terms of the punishment included a bonus kick on the way out: Wheeler was not able to profit from his crimes for these ten years, far past the likely expiration of his fifteen minutes of notoriety. Tough state-mandated love for a cocky youngster who'd gone too far? Spin it that way if you must. More important, though, was the no-profit rider's efficiency in sparing the Harvard brand from the more explosive humiliations, presented in all their naked detail, that could surface in the would-be tell-all, *My Story: How I Played Those Harvard Suckers Good and You Can Too*, by Adam Wheeler.

Further examples of Wheeler's fraud, fakery, and amateurish self-parody abound, but the simplest way to put the episode in perspective is to imagine that someone was running across Harvard Yard in an unmissable neon suit screaming "I'M A FRAUD WHO HAS LIED ABOUT EVERYTHING," around the clock, for two years, until one professor finally suspected that something was *most decidedly off* about this young man whose Rhodes scholarship application he'd been reviewing and intending to accept.

To be fair, every incoming Ivy League class since the dawn of time has had its share of opportunistic tools who arrive at campus embracing the well-known snob stereotypes that recruiters had sworn were the stuff of mythology. When I arrived for my freshman year at Penn—yes, reader, I, too, once was an ambitious young know-it-all from a mid-Atlantic suburb who'd heeded the siren song of a lesser Ivy to launch me into the stratosphere of the great American meritocracy—there was a first-year student in the Wharton School of Business who lived down my hall. And he'd Scotch-taped above his computer monitor a dollar bill, on which was written "FOCUS." He would improve.

But it's hard to ignore the chilling way in which Wheeler's shtick—all of it—reflects on Harvard's administration, admissions office, faculty, students, and others who'd interacted with him for years, sucking up one fakery after another. Did they really believe such a person could exist? Yes, they did; not only did they, but they showered this such person with awards and honors and cash, rewarding the young man for making them feel great about themselves for attracting and forging such a person. They *adored* him. Grandiosity, even of the bizarre strain that Wheeler had taught himself to practice, sustains itself, multiplies, and warps minds only when no one bothers to roll down a window.

Many of the media analyses that followed Wheeler's unraveling took the same path to nowhere, and missed the point all over again: From what diagnosable mental affliction must this young man suffer? Psychopathy? Sociopathy? (Is that different from psychopathy?) Depression? *Manic* depression? Schizophrenic-hyper-lunatic-madness-disorder thing? In the usual journalistic procedure, self-appointed experts were contacted, and duly quoted, to offer commonsense observations branded with the seal of science. Narcissistic personality disorder was the closest they came to a consensus. This sounded about right to many online commenters. *Narcissist, yes.* That is the one.

But like many forms of overeager armchair diagnosis, the pathologized version of the Wheeler saga reveals at least as much about the diagnosticians as it does about the patient. While the complexity, thoroughness, and attention to detail evident in Wheeler's schemes put him in a rare class that may well merit psychiatric forensics, the cultural game that essentially licenses everyone and their mother to pin him with the proper chilling medical acronym comes close to violating the no-profit clause of Wheeler's probation agreement. It conveniently allows us to ignore the broader, uncomfortable class issues that might arise through the application of critical thought. If we can say that that guy over there did what he did because of severe narcissistic personality disorder, then, phew—he's just out of his mind, *unlike you and me.*

Only afterward, in an article such as the *Christian Science Monitor*'s "Harvard Hoax: Adam Wheeler Case Points to Rise of Student Fraud," do we begin to broach the issue of the prevailing trends that could induce normal folk—people like you and me!—to masquerade as overachieving Ivy Leaguers. The *Monitor* story quotes Barmak Nassirian, an associate executive director for the American Association of Collegiate Registrars and Admissions Officers and this piece's dial-an-expert of choice, finally saying the obvious goddamn thing:

"As the economic value of higher education has taken center stage in people's minds, we are seeing more often people trying to get ahead by whatever means necessary."

Amid the smoldering ruin of the post-meltdown American scene, the popular mind now sees one last means of ascending the ladder of social mobility: obtaining a four-year college degree. As more and more rush to climb it, scarcity sets in, and tuition spirals. You, the graduate, soon recognize that there aren't many jobs out there paying enough to allow you to service your six-figure debt load. College may be worth it now only if you can get accepted into what we call top-tier schools. But they've got no space for you—the children born into upper-middle-class families have taken those spots, and they've kicked down the ladder behind them. They will hoover up your money, present and future, and, eventually, they will lose it all playing financial computer games. The crimes of larceny, fraud, embezzlement, tax evasion, and bad taste will not apply to them. They will blame you for taking out loans that you couldn't afford, even though they were the ones who approved them and pushed them on you.

So, what else is there to do if you're a student from a rural Delaware public high school hoping to realize your God-given right to American social mobility as the byproduct of hard work? Student fraud, baby. It's the last hurrah. You went to Andover, you aced your SATs, you're transferring from MIT, you speak Old Persian and Old English and you've coauthored four books. You'll go to jail if they catch you, so don't get caught.

For all the rival diagnoses of Wheeler's psychiatric maladies caroming around the courts and the media, maybe his real problem was bad timing. Maybe he saw what he needed, far in the distance, and jumped too soon. Maybe in another generation or two, Harvard admissions officials will have caught up with the vanguard trends and grace a future Adam Wheeler with a full scholarship for the ingenious fabrications he will lay at their feet, instead of dispatching him to the correctional facility.

And by then, future Adam Wheelers will be bedding down in dorms named after Larry Summers, that greatest hustler among the great Harvard meritocrats, who rose to the top of the American elite from a hardscrabble childhood in nowheresville, with nowhere to go, no hope for a better life, only two prominent economists as parents and two of the greatest economists of the twentieth century as uncles. But he dared to dream against all odds.

You, meanwhile, will have to figure something else out.

The Missionary Position

BARBARA EHRENREICH

Most critics have regarded Ridley Scott's *Prometheus* in much the same way that Arthur Miller probably thought of Marilyn Monroe—gorgeous, but intellectually way out of her depth. No one denies the film's visual glory, which begins the moment a giant chalk-white alien strides out into the Icelandic wasteland, guzzles some gunk from a can, and splits open to release thousands of wriggling worm-like DNA strands into a waterfall. But when it comes to metaphysical coherence, the critical consensus is that *Prometheus* has nothing to offer. "There are no revelations," the *New York Times* opines, "only what are called, in the cynical jargon of commercial storytelling, 'reveals,' bits of momentarily surprising information bereft of meaning or resonance." In its refusal to offer an adequate accounting of the universe and our place in it, the film can even be accused of anti-intellectualism. "We were never really in the realm of working out logical solutions to difficult problems," Geoffrey O'Brien complains in the *New York Review of Books*, just a "cauldron" of "juicily irrational ingredients."

But *Prometheus* does have a clear-cut metaphysical proposition to offer, one so terrible as to be almost inadmissible. Consider the basic plot, minus the many alien invasions of human flesh, the references to corporate greed and alien WMDs, and the enigma of the devious HAL-like android: Guided by archaeological clues found in prehistoric rock art, a group of humans set out on a trillion-dollar expedition to visit the planet (actually

From *The Baffler*, no. 21

a moon) that the giant white alien came from. There, among innumerable horrors, since under its bleak surface this moon seems to be a breeding ground for lethal predators of the dark and squirmy variety, they find a cryogenically preserved clone or sibling of that original alien "creator" who seeded earth with DNA. The humans foolishly awaken him, perhaps expecting some sort of seminar on the purpose of life. Instead, the alien starts knocking heads off and strides away to resume his pre-nap project of traveling to and destroying the planet Earth. This, and not the DIY abortion of a squid-like alien fetus, is the emotional climax of the film, the point when Noomi Rapace screams at the homicidal alien, "I need to know why! What did we do wrong? Why do you hate us?"

True, we don't know whether the big white aliens are gods, manifestations of a single God, or operatives working for some higher power. But just how much theological clarity can you expect from a Hollywood action film? It doesn't take any great imaginative leap to see that Scott and his writers are confronting us with the possibility that there may be a God, and that He (or She or It or They) *is not good.*

This is not atheism. It is a strand of religious dissidence that usually flies well under the radar of both philosophers and cultural critics. For example, it took about five years before the critics noticed that Philip Pullman's popular trilogy *His Dark Materials* was not just about a dodgy or unreliable God, but about one who is actively malevolent. Atheism has become a respectable intellectual position, in some settings almost de rigueur, but as Bernard Schweizer explains in his enlightening 2010 book *Hating God: The Untold Story of Misotheism*, morally inspired *opposition* to God remains almost too radical to acknowledge. How many of Elie Wiesel's admirers know that he said, "Although I know I will never defeat God, I still fight him"? Or that Rebecca West declaimed that "the human will should [not] be degraded by bowing to this master criminal," and that she was echoing a sentiment already expressed by Zora Neale Hurston?

Barred from more respectable realms of speculation, the idea of an un-good God has been pretty much left to propagate in the fertile wetlands of science fiction. One of the early sci-fi classics of the twentieth century, H. P. Lovecraft's 1931 *At the Mountains of Madness*, offers a plotline that eerily prefigures *Prometheus*. An Antarctic expedition uncovers the ruins of a millions-of-years-old civilization created by extraterrestrial aliens, who awaken and kill most of the explorers. A couple of humans survive to determine, through a careful study of the ruins, that the aliens had "filtered down from the stars and concocted earth life as a joke or mistake." Not all sci-fi deities are so nasty. C. S. Lewis offered a Christlike lion god in the Narnia series; *Battlestar Galactica*'s climax featured a vision of a benevolent, and oddly Luddite, god. But many of the great sci-fi epics derive their philosophical frisson from a callous or outright wicked deity: the impertinent Vulcan god of *Star Trek V: The Final Frontier*, the tyrannical worm-god of *God Emperor of Dune*, the trickster sea god of *Solaris*.

There are less satanic sci-fi gods too—more ethereal, universal, and even intermittently nonviolent. Olaf Stapledon's 1937 *Star Maker* ends with its far-traveling human protagonist encountering the eponymous "eternal spirit": "Here was no pity, no proffer of salvation, no kindly aid. Or here were all pity and all love, but mastered by a frosty ecstasy." In Arthur C. Clarke's 1953 short story "The Nine Billion Names of God," Tibetan monks who have set themselves the task of generating all the possible names of God finally get some assistance from a computer brought to them by Western technicians. As the technicians make their way back down the mountainside from the monastery, they look up at the night sky to see that "without any fuss, the stars were going out." The monks had been right: the universe existed for the sole purpose of listing the names of God and, once this task was accomplished, there was no reason for the universe to go on. The theme of an über-Being who uses humans for its own inscrutable purposes is developed more fully in Clarke's novel *Childhood's End*, in which an "Overmind" of remote extraterrestrial provenance sets humans on a course toward ecstatic communion with each other—and, somehow, at the same time, with it. When that goal is achieved, the earth blows itself up, along with the last human on it, after which the Overmind presumably moves on to find a fresh planet—and species—to fulfill its peculiar cravings.

The idea of an un-good God, whether indifferent or actively sadistic, flies in the face of at least two thousand years of pro-God PR, much of it irrational and coming from professed "people of faith." God is perfectly good and loving, they assert with an almost infantile sense of entitlement; he "has a plan" for us, no matter how murky or misguided that plan often seems. Otherwise, they ask, as if evaluating a health care provider, what comfort does he have to offer us? Or they petulantly demand a "perfect" God—all-good, omnipotent, and omniscient—in the name of what amounts to human vanity. If we, the top dogs on our planet, are to worship some invisible Other, he (or it) had better be unimaginably perfect.

But you don't have to be a theist to insist on the goodness of God. Generations of secular social scientists and others writing in the social-science tradition have insisted that a good God, whether he exists or not, is good *for us*. The argument takes the form of a historical narrative: in the ancient past—and its seeming equivalent in small-scale or "primitive" societies—deities were plural, female as well as male, and often of no detectable moral valence. The ancient deities of Mediterranean peoples, for example, a pantheon that ranges from Zeus to Yahweh and Baal, were psycho-gods—insatiable consumers of blood sacrifice, abettors of genocide, even, in the case of Zeus, a serial rapist. They offered no rationales for their behavior, and when Job insisted on an explanation for the travails visited upon him, he was told, in effect, "Because I can." Further back, in prehistory, lurk deities too wild and bloody minded to take fully human form. They were predatory animals like Sekhmet, the lion-headed goddess of ancient Egypt, and the man-eating goddess Kali, who wears a tiger skin.

Then, the official narrative continues, somewhere between 900 and 200 BCE, the so-called "Axial Age," God underwent a major

MARK S. FISHER

makeover. Blood sacrifice was gradually abandoned; diverse and multiple gods fused into a single male entity; a divine concern for peace and order supposedly came to permeate the universe. In the often-told story of divine redemption, Yahweh matures into the kindly shepherd of the Psalms and finally into the all-loving person of Jesus, who is himself offered up as a sacrifice. Comparable changes occur outside the Mediterranean world, including in persistently polytheistic Hinduism, which gives up animal sacrifice and reaches for a sublime über-deity. What brought about this transformation?

Religious historian Karen Armstrong, probably the best-known living celebrant of axial progress, proposes in her 2006 book *The Great Transformation* that people simply got tired of the bad old gods' violence and immorality. Speaking of the late Vedic period in India, she writes that the traditional gods "were beginning to seem crude and unsatisfactory," leading to the search for a god "who was more worthy of worship." As people became nicer and more sensitive, they lost interest in the grand spectacles of animal sacrifice that constituted pre-axial religious ritual and sought a more "spiritual" experience. (She also mentions, but only in passing, that in some parts of the world people had a less exalted reason for abandoning blood sacrifice: they were running out of animals to sacrifice.) To Armstrong, the axial transformation had only one flaw—its "indifference to women," which is a pretty wan way to describe a theological shift that eliminated most of the planet's goddesses. But she humbly accepts the limits set by patriarchal monotheism: "Precisely because the question of women was so peripheral to the Axial Age, I found that any sustained discussion of this topic was distracting."

In his 2009 book *The Evolution of God*, polymathic scholar Robert Wright offered what promised to be an even more objective and secular explanation for God's "transformation." He argues that, for various reasons, people, or at least key peoples, were becoming more cosmopolitan and tolerant, hence in need of a single, universal, morally admirable deity. This seems like a useful approach, until you recall that the ultracosmopolitan and theologically tolerant Romans readily absorbed the gods of conquered peoples into their own polytheistic pantheon. But Wright hardly needs any concrete historical forces, because "moral progress . . . turns out to be embedded in the very logic of religion as mediated by the basic direction of social evolution"—which I suppose is a way of saying that things could only get better, because such is their "logic" and "basic direction." As Wright informs us, "cultural evolution was all along pushing divinity, and hence humanity, toward moral enlightenment."

The "New Atheists"—Christopher Hitchens, Richard Dawkins, Sam Harris, and Daniel Dennett—easily flicked away the argument that God's axial upgrade was accompanied by a general increase in human goodness and mercy. They note that the new-model deities, with prophets like Jesus and Muhammad, have proved just as effective at abetting cruelty and war as the old ones. If the gods have any of their reputed powers, and if they got nicer while humans did not, then we have to question the depth and sincerity of the gods' transformation—or whether it occurred at all. Interestingly, though, neither Armstrong nor Wright cedes any power or agency to the God whose growing goodness they applaud: to do so would be to give up their own claims to scholarly detachment. Their God is presented as nothing more than a projection of human needs and desires, an assessment no atheist could disagree with.

There is another theory of how humans became attached to "good" and increasingly monotheistic gods—and one that is refreshingly free of sweetness and optimism. As Jürgen Habermas and, more recently, in rich historical detail, Robert Bellah have pointed out, the "Axial Period" was a time of endemic warfare, intensified by the introduction of iron weapons across Eurasia. The maintenance of armies and the practice of war require strong central authorities—kings and eventually emperors—who discover that it is both risky and inefficient to try to rule their domestic populations entirely by force. Far easier to persuade the public that the king or the emperor is *deserving* of obedience because the deity he represents, or even embodies, is himself so transcendentally good. The autocrat who rules by divine right—from Constantine to Hirohito, the God-emperor of Japanese State Shintoism—demands not only obedience, but gratitude and love.

The good, post-axial God has not, of course, always been a reliable ally of tyrants. Christianity has again and again helped inspire movements against the powerful, such as, for example, the abolitionists and the twentieth-century Civil Rights movement. But this does not mean that the good God is necessarily good for us, or at least for the downtrodden majority of us. The unforgivable crime of the post-axial religions is to encourage the conflation of authority and benevolence, of hierarchy and justice. When the pious bow down before the powerful or, in our own time, the mega-churches celebrate wealth and its owners, the "good" God is just doing his job of what Habermas called "legitimation."

In 1974 Philip K. Dick experienced a theophany—a "self-disclosure by the divine"—which deftly summarizes science fiction's contribution to theology. It was a shattering revelation, leaving him feeling more like "a hit-and-run accident victim than a Buddha." He disintegrated into mental illness, at least to the point of earning a bed in a locked psychiatric ward for several weeks. As related in his novel *Valis*, in which the author figures as the protagonist, he fought back by working obsessively to understand and communicate his encounter with a deity of extraterrestrial origin that was "*in no way like mortal creatures*" (his italics). This deity or deities—for there may be at least a half dozen of them in Dick's idiosyncratic cosmogony—bear some resemblance to biological creatures: they have their own agendas, and what they seek, through their self-disclosures to humans, is "interspecies symbiosis."

If God is an alternative life-form or member of an alien species, then we have no reason to believe that It is (or They are), in any humanly recognizable sense of the word, "good." Human conceptions of morality almost all derive from the intensely social nature of the human species: our young require years of caretaking, and we have, over the course of evolution, depended on each other's cooperation for mutual defense. Thus we have lived, for most of our existence as a species, in highly interdependent bands that have had good reasons to emphasize the values of loyalty and heroism, even altruism and compassion. But these virtues, if not unique to us, are far from universal in the animal world (or, of course, the human one). Why should a Being whose purview supposedly includes the entire universe share the tribal values of a particular group of terrestrial primates?

Besides, Dick may have been optimistic in suggesting that what the deity hungers for is "interspecies symbiosis." Symbiosis is not the only possible long-term relationship between different species. Parasitism, as hideously displayed in Ridley Scott's *Alien* series, must also be considered, along with its quicker-acting version, predation. In fact, if anything undermines the notion of a benevolent deity, it has to be the ubiquity of predation in the human and nonhuman animal worlds. Who would a "good" God favor—the antelope or the lion with hungry cubs waiting in its den, the hunter or the fawn? For Charles Darwin, the deal-breaker was the Ichneumon wasp, which stings its prey in order to paralyze them so that they may be eaten alive by the wasp's larvae. "I cannot persuade myself," wrote Darwin, "that a beneficent and omnipotent God would have designedly created the Ichneumonidae with the express intention of their feeding within the living bodies of Caterpillars, or that a cat should play with mice." Or, as we may ask more generally: What is kindness or love in a biological world shaped by interspecies predation? "Morality is of the highest importance," Albert Einstein once said, "but for us, not for God."

In *Prometheus*, the first alien releases DNA on earth about five hundred million years ago, on the eve, in many viewers' interpretation, of what has been called the Precambrian evolutionary explosion. If so, it was not life that the alien initiated on earth, because life predated the Precambrian. What he did may have been far worse; he may have infected the earth with the code or script for interspecies predation. Before the "explosion," terrestrial life was mostly unicellular and, judging from the low frequency of claws, shells, and other forms of weaponry found in the fossil record, relatively peaceful. Afterwards, living creatures became bigger, more diverse, better armed, and probably either meaner or a lot more frightened: the "arms race" between predator and prey had begun. The causality remains in question here, with scientists still puzzling over the origins of predation and its role in triggering the runaway evolutionary process that led, from the Cambrian on, to humans, to science fiction, and to the idea of God.

If the doughy aliens are not the ultimate deities whose morality we need to assess, then who or what is? Who do these aliens work for—or against? At the end of the movie, with all of their human comrades dead, the android and the Noomi Rapace character rebuild an alien space ship and set off to find the planet that, according to the android's research, the aliens themselves originally came from. The possibility of a good God or gods, signaled by the cross Noomi wears around her neck, remains open—as it must, of course, for the sequel.

But, contra so many of the critics, we have learned an important lesson from the magnificent muddle of *Prometheus*: if you see something that looks like a god—say, something descending from the sky in a flaming chariot, accompanied by celestial choir sounds and trailing great clouds of star dust—do not assume that it is either a friend or a savior. Keep a wary eye on the intruder. By all means, do not fall down on your knees.

MARK S. FISHER

PART THREE

POSITIVE THINKING

Facebook Feminism, Like It or Not

SUSAN FALUDI

The congregation swooned as she bounded on stage, the prophet sealskin sleek in her black skinny ankle pants and black ballet flats, a lavalier microphone clipped to the V-neck of her black button-down sweater. "All right!! Let's go!!" she exclaimed, throwing out her arms and pacing the platform before inspirational graphics of glossy young businesswomen in managerial action poses. "Super excited to have all of you here!!"

"Whoo!!" the young women in the audience replied. The camera, which was livestreaming the event in the Menlo Park, California, auditorium to college campuses worldwide, panned the rows of well-heeled Stanford University econ majors and MBA candidates. Some clutched copies of the day's hymnal: the speaker's new book, which promised to dismantle "internal obstacles" preventing them from "acquiring power." The atmosphere was TED-Talk-cum-tent-revival-cum-Mary-Kay-cosmetics-convention. The salvation these adherents sought on this April day in 2013 was admittance to the pearly gates of the corporate corner office.

"Stand up," the prophet instructed, "if you've ever said out loud, to another human being—and you have to have said it out loud—'I am going to be the number one person in my field. I will be the CEO of a major company. I will be governor. I will be the number one person in my field.'" A small, although not inconsiderable, percentage of the young women rose to their feet.

The speaker consoled those still seated; she,

From *The Baffler*, no. 23

too, had once been one of them. When she was voted "most likely to succeed" in high school, she confided, she had begged a yearbook editor to delete that information, "because most likely to succeed doesn't get a date for the prom." Those days were long gone, ever since she'd had her conversion on the road to Davos: she'd "leaned in" to her ambitions *and* enhanced her "likability"—and they could do the same. What's more, if they took the "lean in" pledge, they might free themselves from some of those other pesky problems that hold women back in the workplace. "If you lean forward," she said, "you will get yourself into a position where the organization you're with values you a lot and is therefore willing to be more flexible. Or you'll get promoted and then you'll get paid more and you'll be able to afford better child care." If you "believe you have the skills to do anything" and "have the ambition to lead," then you will "change the world" for women. "We get closer to the goal of true equality with every single one of you who leans in."

The pitch delivered, Lean In founder and Facebook chief operating officer Sheryl Sandberg summoned her deacon to close the deal. Rachel Thomas hustled onstage, a Sandberg Mini-Me in matching black ensemble (distinguished only by the color of her ballet flats and baubled necklace, both of which were gold). She's Lean In's president. (Before *Lean In* hit the bookstores, it was already a fully staffed operation, an organization purporting to be "a global community committed to encouraging and supporting women leaning in to their ambitions.") "I *really* want to invite you to join our community!" Thomas told the assembled. "You'll get daily inspiration and insights."

Joining "the community" was just a click away. In fact, the community was already uploaded and ready to receive them; all they had to do was hit the "Lean In Today" button on their computer screen . . . and, oh yeah, join Facebook. (There is no entry into Lean In's Emerald e-Kingdom except through the Facebook portal; Sandberg has kept her message of liberation confined within her own corporate brand.)

Thomas enumerated the "three things" that Lean In offered. (In the Lean In Community, there are invariably three things required to achieve your aims.) First, Thomas instructed, "Come like us on

Facebook" (and, for extra credit, post your own inspirational graphic on Lean In's Facebook "photo gallery" and "tag your friends, tell them why you're leaning in!"). Second, watch Lean In's online "education" videos, twenty-minute lectures from "experts" (business school professors, management consultants, and a public speaking coach) with titles like "Power and Influence" and "Own the Room." Third, create a "Lean In Circle" with eight to ten similarly aspirational young women. The circles, Lean In literature stresses, are to promote "peer mentorship" only—*not* to deliver aid and counsel from experienced female elders who might actually help them advance. Thomas characterized the circle as "a book club with a purpose." All they had to do was click on the "Create a Circle" button on LeanIn.org and follow the "three easy steps." "We provide everything that you need to do it," Thomas assured. "All the materials, all the how-to information, and a very cool technology platform called Mightybell." Mightybell's CEO, it so happens, is Gina Bianchini, cofounder of Lean In. "So it's really easy to do, and don't wait!" Thomas said. "Go do it for yourself today!"

Since its unveiling in spring 2013, the Lean In campaign has been reeling in a steadily expanding group of tens of thousands of followers with its tripartite E-Z plan for getting to the top. But the real foundation of the movement is, of course, Sheryl Sandberg's bestselling book, *Lean In: Women, Work, and the Will to Lead,* billed modestly by its author as "sort of a feminist manifesto." Sandberg's mantra has become the feminist rallying cry of the moment, praised by notable figures such as Gloria Steinem, Jane Fonda, Marlo Thomas, and *Nation* columnist Katha Pollitt. A *Time* magazine cover story hails Sandberg for "embarking on the most ambitious mission to reboot feminism and reframe discussions of gender since the launch of *Ms.* magazine in 1971." Pretty good for somebody who, "as of two and a half years ago," as Sandberg confessed on her book tour, "had never said the word woman aloud. Because that's not how you get ahead in the world."

The lovefest continues on LeanIn.org's "Meet the Community" page, where tribute is paid by Sandberg's high-powered network of celebrities, corporate executives, and media moguls (*many* media moguls), among them Oprah Winfrey, *New York Times* executive editor Jill Abramson, *Newsweek* and *Daily Beast* editor in chief Tina Brown, *Huffington Post* founder Arianna Huffington, *Cosmopolitan* editor in chief Joanna Coles, former *Good Morning America* coanchor Willow Bay, former first lady Laura Bush (and both of her daughters), former California first lady and TV host Maria Shriver, U.S. senators Barbara Boxer and Elizabeth Warren, Harvard president Drew Gilpin Faust, Dun & Bradstreet CEO Sara Mathew, Yahoo CEO Marissa Mayer, Coca-Cola marketing executive Wendy Clark, fashion designer Diane von Furstenberg, supermodel Tyra Banks, and actor (and Avon "global ambassador") Reese Witherspoon.

Beneath highly manicured glam shots, each "member" or "partner" reveals her personal "Lean In moment." The accounts inevitably have happy finales—the Lean In guidelines instruct contributors to "share a positive ending." Tina Brown's Lean In moment: getting her parents to move from England to "the apartment across the corridor from us on East 57th Street in New York," so her mother could take care of the children while Brown took the helm at *The New Yorker*. If you were waiting for someone to lean in for child care legislation, keep holding your breath. So far, there's no discernible groundswell.

When asked why she isn't pushing for structural social and economic change, Sandberg says she's all in favor of "public policy reform," though she's vague about how exactly that would work, beyond generic tsk-tsking about the pay gap and lack of maternity leave. She says she supports reforming the workplace—but the particulars of comparable worth or subsidized child care are hardly prominent elements of her book or her many media appearances.

Sandberg began her TED Talk in December 2010, the trial balloon for the Lean In campaign, with a one-sentence nod to "flex time," training, and other "programs" that might advance working women, and then declared, "I want to talk about none of that today." What she wanted to talk about, she said, was "what we can do as individuals" to climb to the top of the command chain.

This clipped, jarring shift from the collective grievances of

ELEANOR DAVIS

working women to the feel-good options open to credentialed, professional types is also a pronounced theme in *Lean In*, the book. In the opening pages, Sandberg acknowledges that "the vast majority of women are struggling to make ends meet," but goes on to stress that "each subsequent chapter focuses on an adjustment or difference that we can make ourselves." When asked in a radio interview in Boston about the external barriers women face, Sandberg agreed that women are held back "by discrimination and sexism and terrible public policy" and "we should reform all of that," but then immediately suggested that the concentration on such reforms has been disproportionate, arguing that "the conversation can't be only about that, and in a lot of ways the conversation on women is usually *only* about that." Toward the end of the Q&A period at the Menlo Park event, a student watching online asked, "What would you say to the critics who argue that lower socioeconomic status makes it difficult to lean in?" Sandberg replied that leaning in might be even "more important for women who are struggling to make ends meet," and then offered this anecdote as evidence: She had received a fan email from a reader who "never graduated from college" and had gone back to work in 1998 after her husband lost his job. "Until she read *Lean In*, she had never asked for a raise. And last week, she asked for a raise." Pause for the drum roll. "*And she got it*! That's what this is about."

Lean In's rank-and-file devotees don't get the marquee billing accorded the celebrity and executive set on the handpicked "Meet the Community" page. Nevertheless, they seem eager to "join the community": as of July 12, 2013, they had "liked" Lean In 237,552 times. Their online participation on Lean In's Facebook page is limited to making comments in response to the organization's announcements of the latest Lean In marketing triumphs. ("Very excited that Lean In is #1 on The New York Times Book Review - Six weeks in a row!"; "Very excited to see Sheryl Sandberg on the TIME 100 list of the most influential people in the world!"; "We're excited to watch Sheryl Sandberg Lean In with Oprah this weekend. Tune in to watch Oprah's Next Chapter on Sunday, March 24 at 9 p.m. ET/PT on OWN: Oprah Winfrey Network!")

Evidently the "likers" are excited too: they cheer the media conquests of the Leaner-In-in-chief, whose success began at the top (thanks not to "peer mentoring" but to her powerful college adviser, former Harvard University president Larry Summers) and who has remained there ever since—a stratospheric hurtle from Harvard to the World Bank to the U.S. Treasury Department to Google to Facebook. The comments read like a Sandbergian amen corner: "Congratulations Sheryl! You diserve [*sic*] it! ♥"; "This is such an awesome book! It has really energized me with refocusing on my career goals"; "am reading book on my kindle now, awesome so far!"; "Awesome talk!!!"; "God Bless! And lets [*sic*] continue to spread this message and lean in!"; "Sheryl is igniting the new feminine movement!"; "THANK YOU FOR LEADING THE REVOLUTION!!!!☺"; "sheryl is inspirational! I missed zumba for this and happy I did!"

The scene at the Menlo Park auditorium, and its conflation of "believe in yourself" faith and material rewards, will be familiar to anyone who's ever spent a Sunday inside a prosperity-gospel megachurch or watched Reverend Ike's vintage "You Deserve the Best!" sermon on YouTube. But why is that same message now ascendant among the American feminists of the new millennium?

Sandberg's admirers would say that Lean In is using free-market beliefs to advance the cause of women's equality. Her detractors would say (and have) that her organization is using the desire for women's equality to advance the cause of the free market. And they would both be right. In embodying that contradiction, Sheryl Sandberg would not be alone and isn't so new. For the last two centuries, feminism, like evangelicalism, has been in a dance with capitalism.

All As One

In 1834 America's first industrial wage earners, the "mill girls" of Lowell, Massachusetts, embarked on their own campaign for women's advancement in the workplace. They didn't "lean in," though. When their male overseers in the nation's first large-scale planned industrial city cut their already paltry wages by 15 to 20 percent, the textile workers declared a "turn-out," one of the nation's earliest industrial strikes. That first effort failed, but its participants did not concede defeat. The Lowell women would stage another turn-out two years later, create the first union of working women in American history, lead a fight for the ten-hour work day, and conceive of an increasingly radical vision that took aim at both corporate power and the patriarchal oppression of women. Their bruising early encounter with American industry fueled a nascent feminist outlook that would ultimately find full expression in the first wave of the American women's movement.

Capitalism, you could say, had midwifed feminism.

And capitalism, Sandberg would say, still sustains it. But what happened between 1834 and 2013—between "turn-out" and "lean in"—to make Lean In such an odd heir to the laurels of Lowell? An answer lies in the history of those early textile mills.

The Lowell factory owners had recruited "respectable" Yankee farmers' daughters from the New England countryside, figuring that respectable would translate into docile. They figured wrong. The forces of industrialization had propelled young women out of the home, breaking the fetters binding them to the patriarchal family, unleashing the women into urban areas with few social controls, and permitting them to begin thinking of themselves as public citizens. The combination of newly gained independence and increasingly penurious, exploitative conditions proved combustible—and the factory owners' reduction in pay turned out to be the match that lit the tinder. Soon after they heard the news, the "mill girls"—proclaiming that they "remain in possession of our unquestionable rights"—shut down their looms and walked out.

From the start, the female textile workers made the connection between labor and women's rights. Historian Thomas Dublin, in his book on the Lowell mill girls, *Women at Work*, cites an account in the Boston *Evening Transcript*. "One of the leaders mounted a pump," the article reported, "and made a flaming Mary Woolstonecroft [*sic*] speech on the rights of women and the iniquities of the '*monied* aristocracy.'" The speech "produced a powerful effect on her auditors, and they determined 'to have their own way if they died for it.'" In a statement the mill workers issued on the first day of the turn-out, titled "Union is Power," they elaborated:

> The oppressing hand of avarice would enslave us, and to gain their object, they gravely tell us of the pressure of the times, this we are already sensible of, and deplore it. If any are in want, the Ladies will be compassionate and assist them; but we prefer to have the dispos-

> ing of our charities in our own hands; and as we are free, we would remain in possession of what kind Providence has bestowed upon us, and remain daughters of freemen still.

The mill proprietors looked on with unease at what they regarded as an "amizonian [*sic*] display" and "a spirit of evil omen."

The Lowell turn-out was a communal endeavor, built on intense bonds of sisterhood forged around the clock: by day on the factory floor, where the women worked in pairs, with the more experienced female worker training and looking out for the newcomer, and by night in the company boarding houses, where they shared cramped quarters, often two to a bed, and embroiled themselves in late-night discussions about philosophy, music, literature, and, increasingly, social and economic injustice. As Dublin observes of the web of "mutual dependence" that prevailed in the Lowell mill workforce, the strike was "made possible because women had come to form a 'community' of operatives in the mill, rather than simply a group of individual workers." An actual community, that is—not an online like-a-thon. Tellingly, the strike began when a mill agent, hoping to nip agitation in the bud, fired one of the more voluble factory workers whom he regarded as the ringleader. The other women immediately walked out in protest over her expulsion. The petition they signed and circulated concluded: "Resolved, That none of us will go back, unless they receive us all as one."

In a matter of years, the Lowell women would become increasingly radical, as crusaders for both worker and gender equality. They had originally been encouraged to write ladylike stories for the mill girls' literary magazine, the *Lowell Offering*, which was launched by a local minister and supported by the textile companies. By the 1840s, many young working women were filing copy instead with the *Voice of Industry*, a labor newspaper published by the Lowell Female Labor Reform Association. The paper's "Female Department," edited by the association's president, Sarah Bagley, featured articles by and about women workers, with a declared mission both to revamp "the system of labor" and "defend woman's rights." "You have been degraded long enough," an article in the *Voice* advised its female readers. "You have sufficiently long been considered 'the inferior'—a kind of 'upper servant,' to obey and reverence, and be in subjection to your equal." No more. "Enter at once upon your privileges," the article exhorted, calling on women to demand their equal rights to education, employment, and respect from men.

The mill workers went on to agitate against an unjust system in all its forms. When Lowell's state representative thwarted the women's statewide battle for the ten-hour day, they mobilized and succeeded in having him voted out of office—nearly eighty years before women had the vote. Mill women in Lowell, and in the decades to come, their counterparts throughout New England, threw themselves into the abolitionist movement (drawing connections between the cotton picked by slaves and the fabric they wove in the mills); campaigned for better health care, safer schools, decent housing, and cleaner water and streets; and joined the fight for women's suffrage. Sarah Bagley went on to work for prison reform, women's rights, and education and decent jobs for poor women and prostitutes. After a stint as the first female telegrapher in the nation (where she pointed out that she was being paid two-thirds of a male telegrapher's salary), she taught herself homeopathic medicine and became a doctor, billing her patients according to her personal proviso: "To the rich, one dollar—to the poor gratis."

Increasingly, the mill girls were joined in these efforts by their middle-class sisters. Cross-class female solidarity surfaced early in Lawrence, Massachusetts, after the horrific building collapse of the Pemberton Mills factory in 1860, which killed 145 workers, most of them women and children. (The mills in Lawrence would later give rise to the famously militant "Bread and Roses" strike of 1912, in which female workers again played a leading role.) In the aftermath of the Pemberton disaster, middle-class women in the region flocked to provide emergency relief and, radicalized by what they witnessed, went on to establish day nurseries, medical clinics and hospitals, and cooperative housing to serve the needs of working women. By the postbellum years, with industrialization at full tide and economic polarization at record levels, a critical mass of middle-class female reformers had come to believe that the key to women's elevation was not, as they once thought, "moral uplift," but economic independence—and that cross-class struggle on behalf of female workers was the key to achieving it.

A host of organizations launched by professional women, like Sorosis and the Women's Educational and Industrial Union (WEIU), sprang up to campaign for the economic advancement of both middle- and working-class women. "From its first days," historian Mari Jo Buhle observes in *Women and American Socialism*, "Sorosis encompassed broader purposes than aid to a handful of aspiring women professionals. All working women, the leaders believed, shared a common grievance and a common need for organization." The WEIU in Boston, like Lean In, held lectures to promote women in business—but it also sent investigative teams to expose poor conditions for women on the factory and retail floor, procured legal services for working women denied their rightful wages, offered job referral services for women of all classes, and set up cooperative exchanges for homebound women to sell their handcrafts so that even they might achieve some measure of fiscal independence from their husbands. In Chicago, the Illinois Woman's Alliance launched a full-bore probe of abusive sweatshops that spawned a congressional investigation, successfully lobbied for a shorter workday for sweatshop workers, and even demanded legal rights for prostitutes, including the right to be free of police harassment.

From the sounds of recent pronouncements, it might seem that efforts to elevate the woman worker have finally paid off. With giddy triumphalism, books like Hanna Rosin's *The End of Men: And the Rise of Women* and Liza Mundy's *The Richer Sex: How the New Majority of Female Breadwinners Is Transforming Sex, Love, and Family* (both published in 2012) celebrate the imminent emergence of a female supremacy. "For the first time in history, the global economy is becoming a place where women are finding more success than men," Rosin declared, noting that twelve of the fifteen jobs projected to grow the fastest in the United States in the next decade "are occupied primarily by women." The female worker, she wrote, is "becoming the standard by which success is measured." Mundy, who called this supremacy the "Big Flip," predicted that, thanks to the new economy, we would soon be living in a world "where women routinely support households and outearn the men they are married to," and that men "will gladly hitch their wagon to a female star."

A star like Sheryl Sandberg, whose feminism seems a capstone of female ascendancy. Never mind that the "fastest-growing" future occupations for women—home health aide, child care worker, customer service representative, office clerk, food service worker—are among the lowest paid, most with few to no benefits and little possibility for "advancement." Progress has stalled for many ordinary women—or gone into reverse. The poverty rate for women, according to the Census Bureau's latest statistics, is at its highest point since 1993, and the "extreme poverty rate" among women is at the highest point ever recorded.

But there seems to be little tangible cross-class solidarity coming from the triumphalists, despite their claims to be speaking for all womankind. "If we can succeed in adding more female voices at the highest levels," Sandberg writes in her book, "we will expand opportunities and extend fairer treatment to all." But which highest-level voices? When former British prime minister Margaret ("I hate feminism") Thatcher died, Lean In's Facebook page paid homage to the Iron Lady and invited its followers to post "which moments were most memorable to you" from Thatcher's tenure. That invitation inspired a rare outburst of *un*-"positive" remarks in the comment section, at least from some women in the United Kingdom. "Really??" wrote one. "She was a tyrant. . . . Just because a woman is in a leadership position does not make her worthy of respect, especially if you were on the receiving end of what she did to lots of people." "So disappointing that Lean In endorses Thatcher as a positive female role model," wrote another. "She made history as a woman, but went on to use her power to work against the most vulnerable, including women and their children."

Even when celebrating more laudable examples of female leadership, Lean In's spotlight rarely roves beyond the uppermost echelon. One looks in vain through its website statements, literature, and declarations at its public events for evidence of concern about how the other half lives—or rather, the other 99 percent. As Linda Burnham observed in a perceptive essay on Portside.org, Lean In "has essentially produced a manifesto for corporatist feminism," a "1% feminism" that "is all about the glass ceiling, never about the floor." The movement originally forged to move the great mass of women has been hijacked to serve the individual (and privileged) girl.

As it turns out, it's a hijacking that's long been under way.

Dream On

The landmark year in the transition from common struggle to individual enhancement was 1920—ironically, the same year that women won the right to vote. In the course of the twenties, an ascendant consumer economy would do as much to derail feminist objectives as advance them. Capitalism, feminism's old midwife, had become its executioner. And a cleverly disguised one: this grim reaper donned a feminist-friendly face.

The rising new forces of consumer manipulation—mass media, mass entertainment, national advertising, the fashion and beauty industries, popular psychology—all seized upon women's yearnings for independence and equality and redirected them to the marketplace. Over and over, mass merchandisers promised women an ersatz version of emancipation, the fulfillment of individual, and aspirational, desire. Why mount a collective protest against the exploitations of the workplace when it was so much more gratifying—not to mention easier—to advance yourself (and only yourself) by shopping for "liberating" products that expressed your "individuality" and signaled your (seemingly) elevated class status?

The message was ubiquitous in 1920s advertising pitched to women. "An Ancient Prejudice Has Been Removed," decreed a Lucky Strike banner, above a picture of an unfettered flapper girl wreathed in cigarette smoke. Enjoy "positive agitation" at home, Hoover vacuum ads entreated, with the new machine's "revolutionary cleaning principle." "Woman suffrage made the American woman the political equal of her man," General Electric cheered. "The little switch which commands the great servant Electricity is making her workshop the equal of her man's." That "workshop," of course, was the domestic bower, to which privileged women were now expected to retire. In 1929, at the behest of the American Tobacco Company, Edward Bernays, the founding father of public relations, organized a procession of debutantes to troop down Fifth Avenue during the Easter Parade, asserting their "right" to smoke in public by puffing "torches of freedom." Women's quest for social and economic freedom had been reenacted as farce.

Where industrial capitalism had driven women as a group to mobilize to change society, its consumer variant induced individual women to submit, each seemingly of her own free will, to a mass-produced culture. They were then encouraged to call that submission liberation. This is the mode that much of American feminism has been stuck in ever since, despite attempts by late-1960s radical feminists to dismantle the female consumer armament of cosmetics, girdles, and hair spray. (The dismantling became quite literal in the 1968 demonstration against the Miss America Pageant, where young radicals hurled "instruments of female torture" into a "Freedom Trash Can.")

In the postindustrial economy, feminism has been retooled as a vehicle for expression of the self, a "self" as marketable consumer object, valued by how many times it's been bought—or, in our electronic age, how many times it's been clicked on. "Images of a certain kind of successful woman proliferate," British philosopher Nina Power observes of contemporary faux-feminism in her 2009 book, *One-Dimensional Woman*. "The city worker in heels, the flexible agency employee, the hard-working hedonist who can afford to spend her income on vibrators and wine—and would have us believe that—yes—capitalism is a girl's best friend."

In the 1920s male capitalists invoked feminism to advance their brands of corporate products. Nearly a century later, female marketers are invoking capitalism to advance their corporate brand of feminism. Sandberg's "Lean In Community" is Exhibit A. What is she selling, after all, if not the product of the company she works for? Every time a woman signs up for Lean In, she's made another conquest for Facebook. Facebook conquers women in more than one way. Nearly 60 percent of the people who do the daily labor on Facebook—maintaining their pages, posting their images, tagging their friends, driving the traffic—are female, and, unlike the old days of industrial textile manufacturing, they don't even have to be paid or housed. "Facebook benefits every time a woman uploads her picture," Kate Losse, a former employee of Facebook and author of *The Boy Kings*, a keenly observed memoir of her time there, pointed out to me. "And what is she getting? Nothing, except a constant flow of 'likes.'"

When Losse came to Facebook in 2005, she was only the second woman hired in a company that then had fifty employees. Her job was to answer user-support emails. Low-wage customer support work would soon become Facebook's pink ghetto. Losse recalled the decor that adorned the company walls in those years: drawings of "stylized women with large breasts bursting from small tops." On Mark Zuckerberg's birthday, the women at the company were instructed to wear T-shirts displaying his photo, like groupies.

"It was like *Mad Men*," she writes of the office environment in *Boy Kings*, "but real and happening in the current moment, as if in repudiation of fifty years of social progress." A few years into her tenure, Losse was promoted to oversee the translation of Facebook's site into other languages. The promotion didn't come with an increase in pay. When Losse, like the woman in Sandberg's anecdote, asked for a raise, she was refused. "You've already doubled your salary in a year," her manager told her, "and it wouldn't be fair to the engineers who haven't had that raise"—the engineers (virtually all male) who were already at the top of the pay scale, unlike her. Her final job at Facebook was to serve as Mark Zuckerberg's personal "writer and researcher." The job, or rather "the role," as Zuckerberg called it, required her to write "his" blog entries on Facebook and post "his" updates to the Zuckerberg fan page.

Losse quit in 2010 to become a writer—of her own words, not

her boss's. In March 2013 she wrote a thought-provoking piece about Lean In for *Dissent*, "Feminism's Tipping Point: Who Wins from Leaning In?" The winners, she notes, are not the women in tech, who "are much more likely to be hired in support functions where they are paid a bare minimum, given tiny equity grants compared to engineers and executives, and given raises on the order of fifty cents an hour rather than thousands of dollars." These are the fast-growth jobs for women in high technology, just as Menlo Park's postindustrial campuses are the modern equivalent of the Lowell company town. Sandberg's book proposed to remedy that system, Losse notes, not by changing it but simply by telling women to work harder:

> Life is a race, Sandberg is telling us, and the way to win is through the perpetual acceleration of one's own labor: moving forward, faster. The real antagonist identified by *Lean In* then is not institutionalized discrimination against women, but women's reluctance to accept accelerating career demands.

For her candor, Losse came under instant attack from the Sandberg sisterhood. Brandee Barker, a Lean In publicist and former head of public relations for Facebook, sent Losse the following message: "There's a special place in hell for you." Losse defended herself the only way you can in the age of social media: she took a screenshot of Barker's nastygram and tweeted it. "Maybe sending Hellfire and Damnation messages is part of the Lean In PR strategy," Losse wrote in her tweet. "LEAN IN OR ELSE YOU'RE GOING TO HELL." Other Lean In naysayers have been similarly damned by Lean In devotees. When *New York Times* columnist Maureen Dowd wrote a measured critique of Lean In, Sandberg's fans promptly and widely denounced her. Losse said she's not surprised by the fire-and-brimstone ferocity of the response. "There's this cult-like religiosity to Facebook and Lean In," she told me. "If you're 'in,' you belong—and if you're not, you're going to hell."

That Lean In is making its demands of individual women, not the corporate workplace, is evident in the ease with which it has signed up more than two hundred corporate and organization "partners" to support its campaign. The roster includes some of the biggest American corporations: Chevron, General Electric, Procter & Gamble, Comcast, Bank of America and Citibank, Coca-Cola and Pepsico, AT&T and Verizon, Ford and GM, Pfizer and Merck & Co., Costco and Walmart, and, of course, Google and Facebook. Never before have so many corporations joined a revolution. Virtually nothing is required of them—not even a financial contribution. "There are no costs associated with partnering with Lean In," the organization's manual assures. "We just ask that you publicly support our mission and actively promote our Community to your employees." All the companies have to do is post their logo on Lean In's "Platform Partners" page, along with a quote from one of their executives professing the company's commitment to advancing women. The testimonials are predictably platitudinous:

- Ed Gilligan, American Express president: "At American Express, we believe having more women in senior leadership is critical to fostering an environment that embraces diverse opinions and empowers all employees to reach their full potential. It's this spirit of inclusiveness that helps us make better decisions today to drive our growth for tomorrow."

- Paul Bulcke, Nestlé CEO: "At Nestlé we are committed to enhancing the career opportunities for both men and women, and the knowledge and expertise provided by Lean In will help accelerate our journey."

- Jeff Wilke, Amazon senior vice president, consumer business: "At Amazon, we lean in to challenge ourselves to develop as leaders by building things that matter. We solve problems in new ways and value calculated risk-taking; many decisions are reversible. Bold directions that inspire results help us to think differently and look around corners for ways to serve our customers."

That last statement manages to endorse Lean In without even bothering to mention women. Many of the high-level executives dispensing quotations are male—and a notable number of the female executives are in "communications," "human resources," or "diversity" posts. And funny—or not—how often professed "commitment" to women's advancement fails to bear up under inspection. Run some Platform Partner names through databases that track legal cases, and you will find a bumper crop of recent or pending EEOC grievances and state and federal court actions involving sex discrimination, sexual harassment, pregnancy discrimination, unfair promotion policies, wrongful terminations, and gender-based retaliations against female employees. Here are just a few:

• Lean In Platform Partner Citibank: In 2010 six current and former female employees sued Citibank's parent company, Citigroup, for discriminating against women at all levels, paying them less, overlooking them for promotions, and firing them first in company-wide layoffs. Their federal court complaint held that the company "turns a blind eye" to widespread discrimination against women and detailed the paltry numbers of women in upper management in every division—with the proportion of female managing directors in some divisions as low as 9 percent. All nineteen members of the bank's executive committee are male. "The outdated 'boys club,'" the complaint concluded, "is alive and well at Citigroup."

• Lean In Platform Partner Booz Allen Hamilton: In 2011 Molly Finn, a former partner at the firm who had been fired after serving as its highest-ranking female employee and a star performer, sued for sex discrimination. She charged the company with creating an unwelcome environment for women and intentionally barring them from top leadership posts. During a review for a promotion (which she was subsequently denied), she was told to stop saying "pro-woman, feminist things," she recalled.

Soon after Finn's suit, a second longtime partner and leading moneymaker, Margo Fitzpatrick, sued the company for sex discrimination and retaliatory termination. In court papers, she charged that the firm has "maintained a 'glass ceiling' that intentionally excludes highly-qualified women." The complaint went on to note, "Currently, The Firm has no female partners in the pipeline for Senior

Partner." With the termination of Fitzpatrick and Finn, "the number of females in the partnership has dwindled to 21—or only 18%."

• Lean In Platform Partner Wells Fargo: In 2011 the bank reached a class-action settlement with 1,200 female financial advisers for $32 million. The sex discrimination suit charged that the bank's brokerage business, Wells Fargo Advisors (originally Wachovia Securities), discriminated against women in compensation and signing bonuses, denied them promotions, and cheated them out of account distributions, investment partnerships, and mentoring and marketing opportunities.

• Goldman Sachs (whose philanthropic arm, the Goldman Sachs Foundation, is a Lean In Platform Partner): In 2010 former employees of Goldman Sachs filed a class-action suit against the company, accusing Wall Street's most profitable investment bank of "systematic and pervasive discrimination" against female employees, subjecting them to hostile working conditions and treating them "like disposable, second-class citizens."

• Lean In Platform Partners Mondelez and Nestlé: In 2013 an Oxfam investigation in four countries where the two companies outsourced their cocoa farms found that the women working in the cocoa fields and processing plants that the companies relied on "suffer substantial discrimination and inequality." When women at a cocoa processing factory demanded equal treatment and pay, the investigation noted, all of the female workers were fired. The same companies that "put women first in their advertisements," Oxfam concluded, "are doing very little to address poor conditions faced by the women who grow cocoa."

• Lean In Platform Partner Costco: In 2012 a federal judge approved a huge class-action lawsuit that alleges Costco discriminated against about seven hundred women and denied them promotions. The company, the suit charged, maintains a "glass ceiling" that prevents women from advancing to assistant manager and general manager positions. Costco's senior management, the complaint observed, is virtually all male, and less than 16 percent of general managers nationwide are

> women. Costco cofounder and longtime CEO Jim Sinegal (who retired in 2011), has argued that women don't want warehouse management posts because "women have a tendency to be the caretakers and have the responsibility for the children and for the family."

And then there's Lean In Platform Partner Walmart. In 2011 the world's largest retailer famously managed to dodge one of the largest class-action sex-discrimination suits in U.S. history (involving 1.5 million women) after the U.S. Supreme Court ruled on technical grounds that the case didn't constitute a single class action. In preparation for a second round of individual and regional class-action proceedings, thousands of female employees have already refiled sex-discrimination grievances in forty-eight states.

Here's what Mike Duke, Walmart CEO and president, had to say in his statement on Lean In's Platform Partner page: "As we lean in to empower women, it helps us to better serve our customers, develop the best talent, and strengthen our communities."

And what about Facebook? When asked about women's representation at the company during media appearances for her book tour, Sandberg was vague. "We're ahead of the industry," she told one interviewer, noting that a woman heads Facebook's "global sales" and another is "running design," before briskly changing the subject.

I contacted Facebook's press office and submitted questions about the numbers and percentage of women in management, engineering, and so on. Ashley Zandy, media spokeswoman at Facebook, emailed me back, thanking me "for reaching out" and offering a "chat." The chat was off the record and, in any case, provided no additional information on women's representation at the company. Then she offered me an "off the record" conversation with Sandberg, which I declined: off the record meant I couldn't repeat what Sandberg told me—and, considering Sandberg's polish and power, I didn't understand her reticence. Zandy said she'd try to get the figures I'd requested and arrange interviews, including ones with Sandberg and Facebook's head of human resources.

Two days later, she sent me a second email. "I appreciate you reaching out," she wrote. "Unfortunately, I won't be able to arrange any of the interviews you requested." Nor provide statistics. "Unfortunately, we don't share much of the detailed and quantitative data you have asked for." She was able to tell me the following:

> • The names of Facebook's top executives (which the company, by law, has to disclose in its annual report). Except for Sandberg, they were all male.
>
> • Names of "female leaders in operational roles." Of the nine, only one was on the engineering side of the aisle; the others were mostly in traditionally "female" roles like communications, consumer marketing, and human resources.
>
> • Examples of Facebook's "incredible benefits" (a generous four-month paid parental leave and a $4,000 "baby cash" payment) and "strong resources for ALL employees—and for women" ("Women Leadership Day," "hosting speakers and mentoring student groups," etc.).
>
> • And finally, "a FB statement in lieu of an interview": "Statement: Facebook supports the message of Lean In—that women should pursue their goals with gusto, no matter what they may be. We work hard to create a work environment that supports women and gives them the opportunities to have impact and lead. Our management and employees are incredibly passionate about not just recruiting and retaining women, but developing the right leadership, policies and support to create a culture and workplace where they can thrive."

I wrote back to say I appreciated the information and still wished to talk to Sandberg. "Though some of my questions are skeptical," I said, "I hoped that they might open an actual and meaningful dialogue on a subject both she and I care about." I presented four questions for Sandberg. Here are the first two:

> **1.** A number of Lean In's corporate Platform Partners seem to have a woman problem—most notably (though not alone), the sex-discrimination legal actions against Walmart and Costco. How do you ensure

> that corporate partners are not signing up as a way of whitewashing (agreeing publicly with the concept of women's advancement, and securing Lean In's imprimatur, to avoid addressing more systemic problems)? Is there an instance where you've said to such a company that you'd be glad to have it as a partner, but only *after* it cleans up its act? Wouldn't such a demand be an example of what you champion—that having women in power will benefit ordinary women?
>
> **2.** Lean In Circles have been described as peer mentoring and as a sort of consciousness-raising for our times. If a Lean In Circle decides that members of its group have actual grievances with the companies they work for that require a political response, would Lean In be supportive of them taking political or legal action against those companies? Would you, for example, encourage a Lean In Circle to picket a discriminatory employer?

Zandy replied: "As I mentioned before, I do think an off the record conversation between you and Sheryl would be a great place to start the dialogue. Let me know if you would reconsider that." I again declined.

In the middle of the next week, I received an email from another media spokesperson, this one with Lean In. Andrea Saul (formerly the press secretary for Mitt Romney's 2012 presidential campaign) informed me, "Unfortunately, an interview will not be possible." Instead, she sent me written answers to my questions, evidently drafted by Lean In's public relations apparatus (see box, p. 222), and "a quote for your use":

> Lean In is a global community committed to encouraging and supporting women leaning in to their ambitions. We're incredibly grateful to our community and the individuals, and institutions, who have already made progress changing the conversation on gender. But we know there is so much more to do before we live in an equal world. That's why we're not just encouraging, but supporting, everyone and every company that wants to lean in. It's time to change the world, not just the conversation.

Upstairs, Downstairs

One Saturday several weeks into Sandberg's protracted multimedia tour, I drove to the mother root of American industry, the city that, as its historical literature puts it, "gave birth to the modern corporation." So many of New England's old textile factories have been gutted and converted into boutique and condo space. But in the 1970s Lowell, Massachusetts, turned over millions of square feet of abandoned mills to the National Park Service. The 141 acres of factories, boardinghouses, and power canals are now the preserve of the Lowell National Historical Park.

Its centerpiece is the Boott Cotton Mills, "the cathedral of industry," a red brick behemoth that sits alongside the Merrimack River like a medieval fortress, ensconced within a rampart of thick red brick walls, accessible only by a single bridge spanning a deep-water canal. A huge bell tower presides over the courtyard: for decades, its 4:30 a.m. toll summoned a nearly all-female workforce to a fourteen-hour day. The Boott Mills is now a museum, its exhibition space a reminder of the vast divide between the men who owned it and the women who labored there.

Upstairs, a wing is adorned with large oil portraits of the gentlemen mill proprietors who formed the WASPy Boston Associates. Downstairs, the "weave room," a sprawling factory floor, has been restored to its early glory (minus the humid, lint-choked air that incubated spectacular rates of tuberculosis and other lung diseases, and minus the mass infestation of cockroaches that swarmed over employees' clothes and lunch pails). During visiting hours, museum staffers run a portion of the eighty-eight power looms to provide visitors with a modest sense of the earsplitting cacophony. (Even at reduced levels, the museum must dispense earplugs.) On the day I visited, two middle-aged women were operating the clanking looms. As I stood, half-hypnotized by a power shuttle flinging itself back and forth between the warp threads, they came over to ask if I had questions. Several minutes into our conversation, it was apparent that they were no ordinary docents. Francisca DeSousa and Cathy Randall were lifelong mill workers.

My Questions for Sheryl Sandberg ... and the Answers from Her PR Department

Q: A number of Lean In's corporate Platform Partners seem to have a woman problem—most notably (though not alone), the sex-discrimination legal actions against Walmart and Costco. How do you ensure that corporate partners are not signing up as a way of whitewashing (agreeing publicly with the concept of women's advancement, and securing Lean In's imprimatur, to avoid addressing more systemic problems)? Is there an instance where you've said to such a company that you'd be glad to have it as a partner, but only after it cleans up its act? Wouldn't such a demand be an example of what you champion—that having women in power will benefit ordinary women?

A: We reject this premise. There are over 200 companies who have joined as platform partners, and it seems early to judge their motivations. We are not setting up a watchdog organization or an audit function. Rather, we are providing high-quality educational materials and technology at scale that companies can use to improve their understanding of gender bias. We want to make these materials available to everyone—because every company can get better, and we want them to.

Q: Lean In Circles have been described as peer mentoring and as a sort of consciousness-raising for our times. If a Lean In Circle decides that members of its group have actual grievances with the companies they work for that require a political response, would Lean In be supportive of them taking political or legal action against those companies? Would you, for example, encourage a Lean In Circle to picket a discriminatory employer?

A: Lean In Circles are a starting point, not an endpoint. We are encouraging people to set up Circles and take them where they will through an open and constructive dialogue—and share their learnings with other Circles. Lean In provides a framework but we want each Circle to decide what it does or focuses on, because each Circle is different and has different needs.

Q: Lean In has described itself as a "movement." Social movements in my experience are all about solidarity and confrontation—that is, a collective response that confronts powerful institutions and people who are holding a group down. What is the confrontation here, and who or what is being confronted? Or does the sort of self-awareness endorsed by Lean In Circles stop where external confrontation begins? Put another way, is the confrontation all with one's self, to appeal to the corporation?

A: Again, we reject this premise. We are a community that seeks to promote awareness and empower individual, as well as collective, action. Lean In is made up of individuals and organizations coming together to further the common aim of understanding gender bias and helping other women achieve their goals.

Q: Lean In emphasizes individual solutions to problems of individual advancement. How do you keep this focus on individual initiative from undermining an alternative group awareness necessary to fuel an actual movement?

A: This is not a zero-sum solution. It takes both individual and collective initiative. In fact, Lean In makes clear that individuals can facilitate institutional reform. The more people are focused on issues for gender, the more of both there will be. We think Lean In is already demonstrating results—individuals taking action, women asking for and getting raises, companies changing policies. The question we would ask back is: "Has overall group awareness of these important issues increased since Lean In launched?" Our answer is that while there is so much more to do, changes have begun.

The textile factory where DeSousa had worked for more than a quarter century had hightailed it to Mexico, and she'd taken the job at the museum. Randall has continued to work in the few remaining mills, including for a time at one that has made certain adjustments to the times: it weaves carbon fiber for microchips. She was working, that is, at the industrial production end of the empire that Sheryl Sandberg presides over as chief operating officer.

DeSousa, like Randall, started at $3 an hour. Later, she recalled, "they paid you four to five cents per piecework—to make you work faster." In the course of her employment, she and her husband, who also worked full time, had four children. After she gave birth, "I took one week off, unpaid," she said. "You didn't dare take more than that—you'd get fired."

"There was no vacation time," Randall recalled of her first job, "no health insurance, no benefits, and no sick days." After eleven years, she was making $11 an hour. "Now they just don't give you the forty hours," she said, "so they don't have to pay you benefits."

DeSousa and Randall, like so many mill workers, saw many accidents: women who were mauled, women who lost body parts, women nearly scalped when the loom mechanism seized their hair. On the factory floor one day, Randall witnessed an "amputation": a young woman's arm was sucked into the machinery. The memory still haunts her. "She was one of the ones I trained," she said.

None of these jobs were unionized. At the first mill Randall worked for, she became involved in an organizing effort. The union campaign never came to a vote. "People were too afraid," she said, recalling how one of the women "came to me crying, 'Don't do this, I can't lose my job.'"

DeSousa led two ad hoc protest efforts of her own. The first was in response to a company announcement that the workers would no longer be given a lunch hour—which was actually a lunch *half* hour. "I told them we are going to sit down for half an hour, because we deserve it," she said. At first, her coworkers were leery of taking a stand. "It was hard keeping people together. I mean, I was scared, too—my God, what were they going to do to us?" But finally she convinced her colleagues. "I told them, 'Listen, if we stick together, they can't fire all of us.'" After two weeks of sit-downs, the company relented. Then the company announced that mill workers would be required to work overtime on Saturdays. While the women were glad for the extra money, many were single mothers with no weekend day care. "If you didn't show up on Saturday, they'd give you a yellow slip," DeSousa recalled, "and after you got several of them, they could fire you." DeSousa and another mill worker proposed a plan: "We stop all the looms—it's the only way to get their attention." The workers did, and a few minutes later, their overlords rushed in. "Even the big bosses from the main office came running." After a tense negotiation, the women won their fight. DeSousa's supervisor, though, let her know that she better not try for a third victory. "My boss came over," DeSousa recalled, "and he said to me, 'Some day, Norma Rae, I'm going to *get you*.'"

I asked the two women if they had heard of Lean In. Randall said she had seen a couple of Sandberg's TV appearances, but didn't quite understand the message. I told her that Lean In argues that women need to break down "internal obstacles" within themselves that are preventing them from moving up the work ladder. "There *are* a lot of barriers women face," Randall said. She ticked off a few: lousy pay, no benefits, no sick leave, no unions, sexism, and a still highly sex segregated workforce. "There are lots of jobs that are still considered women's work," she said. "In one of the mills, I was actually referred to as 'the girl.'"

What Randall described is what most American working women face. And they are also the sort of problems that the advocates of Lean In and its sister impulses must address if they are not to be seen as individual women empowering themselves by deserting other women—if they are to be called, as Sheryl Sandberg calls herself, feminist.

What about "internal obstacles," I asked Randall—the sort of obstacles that cause women to curb their ambitions because they're afraid they won't be likable? She pondered the question for a time. "I don't know," she said finally. "That's just not the world I came from."

All LinkedIn with Nowhere to Go

ANN FRIEDMAN

In a jobs economy that has become something of a grim joke, nothing seems quite so bleak as the digital job seeker's all-but-obligatory LinkedIn account. In the decade since the site launched publicly with a mission "to connect the world's professionals to make them more productive and successful," the glorified résumé-distribution service has become an essential stop for the professionally dissatisfied masses. The networking site burrows its way into users' inboxes with updates spinning the gossamer dream of successful and frictionless advancement up the career ladder. Just add one crucial contact who's only a few degrees removed from you (users are the perpetual Kevin Bacons in this party game), or update your skill set in a more market-friendly fashion, and one of the site's 187 million or so users will pluck you from a stalled career and offer professional redemption. LinkedIn promises to harness everything that's great about a digital economy that so far has done more to limit than expand the professional prospects of its user-citizens.

In reality, though, the job seeker tends to experience the insular world of LinkedIn connectivity as an irksome ritual of digital badgering. Instead of facing the prospect of interfacing professionally with a nine-figure user base with a renewed spring in their step, harried victims of economic redundancy are more likely to greet their latest LinkedIn updates with a muttered variation of, "Oh shit, I'd better send out some more résumés." At which point, they'll typically mark the noisome

From *The Baffler*, no. 23

email nudge as "read" and relegate it to the trash folder.

Which is why it's always been a little tough to figure out what LinkedIn is for. The site's initial appeal was as a sort of self-updating Rolodex—a way to keep track of ex-coworkers and friends-of-friends you met at networking happy hours. There's the appearance of openness—you can "connect" with anyone!—but when users try to add a professional contact from whom they're more than one degree removed, a warning pops up. "Connecting to someone on LinkedIn implies that you know them well," the site chides, as though you're a stalker in the making. It asks you to indicate how you know this person. Former coworker? Former classmate? Fine. "LinkedIn lets you invite colleagues, classmates, friends and business partners without entering their email addresses," the site says. "However, recipients can indicate that they don't know you. If they do, you'll be asked to enter an email address with each future invitation."

You can try to lie your way through this firewall by indicating you've worked with someone when you haven't—the equivalent of name-dropping someone you've only read about in management magazines. But odds are, you'll be found out. I'd been confused, for instance, about numerous LinkedIn requests from publicists saying we'd "worked together" at a particular magazine. But when I clicked through to their profiles, I realized why they'd confidently asserted this professional alliance into being: the way to get to the next rung is to pretend you're already there. If you don't already know the person you're trying to meet, you're pretty much out of luck.

This frenetic networking-by-vague-association has bred a mordant skepticism among some users of the site. Scott Monty, head of social media for the Ford Motor Company, includes a disclaimer in the first line of his LinkedIn bio that, in any other context, would be a hilarious redundancy: "Note: I make connections only with people whom I have met." It's an Escher staircase masquerading as a career ladder.

On one level, of course, this world of aspirational business affiliation is nothing new. LinkedIn merely digitizes the core, and frequently cruel, paradox of networking events and conferences. You show up at such gatherings because you want to know more import-

J.D. KING

ant people in your line of work—but the only people mingling are those who, like you, don't seem to know anyone important. You just end up talking to the sad sacks you already know. From this crushing realization, the paradoxes multiply on up through the social food chain: those who are at the top of the field are at this event only to entice paying attendees, soak up the speaking fees, and slip out the back door after politely declining the modest swag bag. They're not standing around on garish hotel ballroom carpet with a plastic cup of cheap chardonnay in one hand and a stack of business cards in the other.

LinkedIn does have some advantages over the sad old world of the perennially striving, sweating minor characters in *Glengarry Glen Ross*. After all, it doesn't require a registration fee or travel to a conference center. Sometimes there *are* recruiters trolling the profiles on the site. It's a kinder, gentler experience for the underemployed. It distills the emotionally fraught process of collapsing years of professional experience onto a single 8½ x 11 sheet of paper into the seemingly more manageable format of the online questionnaire. In the past year, the site has made the protocols of networking even more rote, allowing users to select from a list of "skills" and, with a few clicks, declare their proficiency. "You can add up to 50 relevant skills and areas of expertise (like ballet, iPhone and global business development)," chirps an infobox on the site.

A century or so ago, critics worried that the rise of scientific management in the industrial workplace would deskill the American worker; now, in the postindustrial order of social-media-enabled employment, skills (or, you know, quasi-skills) multiply while jobs stagnate. Sure, you probably won't get hired at most places on the basis of your proficiency in ballet—but if you're so inclined, you can spend some of your ample downtime on LinkedIn endorsing the iPhone skills of select colleagues and acquaintances.

These Thoughts for Hire

LinkedIn's architects are self-aware enough to know that, even in the age of social-media following, some of us must be leaders. In October 2012, the site enabled users to "follow" a handpicked set of "thought leaders." LinkedIn has given this "select group" permission "to write long-form content on LinkedIn and have their words and sharing activity be followed by our 187 million members." So far, 190 leaders have made the cut. The "most-followed influencers" are familiar names to anyone who's ever killed time in an airport bookstore: Richard Branson, Deepak Chopra, Arianna Huffington, Tony Robbins.

The animating vision behind the thought leader initiative is that great digital-economy will-o'-the-wisp known as the flattened hierarchy. "It used to be that the only way to hear what someone had to say on LinkedIn was to ask to connect with them. And you're supposed to only do that with people you know and have done business with," Isabelle Roughol, one of LinkedIn's editors, wrote me in an email. "The average professional won't chat at the coffee machine with someone like [Virgin Group founder] Richard Branson, but we still want to know how he got his start in business, how he manages his team or why he thinks private space travel is the future. That's the space our 'Influencers' program fills."

Still, there's a distinctly perfunctory quality to the offerings of the charmed circle of "influencers." They often simply repost things on LinkedIn that they've written (or had ghostwritten, in some cases) for their personal sites. Their advice—on LinkedIn, "thoughts" almost always equal "advice"—ranges from the semipractical (embrace three digital media trends; get all of your employees on social media) to the lofty (be on a mission that doesn't suck; search for a noble purpose) to the downright confusing (how to create time; how do careers really work?). The worst of the bunch reads like management-speak Mad Libs, such as this bit of gobbledygook about the career success ladder: "Failure to make a decision is often worse than making the wrong one. This ability is developed and honed over time based on both successes and failures," writes one thought leader, who includes a complicated chart that is in no way ladder-like. Cue the vacuous, grammar-challenged sloganeering: "High-level thinking, problem-solving and critical decision-making is the cornerstone of long-term success."

A few influencers venture into the realm of politics, where apparently the appeal of conventional wisdom is just as strong as in the business world. How does the CEO of Panera Bread suggest we end gridlock in Congress? Heed a few Thomas Friedman quotes about how bad partisanship is, and then throw our support behind the "nonpartisan" advocacy group No Labels, which promotes relentlessly centrist agendas in the service of publicizing reliably unelectable centrist candidates. Even this wan brand of opinion-making is suffused with LinkedIn's trademark brand of acute striver-anxiety. On the one hand, it seems risky to put forth political views on a networking site, where the goal is to appeal to as many potential employers (or followers) as possible. On the other hand, weighing in on topics beyond the realm of management is also a way to prove you're justified in using such profile buzzwords as "creative" and "analytical." The higher synthesis, of course, is a weirdly totalizing kind of centrism: keep your political ideas as anodyne as your business aphorisms, and all the recruiters and CEOs out there will be reassured that you are safely tucked into the zone of acceptable consensus.

Still, most of the thought-leading counsel on offer at LinkedIn boils down to search-engine-friendly, evergreen nuggets of business advice. An article titled "Three Pieces of Career Advice That Changed My Life" is illustrated with stock photos showing street signs at the corner of "Opportunity Blvd." and "Career Dr." At this very promising intersection, LinkedIn CEO Jeff Weiner explains that readers can do anything they put their minds to, that technology will come to rule everything, and that changing lives is a better goal than merely pushing paper around. This set of warmed-over management nostrums is one of the all-time top five "influencer posts" on the site. Sure, the post's author is the site's CEO. But the appeal runs deeper than that. Listicles take the LinkedIn promise of a cleaner, neater networking experience and apply it to your entire career. Their reassuring, vague steps provide comfort and the illusion of control, in just the same way that we call on carnival fortunetellers or syndicated astrologists to dispense useless vagaries that sound concrete, helpful, and familiar. This brand of advice makes even more sense on LinkedIn than it does in business-to-business publications or corporate newsletters, since it provides a perfect antidote to the inherent depression of the fruitless job search.

And in the frenetic world of just-in-time professional connectivity, LinkedIn's vision of the listicled life is more and more the norm. Just take, for example, another recent influencer post by another social media guru, Dave Kerpen, who helms a network concern bearing the ominously bland name of Likeable Local. In reviewing his own tenure as a regular contributor to the LinkedIn news site, *LinkedIn Today*, Kerpen runs the pageview numbers and, in short order, blows his own mind. The twenty-eight posts he has contributed since the fall of 2012, Kerpen reports, "have generated over 5 million page views, a staggering number by any standard." But the real wonderment here, he observes, is the ridiculously high level of reader engagement he's earned in the site's "new media empire": on average, he's logged "over 600 comments and over 10 thousand shares per post. My top post, '11 Simple Concepts to Become a Better Leader,' has generated over 5 thousand comments."

Of course it has. If you click over to Kerpen's all-time most-commented post, you see yet another listicle culled from the chapter headings of his book *Likeable Business*. There's this comically self-deconstructing morsel from Oprah Winfrey, for instance: "I had no idea that being your authentic self could make me as rich as I've become. If I had, I'd have done it a lot earlier." Or perhaps you'd prefer something more aggressive and imperial in the way of business advice, such as this Navy SEAL mantra: "Individuals play the game, but teams beat the odds." Not quite spiritual enough? All right, how about G. K. Chesterton, reminding you that "gratitude is happiness doubled by wonder"?

Kerpen's self-singing fable of media success, in other words, ultimately has a chilling moral—you can achieve unparalleled likeability on LinkedIn's mammoth media platform, but at the considerable cost of surrendering anything that might remotely resemble a coherent or challenging message to the LinkedIn masses.

An entire subgenre of thought leadership is devoted to the cult of Apple. (Kerpen's mandatory inspirational quote from Steve Jobs: "The only way to do great work is to love the work you do.") A post by "Technology Futurist, Innovation Expert, Business Strategist, Bestselling Business Author, & Keynote Speaker" Daniel Burrus instructs would-be Steve Jobses to "take the time to think both short-term and long-range. Build your future by competing on things other than price, and by asking the right questions, especially when it comes to consumers." Never mind that Burrus hasn't built an Apple-like company; such perorations are like the incantation of a devotional prayer: they call down the mercies of a remote techno-deity in order to ritually cleanse the grubbier aspirations of the business-strategizing, keynote-speaking class. And in the same circular fashion, the point of encouraging users to connect and follow and exchange points of view on LinkedIn is to marshal those users behind the simple, world-conquering faith in networked connectivity. The thoughts that lead the LinkedIn experience, in other words, are usually subtle advertisements for the LinkedIn experience. Or not-so-subtle come-ons: one post promises to help people answer the question "What should I do with my life?" in three steps—by using LinkedIn.

The most hectically advertised spiritual advisers on the site all support some version of this worldview. According to the site's leaderboard, Virgin founder Branson was the first thought leader to crack one million followers. Branson's most shared and commented post is tantalizingly headlined "Five Top Tips to Starting a Successful Business." It's not crazy that people on all rungs of the career ladder would want to hear from Branson: the billionaire has undoubtedly learned a few things during his rise to the top. But take the click-bait and you get a list of bland encouragements rather than practical advice. Listen more than you talk. Keep it simple. Take pride in your work. Have fun. And, if you should fail, rip it up and start again.

Who's to say whether the followers of these tirelessly flogged thought leaders—the folks eagerly inviting others to connect—find this information useful? Surely the gospel of LinkedIn life improvement isn't dramatically enhancing their immediate job search. But on the devotional level, it probably fuels their fantasies of conquering their cluttered professional playing fields in the fashion of that great business demigod Steve Jobs. If the poor, as John Steinbeck once observed, see themselves as temporarily embarrassed millionaires, it seems fair to assume that on LinkedIn, followers see themselves as temporarily embarrassed thought leaders.

How to Click Friends and Influence People

To understand the appeal of the site, it's necessary to reach back to the beginnings of the modern American gospel of success. The roots of the LinkedIn vision of prosperity-through-connectivity lie in the circular preachments of the positive-thinking industry, a singularly American gloss on the sunny doctrine of achieving personal success through inoffensive sociability. This modern branch of the thought-leading discipline began about a century ago, in true rags-to-riches fashion, when an unsuccessful door-to-door salesman named Dale Carnegie started teaching courses in public speaking at his local YMCA. Carnegie—Carnegay, actually, as it would be another seven years before he changed his name to match that of the famous industrialist—was an unlikely motivational speaker. He was kind of a loser. After graduating from the Warrensburg State Teachers' College in Missouri in 1908, he sold correspondence courses, bacon, soap, and lard. But he found the work insufficiently glamorous, and after saving up $500, he moved to New York in 1911 to pursue his dream of becoming an actor. He failed. Nor could he make a go of it as a truck salesman or a novelist. He decided that the best path to success was to tell other people how to find it.

Carnegie's lectures at the Y earned him a modicum of success and prompted him to publish *The Art of Public Speaking* in 1915. But it wasn't until the country was in the grip of the Great Depression that Carnegie's ideas began to really catch on. Simon & Schuster published his best-known book, *How to Win Friends and Influence People*, in 1936, the same year Dorothea Lange snapped her iconic photo of a despondent migrant mother named Florence Owens Thompson. The book was an instant success, and the enduring appeal of *How to Win Friends* makes it clear that Carnegie touched a powerful nerve in the nation's professional id: the book spent years on the bestseller list and still sells hundreds of thousands of copies a year in the United States alone.

Carnegie, of course, didn't stop with *How to Win Friends*. He founded a conventional-wisdom empire, churning out books, conferences, and lectures. The pamphlets handed out at Carnegie courses had titles that are indistinguishable from the thought leadership now being followed on LinkedIn: *How to Get Ahead in the World Today*, *How to Put Magic in the Magic Formula*, *How to Make Our Listeners Like Us*, *How to Save Time and Get Better Results in Conferences*, *The Little Recognized Secret of Success*. "The ideas I stand for are not mine," Carnegie once said to critics of *How to Win Friends*. "I borrowed them from Socrates. I swiped them from Chesterfield. I stole them from Jesus. And I put them in a book. If you don't like their rules, whose would you use?"

Carnegie-style aphorisms and self-esteem-boosting quotes were once relegated to the world of management conferences, leadership training seminars, and the business-to-business press. These days, along with everyone else who's publishing the modern equivalent of Oprah-style self-help dressed up as business advice, you can find the Dale Carnegie Training company on LinkedIn.

Wish Fulfillment as Business Model

Nowadays the gospel of motivationalism is so universal that Americans don't even recognize that we live in a golden age of positive thinking. At a time when user-generated content is king and the economy is in the doldrums, there have never been so many aspiring Carnegies with so many outlets permitting them to push their own particular brand of techno-futurism, business essentialism, or practical optimism. In this sense, LinkedIn is much more a thought-following enterprise than a thought-leading one. Outlets such as *Forbes* and the *Harvard Business Review*, which were always home to business tips alongside big-think pieces on the future of American capitalism, have thrown open the gates to amateur motivational speakers and self-styled consultants who bring in pageviews and in exchange are granted the illusion of a rapt audience.

Most are guys like Greg McKeown. It's hard to tell, based on his LinkedIn profile, exactly what he does. Until recently, his profile picture was a photo of his face framed by two artfully held Sharpies—a set piece that conveyed the look and feel of *Office Space*, but without the sarcasm. (It has since been replaced with a photo of him gesticulating in front of a whiteboard.) "I write and speak around the world on the importance of living and leading as an Essentialist," he explains. His personal site bears his own name in the URL but has the branding and plural language of "a company with the strategic intent to inspire 1,000,000 people to take a step toward a higher point of contribution by the end of 2014." His résumé is full of consulting gigs and courtesy titles; in 2010 he cowrote a book called *Multipliers: How the Best Leaders Make Everyone Smarter*. He links out to the website of his one-man consulting company, THIS Inc., which hawks nebulous, though evidently "essential" services; he vows to help clients "Evaluate the trivial many from the vital few, Eliminate the nonessentials and . . . Enable the team to almost effortlessly execute on the essentials." He's a professional thought leader, and LinkedIn has recognized him as such, letting him through the gates to join the ranks of the Chopras and Bransons.

For aspirants such as McKeown, who presumably have yet to accumulate a fortune, thought leadership is a hopeful self-fulfilling prophecy. Just start leading and the thoughts will come. Then the wealth will follow.

If it seems like anyone could do what McKeown is doing, you're right. LinkedIn allows any user to apply to be an influencer. In exchange for a theoretical mass readership of millions upon millions of eager job seekers, all you have to do is provide LinkedIn with content and pageviews. "Our members are looking for professionals who can write engaging original posts and share links to relevant, thought-provoking presentations, articles, polls, SlideShares, videos, infographics, and more," the site says. "Think you've got what it takes? To apply, please complete the form below and we'll be in touch within a week." The form doesn't ask you about your greatest accomplishments or leadership experience. It doesn't require you to list how much money you've made or the companies you've founded. It asks you about which topics you'd blog about and which links you want to share today.

But that's another beautiful thing about thought leadership: unlike many of the jobs you might pursue on LinkedIn, no experience is required for the gig. Sure, according to *Forbes*, "it's a truism that thought leaders tend to be the most successful individuals or firms in their respective fields." But *Forbes* itself is run by a silver-spoon publishing scion whose only real achievement has been a pair of laughably overfunded, failed runs at the GOP presidential nomination. In the same vein, actual business acumen and leadership skills usually take a back seat in the LinkedIn system to simple digital renown. Some of the best-known gurus on the site have had the most success in the realm of . . . thinking about stuff. Take the case of one of the most popular thought leaders on LinkedIn: Newark mayor Cory Booker. He has 1.3 million Twitter followers. He's appeared on *The Daily Show*. He wrote a bestselling book. His picture is highlighted alongside other LinkedIn-approved thought leaders like Barack Obama, Guy Kawasaki, and Ari Emanuel. Meanwhile, back in Newark, the city has laid off a thousand workers. Crime and unemployment are up. The city's cash-strapped schools are still struggling, under the control of the state. Newark's "finances remain so troubled that it cannot borrow to fix its antiquated water system," reports the *New York Times*. It's tough to be both a thought leader and an action leader—which is presumably why Booker is now vying for a yet more prominent thought-leading spot, as U.S. senator from New Jersey in a notoriously do-nothing Congress.

Thanks to such fast-and-louche appropriations of the mantle of thought leadership, even its apostles are denouncing the fast-multiplying apostasies that dilute the essence of the one true faith. "In only 15 years we've managed to dumb down the idea of thought leadership from someone who has changed their area of business to someone who can create a marketing plan that implants the idea that they are a thought leader," wrote sales guru Paul McCord in 2009. "When everybody's one, nobody is one."

Every once in awhile, though, you'll run across some decent practical advice on LinkedIn. A post about avoiding frequent-flier miles scams—another one of LinkedIn's top "influencer" posts of all time—has some unwittingly trenchant advice for aspiring thought leaders. "First," author Christopher Elliott explains, "only a few people at the top of the scam benefit in any meaningful way. . . . And second, many of those elite program apologists will do anything to defend the system that has rewarded them." You don't say.

The Meme Hustler

Tim O'Reilly's crazy talk

EVGENY MOROZOV

While the brightest minds of Silicon Valley are "disrupting" whatever industry is too crippled to fend off their advances, something odd is happening to our language. Old, trusted words no longer mean what they used to mean; often, they don't mean anything at all. Our language, much like everything these days, has been hacked. Fuzzy, contentious, and complex ideas have been stripped of their subversive connotations and replaced by cleaner, shinier, and emptier alternatives; long-running debates about politics, rights, and freedoms have been recast in the seemingly natural language of economics, innovation, and efficiency. Complexity, as it turns out, is not particularly viral.

This is not to deny that many of our latest gadgets and apps are fantastic. But to fixate on technological innovation alone is to miss the more subtle—and more consequential—ways in which a clique of techno-entrepreneurs has hijacked our language and, with it, our reason. In the last decade or so, Silicon Valley has triggered its own wave of linguistic innovation, a wave so massive that a completely new way to analyze and describe the world—a silicon mentality of sorts—has emerged in its wake. The old language has been rendered useless; our pre-Internet vocabulary, we are told, needs an upgrade.

Fortunately, Silicon Valley, that never-drying well of shoddy concepts and dubious paradigms—from wiki-everything to i-something, from e-nothing to open-anything—is ready to help. Like a good priest, it's always there to con-

From *The Baffler*, no. 22

sole us with the promise of a better future, a glitzier roadmap, a sleeker vocabulary.

Silicon Valley has always had a thing for priests; Steve Jobs was the cranky pope it deserved. Today, having mastered the art of four-hour workweeks and gluten-free lunches in outdoor cafeterias, our digital ministers are beginning to preach on subjects far beyond the funky world of drones, 3-D printers, and smart toothbrushes. That we would eventually be robbed of a meaningful language to discuss technology was entirely predictable. That the conceptual imperialism of Silicon Valley would also pollute the rest of our vocabulary wasn't.

The enduring emptiness of our technology debates has one main cause, and his name is Tim O'Reilly. The founder and CEO of O'Reilly Media, a seemingly omnipotent publisher of technology books and a tireless organizer of trendy conferences, O'Reilly is one of the most influential thinkers in Silicon Valley. Entire fields of thought—from computing to management theory to public administration—have already surrendered to his buzzwordophilia, but O'Reilly keeps pressing on. Over the past fifteen years, he has given us such gems of analytical precision as "open source," "Web 2.0," "government as a platform," and "architecture of participation." O'Reilly doesn't coin all of his favorite expressions, but he promotes them with religious zeal and enviable perseverance. While Washington prides itself on Frank Luntz, the Republican strategist who rebranded "global warming" as "climate change" and turned "estate tax" into "death tax," Silicon Valley has found its own Frank Luntz in Tim O'Reilly.

Tracing O'Reilly's intellectual footprint is no easy task, in part because it's so vast.[1] Through his books, blogs, and conferences, he's nurtured a whole generation of technology thinkers, from Clay Shirky to Cory Doctorow. A prolific blogger and a compulsive Twitter user with more than 1.6 million followers, O'Reilly has a knack for writing articulate essays about technological change. His essay on "Web 2.0" elucidated a basic philosophy of the Internet in a way accessible to both academics and venture capitalists; it boasts more than six thousand references on Google Scholar—not bad for a non-academic author. He also invests in startups—the very startups that he celebrates in his public advocacy—through a venture fund, which, like most things O'Reilly, also bears his name.

A stylish and smooth-talking self-promoter with a philosophical take on everything, O'Reilly is the Bernard-Henri Lévy of Route 101, the favorite court philosopher of the TED elites. His impressive intellectual stature in the Valley can probably be attributed to the simple fact that he is much better read than your average tech entrepreneur. His constant references to the learned men of yesteryear, from "Archilochus, the Greek fabulist" to Ezra Pound, make him stand out from all those Silicon Valley college dropouts who don't know their Plotinus from their Pliny. A onetime recipient of a National Endowment for the Arts grant to translate Greek fables—"Socrates is [one of] my constant companions"—he has the air of a man ready to grapple with the Really Big Questions of the Universe (his Harvard degree in classics certainly comes in handy). While he recently told *Wired* that he doesn't "really give a shit if literary novels go away" because "they're an elitist pursuit," O'Reilly is also quick to acknowledge that novels have profoundly shaped his own life. In 1981 the young O'Reilly even wrote a reputable biography of the science fiction writer Frank Herbert, the author of the *Dune* series, in which he waxes lyrical about Martin Heidegger and Karl Jaspers.

Alas, O'Reilly and the dead Germans parted ways long ago. These days, he's busy changing the world; any list of unelected technocrats who are shaping the future of American politics would have his name at the very top. A Zelig-like presence on both sides of the Atlantic, he hobnobs with government officials in Washington and London, advising them on the Next Big Thing. O'Reilly's thinking on "Government 2.0" has influenced many bureaucrats in the Obama administration, particularly those tasked with promoting the amorphous ideal of "open government"—not an easy thing to do in an administration bent on prosecuting whistle-blowers and dispatching drones to "we-can't-tell-you-where-exactly" destinations. O'Reilly is also active in discussions about the future of health care, having strong views on what "health 2.0" should be like.

None of this is necessarily bad. On first impression, O'Reilly seems like a much-needed voice of reason—even of civic spirit—in the shallow and ruthless paradise-ghetto that is Silicon Valley. Compared to ultra-libertarian technology mavens like Peter Thiel and Kevin Kelly, O'Reilly might even be mistaken for a bleeding-heart liberal. He has publicly endorsed Obama and supported many of his key reforms. He has called on young software developers—the galley slaves of Silicon Valley—to work on "stuff that matters" (albeit preferably in the private sector). He has written favorably about the work of little-known local officials transforming American cities. O'Reilly once said that his company's vision is to "change the world by spreading the knowledge of innovators," while his own personal credo is to "create more value than you capture." (And he has certainly captured a lot of it: his publishing empire, once in the humble business of producing technical manuals, is now worth $100 million.) Helping like-minded people find each other, sharpen their message, form a social movement, and change the world: this is what O'Reilly's empire is all about. Its website even boasts of its "long history of advocacy, meme-making, and evangelism." Who says that spiritual gurus can't have their own venture funds?

O'Reilly's personal journey was not atypical for Silicon Valley. In a 2004 essay about his favorite books (published in *Tim O'Reilly in a Nutshell*, brought out by O'Reilly Media), O'Reilly confessed that, as a young man, he had "hopes of writing deep books that would change the world." O'Reilly credits a book of science fiction documenting the struggles of a young girl against a corporate-dominated plutocracy (*Rissa Kerguelen* by F. M. Busby) with helping him abandon his earlier dream of revolutionary writing and enter the "fundamentally trivial business [of] technical writing." The book depicted entrepreneurship as a "subversive force," convincing O'Reilly that "in a world dominated by large companies, it is the smaller companies that keep freedom alive, with economics at least one of the battlegrounds." This tendency to view questions of freedom primarily through the lens of economic competition, to focus on the producer and the en-

PHILIP BURKE

trepreneur at the expense of everyone else, shaped O'Reilly's thinking about technology.

The Randian undertones in O'Reilly's thinking are hard to miss, even as he flaunts his liberal credentials. "There's a way in which the O'Reilly brand essence is ultimately a story about the hacker as hero, the kid who is playing with technology because he loves it, but one day falls into a situation where he or she is called on to go forth and change the world," he wrote in 2012. But it's not just the hacker as hero that O'Reilly is so keen to celebrate. His true hero is the hacker-cum-entrepreneur, someone who overcomes the insurmountable obstacles erected by giant corporations and lazy bureaucrats in order to fulfill the American Dream 2.0: start a company, disrupt an industry, coin a buzzword. Hiding beneath this glossy veneer of disruption-talk is the same old gospel of individualism, small government, and market fundamentalism that we associate with Randian characters. For Silicon Valley and its idols, innovation is the new selfishness.

However, it's not his politics that makes O'Reilly the most dangerous man in Silicon Valley; a burgeoning enclave of Randian thought, it brims with far nuttier cases. O'Reilly's mastery of public relations, on the other hand, is unrivaled and would put many of Washington's top spin doctors to shame. No one has done more to turn important debates about technology—debates that used to be about rights, ethics, and politics—into kumbaya celebrations of the entrepreneurial spirit while making it seem as if the language of economics was, in fact, the only reasonable way to talk about the subject. As O'Reilly discovered a long time ago, memes are for losers; the real money is in epistemes.

O'Reilly got his start in business in 1978, when he launched a consulting firm that specialized in technical writing. Six years later, it began retaining rights to some of the manuals it was producing for individual clients and gradually branched out into more mainstream publishing. By the mid-1990s, O'Reilly had achieved some moderate success in Silicon Valley. He was well-off, having found a bestseller in *The Whole Internet User's Guide and Catalog* and having sold the Global Network Navigator—possibly the first Internet portal to feature paid banner advertising ("the first commercial website" as O'Reilly describes it today)—to AOL.

It was the growing popularity of "open source software" that turned O'Reilly into a national (and, at least in geek circles, international) figure. "Open source software" was also the first major rebranding exercise overseen by Team O'Reilly. This is where he tested all his trademark discursive interventions: hosting a summit to define the concept, penning provocative essays to refine it, producing a host of books and events to popularize it, and cultivating a network of thinkers to proselytize it.

It's easy to forget this today, but there was no such idea as open source software before 1998; the concept's seeming contemporary coherence is the result of clever manipulation and marketing. Open source software was born out of an ideological cleavage between two groups that, at least before 1998, had been traditionally lumped together. In one corner stood a group of passionate and principled geeks, led by Richard Stallman of the Free Software Foundation, preoccupied with ensuring that users had rights with respect to their computer programs. Those rights weren't many—users should be able to run the program for any purpose, to study how it works, to redistribute copies of it, and to release their improved version (if there was one) to the public—but even this seemed revolutionary compared to what one could do with most proprietary software sold at the time.

Software that ensured the aforementioned four rights was dubbed "free software." It was "free" thanks to its association with "freedom" rather than "free beer"; there was no theoretical opposition to charging money for building and maintaining such software. To provide legal cover, Stallman invented an ingenious license that relied on copyright law to suspend its own most draconian provisions—a legal trick that came to be known as "copyleft." GPL (short for "General Public License") has become the most famous and widely used of such "copyleft" licenses.

From its very beginning in the early 1980s, Stallman's movement aimed to produce a free software alternative to proprietary operating systems like Unix and Microsoft Windows and proprietary software like Microsoft Office. Stallman's may not have been the best software on offer, but some sacrifice of technological efficiency was a price worth paying for emancipation. Some discomfort might even be desirable, for Stallman's goal, as he put it in his 1998 essay "Why 'Free Software' is Better Than 'Open Source,'" was to ask "people to think about things they might rather ignore."

Underpinning Stallman's project was a profound critique of the role that patent law had come to play in stifling innovation and creativity. Perhaps inadvertently, Stallman also made a prescient argument for treating code, and technological infrastructure more broadly, as something that ought to be subject to public scrutiny. He sought to open up the very technological black boxes that corporations conspired to keep shut. Had his efforts succeeded, we might already be living in a world where the intricacies of software used for high-frequency trading or biometric identification presented no major mysteries.

Stallman is highly idiosyncratic, to put it mildly, and there are many geeks who don't share his agenda. Plenty of developers contributed to "free software" projects for reasons that had nothing to do with politics. Some, like Linus Torvalds, the Finnish creator of the much-celebrated Linux operating system, did so for fun; some because they wanted to build more convenient software; some because they wanted to learn new and much-demanded skills.

Once the corporate world began expressing interest in free software, many nonpolitical geeks sensed a lucrative business opportunity. As technology entrepreneur Michael Tiemann put it in 1999, while Stallman's manifesto "read like a socialist polemic . . . I saw something different. I saw a business plan in disguise." Stallman's rights-talk, however, risked alienating the corporate types. Stallman didn't care about offending the suits, as his goal was to convince ordinary users to choose free software on ethical grounds, not to sell it to business types as a cheaper or more efficient alternative to proprietary software. After all, he was trying to launch a radical social movement, not a complacent business association.

By early 1998 several business-minded members of the free software community were ready to split from Stallman, so they masterminded a coup, formed their own advocacy outlet—the Open Source Initiative—and brought in O'Reilly to help them rebrand. The timing was right. Netscape had just marked its capitulation to Microsoft in the so-called Browser Wars and promised both that all future versions of Netscape Communicator would be released free of charge and that its code would also be made publicly available. A few months later, O'Reilly organized a much-publicized summit, where a number of handpicked loyalists—Silicon democracy in action!—voted for "open source" as their preferred label. Stallman was not invited.

The label "open source" may have been new, but the ideas behind it had been in the air for some time. In 1997, even before the coup, Eric Raymond—a close associate of O'Reilly, a passionate libertarian, and the founder of a group with the self-explanatory title "Geeks with Guns"—delivered a brainy talk called "The Cathedral and the Bazaar," which foresaw the emergence of a new, radically collaborative way to make software. (In 1999 O'Reilly turned it into a successful book.) Emphasizing its highly distributed nature, Raymond captured the essence of open source software in a big-paradigm kind of way that could spellbind McKinsey consultants and leftist academics alike.

In those early days, the messaging around open source occasionally bordered on propaganda. As Raymond himself put it in 1999, "what we needed to mount was in effect a marketing campaign," one that "would require marketing techniques (spin, image-building, and re-branding) to make it work." This budding movement prided itself on not wanting to talk about the ends it was pursuing; except for improving efficiency and decreasing costs, those were left very much undefined. Instead, it put all the emphasis on *how* it was pursuing those ends—in an extremely decentralized manner, using Internet platforms, with little central coordination. In contrast to free software, then, open source had no obvious moral component. According to Raymond, "open source is not particularly a moral or a legal issue. It's an engineering issue. I advocate open source, because ... it leads to better engineering results and better economic results." O'Reilly concurred. "I don't think it's a religious issue. It's really about how do we actually encourage and spark innovation," he announced a decade later. While free software was meant to force developers to lose sleep over ethical dilemmas, open source software was meant to end their insomnia.

Even before the coup, O'Reilly occupied an ambiguous—and commercially pivotal—place in the free software community. On the one hand, he published manuals that helped to train new converts to the cause. On the other hand, those manuals were pricey. They were also of excellent quality, which, as Stallman once complained, discouraged the community from producing inexpensive alternatives. Ultimately, however, the disagreement between Stallman and O'Reilly—and the latter soon became the most visible cheerleader of the open source paradigm—probably had to do with their very different roles and aspirations. Stallman the social reformer could wait for decades until his ethical argument for free software prevailed in the public debate. O'Reilly the savvy businessman had a much shorter timeline: a quick embrace of open source software by the business community guaranteed steady demand for O'Reilly books and events, especially at a time when some analysts were beginning to worry—and for good reason, as it turned out—that the tech industry was about to collapse.

The coup succeeded. Stallman's project was marginalized. But O'Reilly and his acolytes didn't win with better arguments; they won with better PR. To make his narrative about open source software credible to a public increasingly fascinated by the Internet, O'Reilly produced a highly particularized account of the Internet that subsequently took on a life of its own. In just a few years, that narrative became the standard way to talk about Internet history, giving it the kind of neat intellectual coherence that it never actually had. A decade after producing a singular vision of the Internet to justify his ideas about the supremacy of the open source paradigm, O'Reilly is close to pulling a similar trick on how we talk about government reform.

To understand how O'Reilly's idea of the Internet helped legitimize the open source paradigm, it's important to remember that much of Stallman's efforts centered on software licenses. O'Reilly's bet was that as software migrated from desktops to servers—what, in another fit of buzzwordophilia, we later called the "cloud"—licenses would cease to matter. Since no code changed hands when we used Google or Amazon, it was counterproductive to fixate on licenses. "Let's stop thinking about licenses for a little bit. Let's stop thinking that that's the core of what matters about open source," O'Reilly urged in an interview with *InfoWorld* in 2003.

So what did matter about open source? Not "freedom"—at least not in Stallman's sense of the word. O'Reilly cared for only one type of freedom: the freedom of developers to distribute software on whatever terms they fancied. This was the freedom of the producer, the Randian entrepreneur, who must be left to innovate, undisturbed by laws and ethics. The most important freedom, as O'Reilly put it in a 2001 exchange with Stallman, is that which protects "my choice as a creator to give, or not to give, the fruits of my work to you, as a 'user' of that work, and for you, as a user, to accept or reject the terms I place on that gift."

This stood in stark contrast to Stallman's plan of curtailing—by appeals to ethics and, one day, perhaps, law—the freedom of developers in order to promote the freedom of users. O'Reilly opposed this agenda: "I completely support the right of Richard [Stallman] or any individual author to make his or her work available under the terms of the GPL; I balk when they say that others who do not do so are doing something wrong." The right thing to do, according to O'Reilly, was to leave developers alone. "I am willing to accept any argument that says that there are advantages and disadvantages to any particular licensing method.... My moral position is that people should be free to find out what works for them," he wrote in 2001. That "what works" for developers might eventually hurt everyone else—which was essentially Stallman's argument—did not bother O'Reilly. For all his economistic outlook, he was not one to talk externalities.

According to this Randian interpretation of open source, the goal of regulation and public advocacy should be to ensure that absolutely nothing—no laws or petty moral considerations—stood in the way of the open source revolution. Any move to subject the fruits of developers' labor to public regulation, even if its goal was to promote a greater uptake of open source software, must be opposed, since it would taint the reputation of open source as technologically and economically superior to proprietary software. Occasionally this stance led to paradoxes, as, for example, during a heated 2002 debate on whether governments should be required to ditch Microsoft and switch to open source software. O'Reilly expressed his vehement opposition to such calls. "No one should be forced to choose open source, any more than they should be forced to choose proprietary software. And any victory for open source achieved through deprivation of the user's right to choose would indeed be a betrayal of the principles that free software and open source have stood for," O'Reilly wrote in a widely discussed blog post.

That such an argument could be mounted reveals just how much political baggage was smuggled into policy debates, once "open source software" replaced "free software" as the idiom of choice. Governments are constantly pushed to do things someone in the private sector may not like; why should the software industry be special? Promoting accountability or improving network security might indeed disrupt someone's business model—but so what? Once a term like "open source" entered our vocabulary, one could recast the whole public policy calculus in very different terms, so that instead of discussing the public interest, we are discussing the interests of individual software developers, while claiming that this is a discussion about "innovation" and "progress," not "accountability" or "security."

To weaken Stallman's position, O'Reilly had to show that the free software movement was fighting a pointless, stupid war: the advent of the Internet made Stallman's obsession with licenses obsolete. There was a fair amount of semantic manipulation at play here. For Stallman, licenses were never an end in themselves; they mattered only as much as they codified a set of practices deriving from his vision of a technologically mediated good life. Licenses, in other words, were just the means to enable the one and only end that mattered to free software advocates: freedom. A different set of technological practices—e.g., the move from desktop-run software to the cloud—could have easily accommodated a different means of ensuring that freedom.

In fact, Stallman's philosophy, however rudimentary, had all the right conceptual tools to let us think about the desirability of moving everything to the cloud. The ensuing assault on privacy, the centralization of data in the hands of just a handful of companies, the growing accessibility of user data to law enforcement agencies who don't even bother getting a warrant: all those consequences of cloud computing could have been predicted and analyzed, even if fighting those consequences would have required tools other than licenses. O'Reilly's PR genius lay in having almost everyone confuse the means and the ends of the free software movement. Since licenses were obsolete, the argument went, software developers could pretty much disregard the ends of Stallman's project (i.e., its focus on user rights and freedoms) as well. Many developers did stop thinking about licenses and, having stopped thinking about licenses, they also stopped thinking about broader moral issues that would have remained central to the debates had "open source" not displaced "free software" as the paradigm du jour. Sure, there were exceptions—like the highly political and legalistic community that worked on Debian, yet another operating system—but they were the exceptions that proved the rule.

To maximize the appeal and legitimacy of this new paradigm, O'Reilly had to establish that open source both predated free software and was well on its way to conquering the world—that it had a rich history and a rich future. The first objective he accomplished, in part, by exploiting the ambiguities of the term "open"; the second by framing debate about the Internet around its complex causal connections to open source software.

The term "open source" was not invented by O'Reilly. Christine Peterson, the cofounder of Foresight Institute (a nanotechnology think tank), coined it in a February 1998 brainstorm session convened to react to Netscape's release of Navigator's source code. Few words in the English language pack as much ambiguity and sexiness as "open." And after O'Reilly's bombastic interventions—"Open allows experimentation. Open encourages competition. Open wins," he once proclaimed in an essay—its luster has only intensified. Profiting from the term's ambiguity, O'Reilly and his collaborators likened the "openness" of open source software to the "openness" of the academic enterprise, markets, and free speech. "Open" thus could mean virtually anything, from "open to intellectual exchange" (O'Reilly in 1999: "Once you start thinking of computer source code as a human language, you see open source as a variety of 'free speech'") to "open to competition" (O'Reilly in 2000: "For me, 'open source' in the broader sense means any system in which open access to code lowers the barriers to entry into the market").

"Open" allowed O'Reilly to build the largest possible tent for the movement. The language of economics was less alienating than Stallman's language of ethics; "openness" was the kind of multipurpose term that allowed one to look political while advancing an agenda that had very little to do with politics. As O'Reilly put it in 2010, "the art of promoting openness is not to make it a moral crusade, but rather to highlight the competitive advantages of openness." Replace "openness" with any other loaded term—say "human rights"—in this sentence, and it becomes clear that this quest for "openness" was politically toothless from the very outset. What, after all, if your interlocutor doesn't give a damn about competitive advantages?

Unsurprisingly, the availability of source code for universal examination soon became the one and only benchmark of openness. What the code did was of little importance—the market knows best!—as long as anyone could check it for bugs. The new paradigm was presented as something that went beyond ideology and could attract corporate executives without losing its appeal to the hacker crowd. "The implication of [the open source] label is that we intend to convince the corporate world to adopt our way for economic, self-interested, non-ideological reasons," Eric Raymond noted in 1998. What Raymond and O'Reilly failed to grasp, or decided to overlook, is that their effort to present open source as non-ideological was underpinned by a powerful ideology of its own—an ideology that worshiped innovation and efficiency at the expense of everything else.

It took a lot of creative work to make the new paradigm stick. One common tactic was to present open source as having a much longer history that even predates 1998. Thus, writing shortly after O'Reilly's historic open source summit, Raymond noted that "the summit was hosted by O'Reilly & Associates, a company that has been symbiotic with the Open Source movement for many years." That the term "open source" was just a few months old by the time Raymond wrote this didn't much matter. History was something that clever PR could easily fix. "As we thought about it, we said, gosh, this is also a great PR opportunity—we're a company that has learned to work the PR angles on things," O'Reilly said in 1999. "So part of the agenda for the summit was hey, just to meet and find out what we had in common. And the second agenda was really to make a statement of some kind [that] this was a movement, that all these different programs had something in common."

What they had in common was disdain for Stallman's moralizing—barely enough to justify their revolutionary agenda, especially among the hacker crowds, who were traditionally suspicious of anyone eager to suck up to the big corporations that aspired to dominate the open source scene.

By linking this new movement to both the history of the Internet and its future, O'Reilly avoided most of those concerns. One didn't have to choose open source, because the choice had already been made. As long as everyone believed that "open source" implied "the Internet" and that "the Internet" implied "open source," it would be very hard to resist the new paradigm. As O'Reilly—always the PR man—wrote in a 2004 essay, "It has always baffled and disappointed me that the open source community has not claimed the web as one of its greatest success stories.... That's a PR failure!" To make up for that failure, O'Reilly had to establish some causal relationship between the two—the details could be worked out later on.

"I think there's a paradigm shift going on right now, and it's really around both open source and the Internet, and it's not entirely clear which one is the driver and which one is the passenger, but at least they are fellow travellers," he announced in his *InfoWorld* interview. Compared to the kind of universal excitement generated by the Internet, Stallman's license-talk was about as exciting as performing Mahler at a Jay Z concert. As O'Reilly himself acknowledged, his "emphasis in talking about open source has never been on the details of licenses, but on open source as a foundation and expression of the Internet." When something is touted as both a foundation and an expression of something else, the underlying logic could probably benefit from more rigor.

Telling a coherent story about open source required finding some inner logic to the history of the Internet. O'Reilly was up to the task. "If you believe me that open source is about Internet-enabled collaboration, rather than just about a particular style of software license," he said in 2000, "you'll see the threads that tie together not just traditional open source projects, but also collaborative 'computing grid' projects like SETIAtHome, user reviews on Amazon.com, technologies like collaborative filtering, new ideas about marketing such as those expressed in *The Cluetrain Manifesto*, weblogs, and the way that Internet message boards can now move the stock market." In other words, everything on the Internet was connected to everything else—via open source.

The way O'Reilly saw it, many of the key developments of Internet culture were already driven by what he called "open source behavior," even if such behavior was not codified in licenses. For example, the fact that one could view the source code of a webpage right in one's browser has little to do with open source software, but it was part of the same "openness" spirit that O'Reilly saw at work in the Internet. No moralizing (let alone legislation) was needed; the Internet already lived and breathed open source. What O'Reilly didn't say is that, of course, it didn't have to be this way forever. Now that apps might be displacing the browser, the openness once taken for granted is no more—a contingency that licenses and morals could have easily prevented. Openness as a happenstance of market conditions is a very different beast from openness as a guaranteed product of laws.

One of the key consequences of linking the Internet to the world of open source was to establish the primacy of the Internet as the new, reinvented desktop—as the greatest, and perhaps ultimate, platform—for hosting third-party services and applications. This is where the now-forgotten language of "freedom" made a comeback, since it was important to ensure that O'Reilly's heroic Randian hacker-entrepreneurs were allowed to roam freely. Soon this "freedom to innovate" morphed into "Internet freedom," so that what we are trying to preserve is the innovative potential of the platform, regardless of the effects on individual users.

Stallman had on offer something far more precise and revolutionary: a way to think about the freedoms of individual users in specific contexts, as if the well-being of the mega-platform were of secondary importance. But that vision never came to pass. Instead, public advocacy efforts were channeled into preserving an abstract and reified configuration of digital technologies—"the Internet"—so that Silicon Valley could continue making money by hoovering up our private data.

Lumping everything under the label of "Internet freedom" did have some advantages for those genuinely interested in promoting rights such as freedom of expression—the religious fervor that many users feel about the Internet has helped catalyze a lot of activist campaigns—but, by and large, the concept also blunted our analytical ability to balance rights against each other. Forced to choose between preserving the freedom of the Internet or that of its users, we were supposed to choose the former—because "the Internet" stood for progress and enlightenment.

In the late 1990s, O'Reilly began celebrating "infoware" as the next big thing after "hardware" and "software." His premise was that Internet companies such as Yahoo and E-Trade were not in the software business but in the infoware business. Their functionality was pretty basic—they allowed customers to make purchases or look up something on a map—so their value proposition lay in the information they delivered, not in the software function they executed. And all those fancy Internet services that made infoware possible were patched together with open source software. By showing that infoware was the future and that open source software was its essential component, O'Reilly sought to reassure those who hadn't joined the movement of their pivotal role in the future of computing, if not all human progress.

The "infoware" buzzword didn't catch on, so O'Reilly turned to the work of Douglas Engelbart, the idiosyncratic inventor who gave us the computer mouse and hypertext, to argue that the Internet could help humanity augment its "collective intelligence" and that, once again, open source software was crucial to this endeavor. Now it was all about Amazon learning from its customers and Google learning from the sites in its index. The idea of the Internet as both a repository and incubator of "collective intelligence" was very appealing to Silicon Valley, not least because it tapped into the New Age rhetoric of the 1970s, but the dotcom crash briefly forced O'Reilly to put his philosophizing on hold. When the tech bubble burst, the demand for manuals and conferences—the bulk of O'Reilly's business—shrank, while he also had to deal with some unpleasant litigation concerning his office headquarters in Sebastopol, California. He fired a quarter of his staff, and things looked pretty dire.

Then, in 2004, O'Reilly and his business partner Dale Dougherty hit on the idea of "Web 2.0." What did "2.0" mean, exactly? There was some theoretical ambition to this label—more about that later on—but the primary goal was to show that the 2001 market crash did not mean the end of the web and that it was time to put the crash behind us and start learning from those who survived. Given how much rhetorical capital had been spent on linking the idea of the web with that of open source, the end of the web would also mean the end of so many other concepts. Tactically, "Web 2.0" could also be much bigger than "open source"; it was the kind of sexy umbrella term that could allow O'Reilly to branch out from boring and highly technical subjects to pulse-quickening futurology. "We normally have lots of technical talks focusing on how to use new software, building our conferences for the hackers who are inventing the future, and the early adopters who are taking their work to the next stage," O'Reilly wrote in a blog post announcing his very first Web 2.0 conference. "In contrast, Web 2.0 is our first 'executive conference'—a conference aimed at business people, with the focus on the big picture."

Thus, a high-profile conference was born, aimed explicitly at helping VIPs in the Valley "see the shape of the future," to be followed by many others. O'Reilly soon expanded on the idea of Web 2.0 in an essay that he coauthored with writer and entrepreneur John Battelle. O'Reilly couldn't improve on a concept as sexy as "collective intelligence," so he kept it as the defining feature of this new phenomenon. What set Web 2.0 apart from Web 1.0, O'Reilly claimed, was the simple fact that those firms that didn't embrace it went bust. All Silicon Valley companies should heed the lesson of those few who survived: they must find a way to harness collective intelligence and make it part of their business model. They must become true carriers of the Web 2.0 spirit.

O'Reilly's explanation of the crash is curious. First of all, some tech companies that did go under (Global Crossing comes to mind) couldn't harness collective intelligence, as they were in the telecommunications business. Most memorable dotcom failures—cases like Pets.com—went under because they were driven by foolish business models and overly exuberant investors. (Pets.com would have made an even worse proposition if it had followed O'Reilly's playbook and become a Web 2.0 company.) Furthermore, companies that didn't follow the Web 2.0 mantra—like Barnes & Noble, which O'Reilly singled out as a company that, unlike Amazon, wasn't learning from collective intelligence—didn't go under at all.

By 2007 O'Reilly readily admitted that "Web 2.0 was a pretty crappy name for what's happening." Back in 2004, however, he seemed pretty serious, promoting this concept left and right. The label caught on; like "open source," it was ambiguous and capacious enough to allow many alternative uses and interpretations. O'Reilly's partners in organizing the conference duly trademarked the term "Web 2.0," but this news wasn't well received by their fellow travellers (a similar effort to trademark "open source" by the Open Source Initiative failed). Once "Web 2.0" was established as a term of cultural reference, O'Reilly could venture outside Silicon Valley and establish its relevance to other industries. Much as "open source software" gave rise to "open source politics" and "open source science," so did "Web 2.0" expand its terminological empire. O'Reilly eventually stuck a 2.0 label on anything that suited his business plan, running events with titles like "Gov 2.0" and "Where 2.0." Today, as everyone buys into the 2.0 paradigm, O'Reilly is quietly dropping it. Last year his "Where 2.0" conference on geolocation was rebranded as just "Where." The exceptional has become the new normal.

Sorting through the six thousand or so academic papers that cite O'Reilly's essay on Web 2.0 is no easy feat. It seems that anyone who wanted to claim that a revolution was under way in their own field did so simply by invoking the idea of Web 2.0 in their work: Development 2.0, Nursing 2.0, Humanities 2.0, Protest 2.0, Music 2.0, Research 2.0, Library 2.0, Disasters 2.0, Road Safety 2.0, Identity 2.0, Stress Management 2.0, Archeology 2.0, Crime 2.0, Pornography 2.0, Love 2.0, Wittgenstein 2.0. What unites most of these papers is a shared background assumption that, thanks to the coming of Web 2.0, we are living through unique historical circumstances. Except that there was no coming of Web 2.0—it was just a way to sell a technology conference to a public badly burned by the dotcom crash. Why anyone dealing with stress management or Wittgenstein would be moved by the logistics of conference organizing is a mystery.

O'Reilly himself pioneered this 2.0-ification of public discourse, aggressively reinterpreting trends that had been happening for decades through the prism of Internet history—a move that presented all those trends as just a logical consequence of the Web 2.0 revolution. Take O'Reilly's musings on "Enterprise 2.0." What is it, exactly? Well, it's the same old enterprise—for all we know, it might be making widgets—but now it has learned something from Google and Amazon and found a way to harness "collective intelligence." For O'Reilly, Walmart is a quintessential Enterprise 2.0 company simply because it tracks what its customers are buying in real time.

That this is a rather standard practice—known under the boring title of "just-in-time delivery"—predating both Google and Amazon didn't register with O'Reilly. In a Web 2.0 world, all those older concepts didn't matter or even exist; everything was driven by the forces of open source and the Internet. A revolution was in the making!

This was a typical consequence of relying on Web 2.0 as the guiding metaphor of the age: in the case of Enterprise 2.0, a trend that had little connection to the Internet got reinscribed in the Internet frame, as if attaching the label of 2.0 was all that was needed to establish the logical parallels between the worlds of retail and search. This tendency to redescribe reality in terms of Internet culture, regardless of how spurious and tenuous the connection might be, is a fine example of what I call "Internet-centrism."

And soon Web 2.0 became the preferred way to explain any changes that were happening in Silicon Valley and far beyond it. Most technology analysts simply borrowed the label to explain whatever needed explaining, taking its utility and objectivity for granted. "Open source" gave us "the Internet," "the Internet" gave us "Web 2.0," "Web 2.0" gave us "Enterprise 2.0": in this version of history, Tim O'Reilly is more important than the European Union. Everything needed to be rethought and redone: enterprises, governments, health care, finance, factory production. For O'Reilly, there were few problems that could not be solved with Web 2.0: "Our world is fraught with problems . . . from roiling financial markets to global warming, failing healthcare systems to intractable religious wars . . . many of our most complex systems are reaching their limits. It strikes us that the Web might teach us new ways to address these limits." Web 2.0 was a source of didactic wisdom, and O'Reilly had the right tools to interpret what it wanted to tell us—in each and every context, be it financial markets or global warming. All those contexts belonged to the Internet now. Internet-centrism won.

In his 1976 book *Crazy Talk, Stupid Talk*, Neil Postman pointed to a certain linguistic imperialism that propels crazy talk. For Postman, each human activity—religion, law, marriage, commerce—represents a distinct "semantic environment" with its own tone, purpose, and structure. Stupid talk is relatively harmless; it presents no threat to its semantic environment and doesn't cross into other ones. Since it mostly consists of falsehoods and opinions "given by one fallible human being about the remarks of another fallible human being," it can be easily corrected with facts. For example, to say that Tehran is the capital of Iraq is stupid talk. Crazy talk, in contrast, challenges a semantic environment, as it "establishes different purposes and assumptions from those we normally accept." To argue, as some Nazis did, that the German soldiers ended up far more traumatized than their victims is crazy talk.

For Postman, one of the main tasks of language is to codify and preserve distinctions among different semantic environments. As he put it, "When language becomes undifferentiated, human situations disintegrate: Science becomes indistinguishable from religion, which becomes indistinguishable from commerce, which becomes indistinguishable from law, and so on. If each of them serves the same function, then none of them serves any function. When such a process is occurring, an appropriate word for it is *pollution*." Some words—like "law"—are particularly susceptible to crazy talk, as they mean so many different things: from scientific "laws" to moral "laws" to "laws" of the market to administrative "laws," the same word captures many different social relations. "Open," "networks," and "information" function much like "law" in our own Internet discourse today.

Postman's thinking on the inner workings of language was heavily influenced by the work of Alfred Korzybski, a Polish count now remembered—if at all—for his 1933 book *Science and Sanity*. Korzybski founded a movement called general semantics. While it has inspired many weird and dangerous followers—Scientology's L. Ron Hubbard claimed to have been a fan—it also earned the support of many serious thinkers, from cyberneticians like Anatol Rapoport to philosophers like Gaston Bachelard. For Korzybski, the world has a relational structure that is always in flux; like Heraclitus, who argued that everything flows, Korzybski believed that an object A at time x1 is not the same object as object A at time x2 (he actually recommended indexing every term we use with a relevant numerical in order to distinguish "science 1933" from "science 2013"). Our language could never properly account for the highly fluid and relational structure of our reality or, as he put it in his most famous aphorism, "the map is not the territory."

Korzybski argued that we relate to our environments through the process of "abstracting," whereby our neurological limitations always produce an incomplete and very selective summary of the world around us. There was nothing harmful in this per se—Korzybski simply wanted to make people aware of the highly selective nature of abstracting and give us the tools to detect it in our everyday conversations. He wanted to artificially induce what he called a "neurological delay" so that we could gain more awareness of what we were doing in response to verbal and nonverbal stimuli, understand what features of reality have been omitted, and react appropriately.

To that end, Korzybski developed a number of mental tools meant to reveal all the abstracting around us; he patented the most famous of those—the "structural differential"—in the 1920s. He also encouraged his followers to start using "etc." at the end of their statements as a way of making them aware of their inherent inability to say everything about a given subject and to promote what he called the "consciousness of abstraction."

There was way too much craziness and bad science in Korzybski's theories for him to be treated as a serious thinker, but his basic question—as Postman put it, "What are the characteristics of language which lead people into making false evaluations of the world around them?"—still remains relevant today.

Tim O'Reilly is, perhaps, the most high-profile follower of Korzybski's theories today. O'Reilly was introduced to Korzybski's thought as a teenager while working with a strange man called George Simon in the midst of California's counterculture of the early 1970s.

O'Reilly and Simon were coteaching workshops at the Esalen Institute—then a hotbed of the "human potential movement" that sought to tap the hidden potential of its followers and increase their happiness. Bridging Korzybski's philosophy with Sri Aurobindo's integral yoga, Simon had an immense influence on the young O'Reilly. Simon's rereading of general semantics, noted O'Reilly in 2004, "gave me a grounding in how to see people, and to acknowledge what I saw, that is the bedrock of my personal philosophy to this day." (In 1976 the twenty-two-year-old O'Reilly edited and published notebooks by Simon after the latter died in an accident; even by the highly demanding standards of the 1970s, those notebooks look outright crazy.)

O'Reilly openly acknowledges his debt to Korzybski, listing *Science and Sanity* among his favorite books and even showing visualizations of the structural differential in his presentations. It would be a mistake to think that O'Reilly's linguistic interventions—from "open source" to "Web 2.0"—are random or spontaneous. There is a philosophy to them: a philosophy of knowledge and language inspired by Korzybski. However, O'Reilly deploys Korzybski in much the same way that the advertising industry deploys the latest findings in neuroscience: the goal is not to increase awareness, but to manipulate. If general semanticists aimed to reveal the underlying emptiness of many concepts that pollute the public debate, O'Reilly is applying some of Korzybski's language insights to practice some pollution of his own.

O'Reilly, of course, sees his role differently, claiming that all he wants is to make us aware of what earlier commentators may have overlooked. "A metaphor is just that: a way of framing the issues such that people can see something they might otherwise miss," he wrote in response to a critic who accused him of linguistic incontinence. But Korzybski's point, if fully absorbed, is that a metaphor is primarily a way of framing issues such that we *don't* see something we might otherwise see.

In public, O'Reilly modestly presents himself as someone who just happens to excel at detecting the "faint signals" of emerging trends. He does so by monitoring a group of überinnovators that he dubs the "alpha geeks." "The 'alpha geeks' show us where technology wants to go. Smart companies follow and support their ingenuity rather than trying to suppress it," O'Reilly writes. His own function is that of an intermediary—someone who ensures that the alpha geeks are heard by the right executives: "The alpha geeks are often a few years ahead of their time. . . . What we do at O'Reilly is watch these folks, learn from them, and try to spread the word by writing down (or helping them write down) what they've learned and then publishing it in books or online."

The name of his company's blog—*O'Reilly Radar*—is meant to position him as an independent intellectual who is simply ahead of his peers in grasping the obvious. Some regular contributors to the *Radar* blog have titles like "correspondents," giving the whole operation a veneer of objectivity and disinterestedness, with O'Reilly merely a commentator knowledgeable enough to provide some context to busy Silicon Valley types. An Edwin Schlossberg quotation he really likes—"the skill of writing is to create a context in which other people can think"—is cited to explain his willingness to enter so many seemingly unrelated fields. As Web 2.0 becomes central to everything, O'Reilly—the world's biggest exporter of crazy talk—is on a mission to provide the appropriate "context" to every field.

In a fascinating essay published in 2000, O'Reilly sheds some light on his modus operandi. The thinker who emerges there is very much at odds with the spirit of objectivity that O'Reilly seeks to cultivate in public. That essay, in fact, is a revealing ode to what O'Reilly dubs "meme-engineering": "Just as gene engineering allows us to artificially shape genes, meme-engineering lets us organize and shape ideas so that they can be transmitted more effectively, and have the desired effect once they are transmitted." In a move worthy of Frank Luntz, O'Reilly meme-engineers a nice euphemism—"meme-engineering"—to describe what has previously been known as "propaganda."

The essay's putative goal is to show how one can meme-engineer a new meaning for "peer-to-peer" technologies—traditionally associated with piracy—and make them appear friendly and not at all threatening to the entertainment industry. Leading by example,

O'Reilly invokes his success in rebranding "free software" as "open source." The key to success, he notes, was to "put a completely different spin on what formerly might have been considered the 'same space.'" To make that happen, O'Reilly and his acolytes "changed the canonical list of projects that we wanted to hold up as exemplars of the movement," while also articulating what broader goals the projects on the new list served. He then proceeds to rehash the already familiar narrative: O'Reilly put the Internet at the center of everything, linking some "free software" projects like Apache or Perl to successful Internet startups and services. As a result, the movement's goal was no longer to produce a completely free, independent, and fully functional operating system but to worship at the altar of the Internet gods.

Another apt example of O'Reilly's meme-engineering is his attempt to establish a strong intellectual link between the development of Unix—a proprietary operating system that Stallman sought to replace with free software—and the development of open source and the Internet. Thus, for instance, O'Reilly claimed that Unix was built and improved in the spirit of open source because its academic cheerleaders were already swapping code with each other in the early 1970s. That such exchanges were just a regular part of the freewheeling academic culture and had little to do with philosophical attitudes toward code doesn't weaken the argument; in fact, this is recast as an advantage, as now the open source model can be presented as just a natural extension of the scientific method. (Since O'Reilly himself played an important role in the production of Unix manuals, his own contribution to the Internet and open source suddenly looks even more significant.)

But O'Reilly's meme-engineering around Unix doesn't stop at the purely discursive level. In his talks and writings, O'Reilly often points to one highly technical 1984 book—*The Unix Programming Environment*—as proof that, at least with respect to collaboration, Unix was some kind of proto-Internet. Indeed, the Wikipedia page for the book states that "the book is perhaps most valuable for its exposition of the Unix philosophy of small cooperating tools with standardized inputs and outputs, a philosophy that also shaped the end-to-end philosophy of the Internet. It is this philosophy, and the architecture based on it, that has allowed open source projects to be assembled into larger systems such as Linux, without explicit coordination between developers."

Could it be that O'Reilly is right in claiming that "open source" has a history that predates 1998? Well, Wikipedia won't tell us much here: in a recent Berkeley talk, O'Reilly admitted that he was the one to edit the Wikipedia page for the book. O'Reilly is perfectly positioned to control our technology discourse: as a publisher, he can churn out whatever books he needs to promote his favorite memes—and, once those have been codified in book form, they can be easily admitted into Wikipedia, where they quickly morph into facts. What's not to like about "collective intelligence"?

Seen through the prism of meme-engineering, O'Reilly's activities look far more sinister. His "correspondents" at *O'Reilly Radar* don't work beats; they work memes and epistemes, constantly reframing important public issues in accordance with the templates prophesied by O'Reilly. Recently, for example, O'Reilly has been interested in the meme of "the industrial Internet," forming a partnership with GE to participate in events and cover the company on the blog. Once "the industrial Internet" meme is out of the bag, only a lack of imagination prevents O'Reilly's writers from seeing it absolutely everywhere. Here is how one of them describes a company that might not otherwise fit the boundaries of the meme: "I'm sure [its founder] wouldn't use the words 'industrial Internet' to describe what he and his team are doing, and it might be a little bit of a stretch to categorize 3Scan that way. But I think they are an exemplar of many of the core principles of the meme and it's interesting to think about them in that frame." Five years down the road, would you be surprised if there is, in fact, something called "the industrial Internet" and that the primary goal of most activism around it is to defend the freedom of GE to "innovate" on it as it pleases?

Or take O'Reilly's meme-engineering efforts around cyberwarfare. In a recent post on the subject, he muses on just how narrowly we have defined the idea of "cyberwarfare" and suggests we expand it to encompass conflicts between states and individuals. Now, who stands to benefit from "cyberwarfare" being defined more broadly? Could it be those who, like O'Reilly, can't currently grab a share of the giant pie that is cybersecurity funding? If O'Reilly's meme-engineering efforts succeed, we might end up classifying acts that should be treated as crime, espionage, or terrorism under the ambiguous label of "war." Such reframing would be disastrous for civil liberties and privacy and would only exacerbate the already awful legal prosecution of hacktivists. It probably won't be long before a "cyberwarfare correspondent" is added to O'Reilly's media empire.

In his 2007 bestseller *Words That Work*, Republican operative Frank Luntz lists ten rules of effective communication: simplicity, brevity, credibility, consistency, novelty, sound, aspiration, visualization, questioning, and context. O'Reilly, while employing most of them, has a few unique rules of his own. Clever use of visualization, for example, helps him craft his message in a way that is both sharp and open-ended. Thus, O'Reilly's meme-engineering efforts usually result in "meme maps," where the meme to be defined—whether it's "open source" or "Web 2.0"—is put at the center, while other blob-like terms are drawn as connected to it.

The exact nature of these connections is rarely explained in full, but this is all for the better, as the reader might eventually interpret connections with their own agendas in mind. This is why the name of the meme must be as inclusive as possible: you never know who your eventual allies might be. "A big part of meme engineering is giving a name that creates a big tent that a lot of people want to be under, a train that takes a lot of people where they want to go," writes O'Reilly. Once the meme has been conceived, the rest of O'Reilly's empire can step in and help make it real. His conferences, for example, play a crucial role:

> When you look at any of our events, there's ultimately some rewriting of the meme map in each of them. *Web 2.0* was about distinguishing companies that survived the dotcom bust from those that didn't.

> *Strata* is about defining the new field of data science. *Velocity* is about making clear that the applications of the web depend on people to keep them running, unlike past generations of software that were simply software artifacts.

There is considerable continuity across O'Reilly's memes—over time, they tend to morph into one another. Thus, as he puts it, "'open source' was a great reshaping of the meme for its day, moving us off some of the limitations of 'free software,' but it may not be the end of the story." O'Reilly has gradually lost interest in "open source" and "Web 2.0," moving on to new memes: "government as a platform" and "algorithmic regulation." We can only guess what comes next. Such dexterity not only helps in organizing new events and investing in cool startups; it also, as those six thousand papers that cite Web 2.0 attest, leaves a huge imprint on our culture.

All the familiar pathologies of O'Reilly's thinking are on full display in his quest to meme-engineer his way to "Government 2.0." The free software scenario is repeating itself: deeply political reform efforts are no longer seen as "moral crusades," but are reinvented as mere attempts at increasing efficiency and promoting innovation.

Before O'Reilly went searching for a big-tent meme, there was little cohesion to the many disparate efforts to use technology to transform government. Some hoped that digitization would help reduce bureaucracy and allow everyone to fill out tax returns online. Others awaited the arrival of electronic town halls that would permit citizens to deliberate on the substance of policies that affect them. Yet another group hoped that digitization might make governments more transparent and accountable by forcing them to put some of the documents obtained through the Freedom of Information Act (FOIA) online. Finally, there were those who believed that increasing the availability and liquidity of government information would lead to new entrepreneurial projects and boost the economy.

Many of these efforts started long before the web and had no obvious connection to Internet culture, let alone Web 2.0. Occasionally, these four efforts—aiming at greater efficiency, deliberation, transparency, and innovation—overlapped, but mostly they have been driven by two very different agendas. One cohort, interested in increasing efficiency and spurring innovation, pursued campaigns that were mostly economic in character; these folks were not particularly interested in the political nature of the regimes they were seeking to reform. Singapore—where anyone can file their paperwork in minutes—was their role model.

The other cohort, interested in deliberation and transparency, was primarily concerned with transferring power from governments to citizens and increasing the accountability of public institutions. They argued that citizens have a right to obtain information about how their governments operate. Such explicitly political demands became the cornerstone of various Right to Information campaigns. This second group wouldn't accept authoritarian Singapore as a role model, since most of its e-innovations do very little to promote meaningful citizen participation in policy-making or increase accountability.

Most modern governments, not surprisingly, prefer the economic aspects of digitization reform to the political ones. Innovative schemes, like smart parking systems, can help at election time; lengthy disclosures of government deliberations are likely to cause headaches. Right-leaning governments have an extra reason to celebrate the economism of the first cohort: publishing aggregate information about the performance of individual public service providers may help convince the electorate that those services should be provided by the private sector.

By the early 2000s, as O'Reilly and his comrades were celebrating open source as a new revolutionary approach to everything, their discussions wandered into debates about the future of governance. Thus, a term like "open government"—which, until then, had mostly been used as a synonym for "transparent and accountable government"—was reinvented as a shortened version of "open source government." The implication of this subtle linguistic change was that the main cultural attributes of open source software—the availability of the source code for everyone's inspection, the immense contribution it can make to economic growth, the new decentralized production model that relies on contributions from numerous highly distributed participants—were to displace older criteria like "transparency" or "accountability" as the most desirable attributes of open government. The coining of the "open government" buzzwords was meant to produce a very different notion of openness.

Initially, O'Reilly had little role in this process; the meme of "open source" was promiscuous enough to redefine many important terms without his intervention. But in 2007 O'Reilly hosted yet another summit, attended by technologists and civic hackers, to devise a list of key principles of open government. The group came up with eight principles, all focused on the purely technical issue of how to ensure that, once data was released by the government, nothing would hold it back. As long as this "open data" was liquid and reusable, others could build on it. Neither the political process that led to the release of the data nor its content was considered relevant to openness. Thus, data about how many gum-chewers Singapore sends to prison would be "open" as long as the Singaporean government shared it in suitable formats. Why it shared such data was irrelevant.

With Obama's election, Washington was game for all things 2.0. This is when O'Reilly turned his full attention to government reform, deploying and manipulating several memes at once—"Gov 2.0," "open government," and "government as a platform"—in order to establish the semantic primacy of the economic dimension of digitization. A decade earlier, O'Reilly had redefined "freedom" as the freedom of developers to do as they wished; now it was all about recasting "openness" in government in purely economic and innovation-friendly terms while downplaying its political connotations.

O'Reilly's writings on Gov 2.0 reveal the same talented meme-engineer who gave us open source and Web 2.0. In his seminal essay on the subject, O'Reilly mixes semantic environments without a shred of regret. Both Web 2.0 and Gov 2.0, he argues, return us to earlier, simpler ways, away from the unnecessary complexity of modern institutions. "Web 2.0 was not a new version of the World Wide Web; it was a renaissance after the dark ages of the dotcom bust, a rediscovery of the power hidden in the original design of the World Wide Web," he writes. "Similarly, Government 2.0 is not a new kind of government; it is government stripped down to its core, rediscovered and reimagined as if for the first time."

Once it's been established that new paradigms of government can be modeled on the success of technology companies, O'Reilly can argue that "it's important to think deeply about what the three design principles of transparency, participation, and collaboration mean in the context of technology." These were the very three principles that the Obama administration articulated in its "Open Government Directive," published on the president's first day in office. But why do we have to think about their meaning in "the context of technology"? The answer is quite simple: whatever transparency and participation used to mean doesn't matter any longer. Now that we've moved to an era of Everything 2.0, the meaning of those terms will be dictated by the possibilities and inclinations of technology. And what is technology today if not "open source" and "Web 2.0"?

Here, for example, is how O'Reilly tries to reengineer the meme of transparency:

> The word "transparency" can lead us astray as we think about the opportunity for Government 2.0. Yes, it's a good thing when government data is available so that journalists and watchdog groups like the Sunlight Foundation can disclose cost overruns in government projects or highlight the influence of lobbyists. But that's just the beginning. The magic of open data is that the same openness that enables transparency also enables innovation, as developers build applications that reuse government data in unexpected ways. Fortunately, Vivek Kundra and others in the administration understand this distinction, and are providing data for both purposes.

Vivek Kundra is the former chief information officer of the U.S. government who oversaw the launch of a portal called data.gov, which required agencies to upload at least three "high-value" sets of their own data. This data was made "open" in the same sense that open source software is open—i.e., it was made available for anyone to see. But, once again, O'Reilly is dabbling in meme-engineering: the data dumped on data.gov, while potentially beneficial for innovation, does not automatically "enable transparency." O'Reilly deploys the highly ambiguous concept of openness to confuse "transparency as accountability" (what Obama called for in his directive) with "transparency as innovation" (what O'Reilly himself wants).

How do we ensure accountability? Let's forget about databases for a moment and think about power. How do we make the government feel the heat of public attention? Perhaps by forcing it to make targeted disclosures of particularly sensitive data sets. Perhaps by strengthening the FOIA laws, or at least making sure that government agencies comply with existing provisions. Or perhaps by funding intermediaries that can build narratives around data—much of the released data is so complex that few amateurs have the processing power and expertise to read and make sense of it in their basements. This might be very useful for boosting accountability but useless for boosting innovation; likewise, you can think of many data releases that would be great for innovation and do nothing for accountability. The language of "openness" does little to help us grasp key differences between the two. In this context, openness leads to Neil Postman's "crazy talk," resulting in the pollution of the values of one semantic environment (accountability) with those of another (innovation).

O'Reilly doesn't always coin new words. Sometimes he manipulates the meanings of existing words. Cue his framing of "participation":

> We can be misled by the notion of participation to think that it's limited to having government decision-makers "get input" from citizens. This would be like thinking that enabling comments on a website is the beginning and end of social media! It's a trap for outsiders to think that Government 2.0 is a way to use new technology to amplify the voices of citizens to influence those in power, and by insiders as a way to harness and channel those voices to advance their causes.

It's hard to make sense of this passage without understanding the exact meaning of a term like "participation" in the glossary of All Things Web 2.0. According to O'Reilly, one of the key attributes of Web 2.0 sites is that they are based on an "architecture of participation"; it's this architecture that allows "collective intelligence" to be harnessed. Ranking your purchases on Amazon or reporting spammy emails to Google are good examples of clever architectures of participation. Once Amazon and Google start learning from millions of users, they become "smarter" and more attractive to the original users.

This is a very limited vision of participation. It amounts to no more than a simple feedback session with whoever is running the system. You are not participating in the design of that system, nor are you asked to comment on its future. There is nothing "collective" about such distributed intelligence; it's just a bunch of individual users acting on their own and never experiencing any sense of solidarity or group belonging. Such "participation" has no political dimension; no power changes hands.

Occasionally, O'Reilly's illustrations include activities that demand no actual awareness of participation—e.g., a blog that puts up links to other blogs ends up improving Google's search index—which is, not coincidentally perhaps, how we think of "participation" in the market system when we go shopping. To imply that "participation" means the same thing in the context of Web 2.0 as it does in politics is to do the very opposite of what Korzybski and general semantics prescribe. Were he really faithful to those principles, O'Reilly would be pointing out the differences between the two—not blurring them.

So what are we to make of O'Reilly's exhortation that "it's a trap for outsiders to think that Government 2.0 is a way to use new technology to amplify the voices of citizens to influence those in power"? We might think that the hallmark of successful participatory reforms would be enabling citizens to "influence those in power." There's a very explicit depoliticization of participation at work here. O'Reilly wants to redefine participation from something that arises from shared grievances and aims at structural reforms to something that arises from individual frustration with bureaucracies and usually ends with citizens using or building apps to solve their own problems.

As a result, once-lively debates about the content and meaning of specific reforms and institutions are replaced by governments calling on their citizens to help find spelling mistakes in patent applications or use their phones to report potholes. If Participation 1.0 was about the use of public reason to push for political reforms, with groups of concerned citizens coalescing around some vague notion of the shared public good, Participation 2.0 is about atomized individuals finding or contributing the right data to solve some problem without creating any disturbances in the system itself. (These citizens do come together at "hackathons"—to help Silicon Valley liberate government data at no cost—only to return to their bedrooms shortly thereafter.) Following the open source model, citizens are invited to find bugs in the system, not to ask whether the system's goals are right to begin with. That politics can aspire to something more ambitious than bug-management is not an insight that occurs after politics has been reimagined through the prism of open source software.

Protest is one activity that O'Reilly hates passionately. "There's a kind of passivity even to our activism: we think that all we can do is to protest," he writes. "Collective action has come to mean collective complaint. Or at most, a collective effort to raise money." In contrast, he urges citizens to "apply the DIY spirit on a civic scale." To illustrate the DIY spirit in action, O'Reilly likes to invoke the example of a Hawaiian community that, following a period of government inaction, raised $4 million and repaired a local park essential to its livelihood. For O'Reilly, the Hawaiian example reveals the natural willingness of ordinary citizens to solve their own problems. Governments should learn from Hawaii and offload more work onto their citizens; this is the key insight behind O'Reilly's "government as a platform" meme.

This platform meme was, of course, inspired by Silicon Valley. Instead of continuing to build its own apps, Apple built an App Store, getting third-party developers to do all the heavy lifting. This is the model that governments must emulate. In fact, notes O'Reilly, they once did: in the 1950s the U.S. government built a system of highways that allowed the private sector to build many more settlements around them, while in the 1980s the Reagan administration started opening up the GPS system, which gave us amazing road directions and Foursquare (where O'Reilly is an investor).

O'Reilly's prescriptions, as is often the case, do contain a grain of truth, but he nearly always exaggerates their benefits while obfuscating their costs. One of the main reasons why governments choose not to offload certain services to the private sector is not because they think they can do a better job at innovation or efficiency but because other considerations—like fairness and equity of access—come into play. "If Head Start were a startup it would be out of business. It doesn't work," remarked O'Reilly in a recent interview. Well, exactly: that's why Head Start is not a startup.

The real question is not whether developers should be able to submit apps to the App Store, but whether citizens should be paying for the apps or counting on the government to provide these services. To push for the platform metaphor as the primary way of thinking about the distribution of responsibilities between the private and the public sectors is to push for the economic-innovative dimension of Gov 2.0—and to ensure the private sector always emerges victorious.

O'Reilly defines "government as a platform" as "the notion that the best way to shrink the size of government is to introduce the idea that government should provide fewer citizen-facing services, but should instead consciously provide infrastructure only, with APIs and standards that let the private sector deliver citizen facing services." He believes that "the idea of government as a platform applies to every aspect of the government's role in society"—city affairs, health care, financial services regulation, police, fire, and garbage collection. "[Government as a platform] is the right way to frame the question of Government 2.0."

One person who is busy turning the "government as a platform" meme into reality is David Cameron in the United Kingdom. Cameron's "Big Society" idea is based on three main tenets: decentralization of power from London to local governments, making information about the public sector more transparent to citizens, and paying providers of public services based on the quality of their service, which, ideally, would be measured and published online, thanks to feedback provided by the public. The idea here is that the government will serve as a coordinator of sorts, allowing people to come together—perhaps even giving them seed funding to kick-start alternatives to inefficient public services.

Cameron's motivation is clear: the government simply has no money to pay for services that were previously provided by public institutions, and besides, shrinking the government is something his party has been meaning to do anyway. Cameron immediately grasped the strategic opportunities offered by the ambiguity of a term like "open government" and embraced it wholeheartedly—in its most apolitical, economic version, of course. At the same time that he celebrated the ability of "armchair auditors" to pore through government databases, he also criticized freedom of information laws, alleging that FOI requests are "furring up the arteries of government" and even threatening to start charging for them. Francis Maude, the Tory politician who Cameron put in charge of liberating government data, is on the record stating that open government is "what modern deregulation looks like" and that he'd "like to make FOI redundant." In 2011 Cameron's government released a white paper on "Open Public Services" that uses the word "open" in a peculiar way: it argues that, save for national security and the judiciary, all public services must become open to competition from the market.

Here's just one example of how a government that is nominally promoting Tim O'Reilly's progressive agenda of Gov 2.0 and "government as a platform" is rolling back the welfare state and increasing government secrecy—all in the name of "openness." The reason why Cameron has managed to get away with so much crazy talk is simple: the positive spin attached to "openness" allows his party to hide the ugly nature of its reforms. O'Reilly, who had otherwise praised the Government Digital Service, the unit responsible for the digitization of the British government, is aware that the "Big Society" might reveal the structural limitations of his quest for "openness." Thus, he publicly distanced himself from Cameron, complaining of "the shabby abdication of responsibility of Cameron's Big Society."

But is this the same O'Reilly who once claimed that the goal of his proposed reforms is to "design programs and supporting infrastructure that enable 'we the people' to do most of the work"? His rejection of Cameron is pure PR, as they largely share the same agenda—not an easy thing to notice, as O'Reilly constantly alternates between two visions of open government. O'Reilly the good cop claims that he wants the government to release its data to promote more innovation by the private sector, while O'Reilly the bad cop wants to use that newly liberated data to shrink the government. "There is no Schumpeterian 'creative destruction' to bring unneeded government programs to an end," he lamented in 2010. "Government 2.0 will require deep thinking about how to end programs that no longer work, and how to use the platform power of the government not to extend government's reach, but instead, how to use it to better enable its citizenry and its economy." Speaking to British civil servants, O'Reilly positions open government as the right thing to do in the times of austerity, not just as an effective way to promote innovation.

After *The New Yorker* ran a long, critical article on the Big Society in 2010, Jennifer Pahlka—O'Reilly's key ally, who runs an NGO called Code for America—quickly moved to dismiss any parallels between Cameron and O'Reilly. "The beauty of the government as a platform model is that it doesn't assume civic participation, it encourages it subtly by aligning with existing motivations in its citizens, so that anyone—ranging from the fixers in Hawaii to the cynics in Britain—would be willing to get involved," she noted in a blog post. "We'd better be careful we don't send the wrong message, and that when we're building tools for citizen engagement, we do it in the way that taps existing motivations."

But what kinds of "existing motivations" are there to be tapped? O'Reilly writes that, in his ideal future, governments will be "making smart design decisions, which harness the self-interest of society and citizens to achieve positive results." That, in fact, is how his favorite technology platforms work: users tell Google that some of their incoming email is spam in order to improve their own email experience. In other words, it's self-interest through and through. "The architecture of Linux, the Internet, and the World Wide Web are such that users pursuing their own 'selfish' interests build collective value as an automatic byproduct," writes O'Reilly. This is also how the likes of Eric Raymond explain the motivation of those contributing to open source projects—they do it for strictly selfish reasons. "The 'utility function' Linux hackers are maximizing is not classically economic, but is the intangible of their own ego satisfaction and reputation among other hackers," Raymond writes in *The Cathedral and the Bazaar*. He goes on to say that "one may call their motivation 'altruistic', but this ignores the fact that altruism is itself a form of ego satisfaction for the altruist." If it sounds like Ayn Rand, that's because Raymond explicitly draws on her crazy talk.

When pressed, O'Reilly the good cop refuses to acknowledge that his thinking about open government is not very different from Raymond's thinking about open source software. When in 2013 Nathaniel Tkacz, a media academic, noted these similarities, O'Reilly complained that he was "a bit surprised to learn that my ideas of 'government as a platform' are descended from Eric Raymond's ideas about Linux, since: a) Eric is a noted libertarian with disdain for government b) Eric's focus on Linux was on its software development methodology." Well, perhaps O'Reilly shouldn't act so surprised: as Tkacz points out, O'Reilly's writings on "government as a platform" explicitly credit Raymond as the source of the metaphor. O'Reilly in 2011: "In *The Cathedral & the Bazaar*, Eric Raymond uses the image of a bazaar to contrast the collaborative development model of open source software with traditional software development, but the analogy is equally applicable to government."

But is it really? Applied to politics, all this talk of bazaars, existing motivations, and self-interest treats citizenship as if it were fully reducible to market relations—yet another form of crazy talk. And it doesn't easily square with the aspirations to active citizenship implicit in the "DIY spirit on a civic scale." Of course, with some clever PR, one can say that the Hawaiians who rebuilt their park had some "existing motivations," like having to earn a living to stay alive. But if the bar for "existing motivations" is set so low, then there are no limits to dismantling the welfare state and replacing it with some wild DIY hacker culture. Why do we need an expensive health care system if people have "existing motivations" to self-monitor at home and purchase drugs directly from Big Pharma? Why bother with police if we can print out guns at home—thanks, 3-D printers!—and we are already highly motivated to stay alive?

Once we follow O'Reilly's exhortation not to treat the government as "the deus ex machina that we've paid to do for us what we could be doing for ourselves," such questions are hard to avoid. In all of O'Reilly's theorizing, there's not a hint as to what political and moral principles should guide us in applying the platform model. Whatever those principles are, they are certainly not exhausted by appeals to innovation and efficiency—which is the language that O'Reilly wants us to speak.

The fundamental problem with O'Reilly's vision is that, on the one hand, it's all about having the private sector build new services that were unavailable when the government ran the show. Thus, it's all about citizen-consumers, guided by the Invisible Hand, creating new value out of thin air. But O'Reilly also likes to invoke "DIY spirit on a civic scale" to call on citizens to take on functions that were previously performed by the government (even if poorly); here, we are not building new services—we are outsourcing public services to the private sector. O'Reilly's logic in a nutshell: the government didn't have to build its own Foursquare—hence, disaster response should be delegated to the private sector. Is the government meant to be a platform for providing services or for stimulating innovation? It's certainly both—but the principles that ought to regulate its behavior in each case are certainly different.

For O'Reilly, the memes of "Government 2.0" and "government as a platform" serve one major function: they make him relevant to the conversation about governance and politics, allowing him to expand his business into new territories. The Internet and open source have become universal connectors that can relate anything to anything. "Just as the interstate highway system increased the vitality of our transportation infrastructure, it is certainly possible that greater government involvement in health care could do the same," he writes. Got it? But what if the dynamics of building highways are different from those of providing health care? What then?

O'Reilly's attempts to meme-engineer how we think about politics are all the more disturbing for the deeply reductionist, anti-democratic flavor of his own politics. Positivist to his core, O'Reilly believes that there is just one right answer to policy dilemmas, and that it's the job of the government (for him, it's all just "government") to produce legislation that gets at this "right" answer and then pass the necessary measures to make it happen. The means don't much matter; it's all about the ends—and the ends are perfectly knowable, as long as we have the data.

O'Reilly's latest meme, which he calls "algorithmic regulation," was inspired by—what else?—the Internet. This idea, writes O'Reilly, "is central to all Internet platforms, and provides a fruitful area for investigation in the design of 21st century government." This is how he explained it in a recent talk at the Long Now Foundation:

> If you look at, say, the way spam is regulated on the Internet, that's the beginnings of a kind of an immune system response to a pathogen and works a lot like biology: you recognize the signature of something new and hostile and you fix it. . . . You compare that to how government regulation works, and you go: "It's just badly broken!" Somebody puts out some rules, and there's no method of enforcement.

Not a very sharp definition yet, but this is how many of O'Reilly's memes start. Once he's cornered the meme, his "correspondents" will do the rest, highlighting it in their blog posts and reports. ("In the future, better outcomes might come . . . through adopting what Tim O'Reilly has described as 'algorithmic regulation,' applying the dynamic feedback loops that web giants use to police their systems against malware and spam in government agencies entrusted with protecting the public interest," writes Alex Howard, the "Government 2.0" correspondent of *O'Reilly Radar*.)

Quite appropriately, the only political institution that corresponds to O'Reilly's vision for "algorithmic regulation" is a central bank. Central banks have very clear, numerical targets—they know what's "right" and don't have to bother with deliberations—and they try to meet those targets with just a few specific tools at their disposal. They love feedback and think like Google. According to O'Reilly, the way they regulate is "kind of like the way Google regulates. They kind of say: I have an outcome in mind and a couple of knobs and levers. Periodically, I might get a few new knobs and levers, and I tweak them to get the outcome. I don't just sort of say: This is a rule and I'm going to follow it regardless of whether it has a good outcome or a bad outcome." Central banks are elegant and simple; they just do stuff, instead of succumbing to, well, politics. "[In central banks] we have a couple of levers, and we keep tweaking them to see if we can get where we want to go. And that's really how I would like to see us thinking about government regulatory processes."

Expanding on this notion of "algorithmic regulation," O'Reilly reveals his inner technocrat:

> I remember having a conversation with Nancy Pelosi not long after Google did their Panda search update, and it was in the context of SOPA/PIPA. . . . [Pelosi] said, "Well, you know, we have to satisfy the interests of the technology industry *and* the movie industry." And I thought, "No, you don't. You have to get the right answer." So that's the reason I mentioned Google Panda search update, when they downgraded a lot of people who were building these content farms and putting low quality content in order to get pageviews and clicks in order to make money and not satisfy the users. And I thought, "Gosh, what if Google had said, yeah, yeah, we have to sit down with Demand Media and satisfy their concerns, we have to make sure that at least 30 percent of the search results are crappy so that their business model is preserved." You wouldn't do that. You'd say,

> "No, we have to get it right!" And I feel like, we don't actually have a government that actually understands that it has to be building a better platform that starts to manage things like that with the best outcome for the real users. *[loud applause]*

Here O'Reilly dismisses the entertainment industry as just "wrong," essentially comparing them to spammers. But what makes Google an appropriate model here? While it has obligations to its shareholders, Google doesn't owe anything to the sites in its index. Congress was never meant to work this way. SOPA and PIPA were bad laws with too much overreach, but to claim that the entertainment industry has no legitimate grievances against piracy seems bizarre.

Underpinning O'Reilly's faith in algorithmic regulation is his naive belief that big data, harnessed through collective intelligence, would allow us to get at the right answer to every problem, making both representation and deliberation unnecessary. After all, why let contesting factions battle it out in the public sphere if we can just study what happens in the real world—with our sensors, databases, and algorithms? No wonder O'Reilly ends up claiming that "we have to actually start moving away from the notion that politics really has very much to do with governance. To the extent that we can fix things without politics, we'd be much better off." It's the ultimate conceit of Silicon Valley: if only we had more data and better tools, we could suspend politics once and for all.

The magic "feedback" that O'Reilly touts so passionately is really the voice of the market—and occasionally he lets that slip: "Government programs must be designed from the outset not as a fixed set of specifications, but as open-ended platforms that allow for extensibility and revision by the marketplace. Platform thinking is an antidote to the complete specifications that currently dominate the government approach not only to IT but to programs of all kinds." But we prefer to have complete specifications at the outset not because no one had thought of building dynamic feedback systems before O'Reilly but because this is the only way to ensure that everyone's grievances are addressed before the policies are implemented.

His treatment of feedback as essentially an Internet phenomenon is vintage O'Reilly. As long as "algorithmic regulation" is defined against a notion like Web 2.0, O'Reilly feels no need to engage with the vast body of thought on feedback systems and the sociology of performance indicators. That most of the ideas behind algorithmic regulation were articulated by the likes of Karl Deutsch and David Easton in the 1960s would probably be news to O'Reilly. Nor is his intellectual equilibrium perturbed by the fact that the RAND Corporation was pitching something very similar to "algorithmic regulation" to American cities in the late 1960s in the hopes of making city governance more cybernetic. The plans, alas, didn't work; the models could never account for the messy reality of urban life.

A decade before he wrote *Science and Sanity*, Alfred Korzybski wrote another weird book, *Manhood of Humanity*. He, too, was very keen on feedback. "Philosophy, law and ethics, to be effective in a dynamic world must be dynamic; they must be made vital enough to keep pace with the progress of life and science," he proclaimed. Korzybski's solution, surprisingly, also lay in turning government into an algorithmically driven platform: "A natural first step would probably be the establishment of a new institution which might be called a Dynamic Department—Department of Coordination or a Department of Cooperation—the name is of little importance, but it would be the *nucleus* of the new civilization." Like O'Reilly's "government as a platform," this new department would aspire to enable citizens. "Its functions," wrote Korzybski, "would be those of encouraging, helping and protecting the people in such cooperative enterprises as agriculture, manufactures, finance, and distribution."

Korzybski envisioned this new scientific government to consist of ten sections, which ranged from the Section of Mathematical Sociology or Humanology ("composed of at least one sociologist, one biologist, one mechanical engineer, and one mathematician") to the Section of Mathematical Legislation ("composed of (say) one lawyer, one mathematician, one mechanical engineer") and from the Promoters' Section ("composed of engineers whose duty would be to study all of the latest scientific facts, collect data, and elaborate plans") to the News Section (its task would be "to edit a large daily paper giving true, uncolored news with a special supplement relating to progress in the work of Human Engineering").

For all his insight into the nature of language and reality, Korzybski was a kooky technocrat who believed that science could resolve all political problems. He would certainly agree with O'Reilly that there is one right way to decide on pending legislation and that any issues and controversies that come up in deliberations are just semantic noise—clever meme-engineering by the parties involved. Scientism is still scientism, even when it's clothed in the rhetoric of big data.

At least O'Reilly is perfectly clear about how people can succeed in the future. Toward the end of his Long Now Foundation talk, he admits that

> [the] future of collective intelligence applications is a future in which the individual that we prize so highly actually has less power—except to the extent that that individual is able to create new mind storms. ... How will we influence this global brain? The way we'll influence it is seen in the way that people create these viral storms .... We're going to start getting good at that. People will be able to command vast amounts of attention and direct large groups of people through new mechanisms.

Yes, let that thought sink in: our Mindstormer-in-Chief is telling us that the only way to succeed in this brave new world is to become a Tim O'Reilly. Anyone fancy an O'Reilly manual on meme hustling? ⚜

NOTES

1 In researching this essay, I tried to read all of O'Reilly's published writings: blog posts, essays, tweets. I read many of his interviews and pored over the comments he left on blogs and news sites. I watched all his talks on YouTube. But I decided against interviewing him.

First of all, I don't believe in interviewing spin doctors: the interviewer learns nothing new while the interviewee gets an extraordinary opportunity to spin the story even before it's published.

Second, my goal in writing this essay was not to profile O'Reilly. Of course, I could have told you all about the wonderful jams—plum, blackberry, raspberry, peach—that he likes to make in his spare time. I left out such trivia on purpose, as my main interest has been O'Reilly the thinker, not O'Reilly the human being. Serious thinkers can be judged by their published output alone.

Third, the only two emails that I ever received from him hinted at his penchant for heavy-handed manipulation of the media. The first email arrived long before I started working on this essay. It was a complaint about something I had written about him in the past, a throwaway line in a long essay—a complaint I believe to be without merit. The second email came right after I finished writing the first draft, which, by coincidence, happened to be on the very day that O'Reilly and I had a brief but feisty exchange on Twitter (he initiated it). In that second email, he offered to explain all his positions to me face to face—an opportunity I turned down, having just spent three months of my life reading his tweets, blog posts, and essays.

That said, I have no doubt that everything in this essay will be meme-engineered against me.

MARK S. FISHER

PART FOUR

QUIET ROOMS, DEAD ZONES

Follow the Money

The Washington Post*'s pageant of folly*

CHRIS LEHMANN

Amid the run-up to the general election of 2012, an awkward fact that didn't have any relevance to either of the major party's stratagems nonetheless came to light. As President Obama began aggressively touting the "Buffett Rule" to introduce marginal increases in capital gains taxes, and as advisers such as economic policy czar Gene Sperling launched yet another decorative bid to step up investment in the manufacturing economy, data from the IRS showed that the Obama years have achieved almost nothing to remedy the yawning inequalities in the economy. The top 1 percent of income earners have taken in fully 93 percent of economic gains since the Great Recession, the numbers showed. That share outpaces Bush-era figures by a mile; as the economy emerged from the 2001–02 recession, the top 1 percent claimed a lousy 65 percent of the gains that followed. It's never been a better time to be rich in America.

As the administration's defenders will tell you, there are structural reasons that the post-2008 feints toward recovery have proven so strikingly top-heavy. In the Bush-era recession much of the damage was confined to the investor class, while in 2008 the housing economy was devastated, and along with it, a great deal of the demand that stoked growth in the labor market. A slower recovery in the real economy meant that returns were greater for the 1 percent.

But such explanations are something close to question-begging. If the Obama administra-

From *The Baffler*, no. 20

tion had wanted to spread recovery measures broadly among the earning public, it could have crafted policies accordingly—in much the same fashion that Franklin Roosevelt responded to the last major economic meltdown by using Keynesian stimulus programs, by scrapping the gold standard, and by curbing Wall Street. The chair of Obama's own Council of Economic Advisers through 2010, Christina Romer, repeatedly sought to place job growth at the center of the administration's economic agenda, but Obama ensured that financial policy remained right where it's been over the past generation or so of anemic economic gains for working Americans—in the hands of Wall Street–approved caretakers of the paper economy such as Timothy Geithner, Ben Bernanke, and Lawrence Summers. In an already upward-skewing pattern of income distribution, in a heavily worker-averse economy, this administration is reaping what it has sown.

Except, you know, for the reaping part. This dry and dismal litany of economic fact has come nowhere close to dislodging the rote messaging of the campaign season, whereby the market-appeasing incumbent is feverishly ginning up the impression that he's a populist, deep down, since he has had the good political fortune to draw from the GOP deck a complacent former private equity kingpin as his major-party opponent. Hence his cost-free embrace of the Buffett Rule—a cosmetic simulacrum of serious tax reform (tellingly named for a billionaire) with zero chance of passing Congress.

Amid the campaign-friendly, ritual invocation of the Buffett Rule, scarcely anyone noted the president's craven, and far more consequential, signing of the House Republicans' JOBS Act. Since so few GOP lawmakers have firsthand acquaintance with actual jobs, they have mistaken the word for an acronym, as in "Jumpstart Our Business Startups." The JOBS Act suspends independent accounting requirements and due-diligence reporting protocols for businesses floating new stock offerings—which means, in the mobbed-up climate of today's Wall Street, that it's essentially a license to commit fraud. And like the Clinton administration's spectacularly dumb endorsement of the GOP Congress's repeal of New Deal regulations

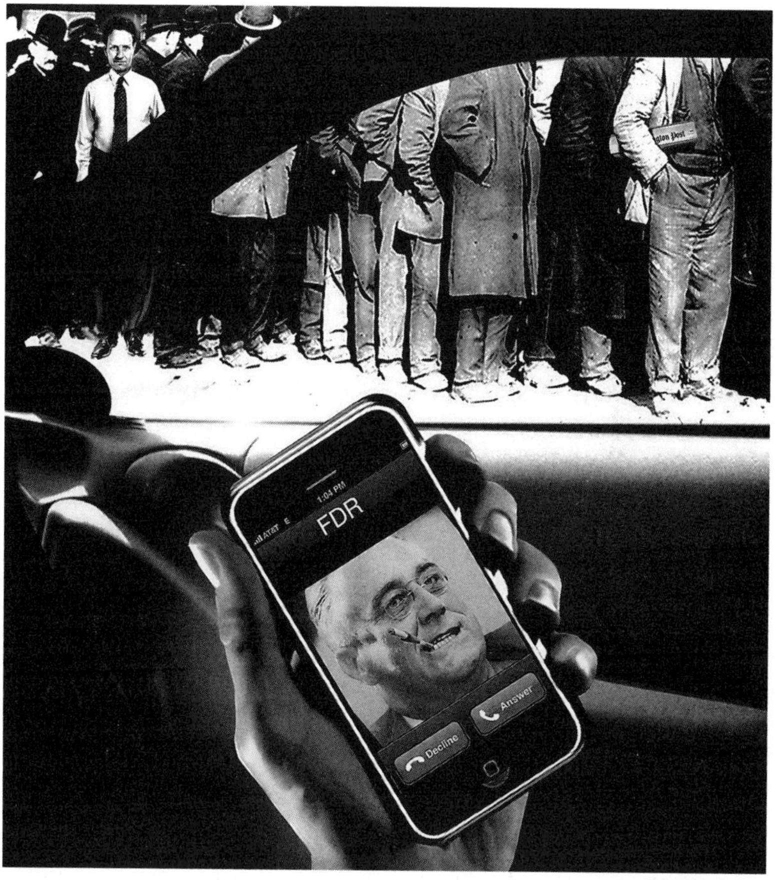

MICHAEL DUFFY

enacted in the 1933 Glass-Steagall law, the JOBS Act effectively wipes out the recent lessons of financial history, rolling back the enhanced accounting standards signed into law after the catastrophic market failures known as Enron and WorldCom.

Such staggeringly cynical displays are the sort of campaign messaging that matters in the orderly conduct of elections under a plutocracy. The JOBS Act serves as an unmistakable reminder to skittish Wall Street donors that all the loose populist talk is just so much telegenic blather for the impressionable 99 percenters, just as the donor class suspected. When it comes to policy, indeed, Obama's message is: don't pay any attention to Warren Buffett's public shows of tax contrition; rather, heed the way that the Berkshire Hathaway baron amassed his fortune—and go and do likewise.

Don't doubt, either, that there's a deeper distemper lurking behind the White House's content-challenged posturing on national economic policy. The steadfast refusal of the administration to advance anything like a serious industrial policy or an agenda to spur (small-*j*) jobs growth reflects the same rear-window outlook that has thwarted administrations back to the Carter years. It reflects, in other words, the backwards vision of American business enterprise that prevails in Washington, a city that has no industrial base to speak of but that collects rentier-style wealth under the rule of a permanent lobbying class. Washington is the only major housing market in America to prosper in the wake of the '08 calamity. This was supposedly so because the center of our national government is "recession proof"; the thinking goes that economic crises spark increased growth in the federal bureaucracy. But the real dosh has been flowing to the exurbs of Metro D.C., where the lords of high-end contract commerce reign, and where your standard GS-4 analyst can't swing a mortgage loan. Loudon County, the horsey Virginia suburban demesne that's home to many a power lobbyist, corporate-cum-political consultant, and defense contractor, is the nation's richest county; nearby Fairfax County is the second richest; and Howard County, Maryland, just across the Potomac, is third.

The chronic distortion of actual productive activity on display in the exurbs has bred an official D.C. discourse almost completely at odds with economic reality. This isn't the case only among the lobbyist-led chorus of lawmakers on Capitol Hill; a singularly surreal vision of economic relations is also, tellingly, the patois of the D.C. media—the reporters, editors, and all-around wise men who are wont to gaze longingly at the real estate listings in Loudon as they lay out in brave, self-regardingly pragmatic detail just what's best for the long-suffering American worker or the out-of-luck single mother.

Consider a remarkable run of coverage assembled in 2012 by the *Washington Post*—the leading organ of meritocratic self-congratulation in a city filled with smug overachievers. As 2011's Occupy protests against economic privilege abated with the onset of colder weather, the *Post*'s arbiters of content programmed a series of essays to get to the bottom of the suddenly hot topics of inequality and public perceptions of the social value of wealth.

The results were textbook studies in near-hysterical journalistic repression. Over at the reliably right-wing Sunday Outlook section, the late social scientist James Q. Wilson—who had been tirelessly denying the larger impact of class inequality in tracts such as *The Marriage Problem* and *The Moral Sense*, together with his now-legendary airing of the since-discredited "broken windows" theory of community policing in the pages of *The Atlantic Monthly*—took a look at the uproar over inequality in these United States and serenely pronounced it a nonproblem.

Wilson's waspish dispatch—titled, of course, "Angry About Inequality? Don't Blame the Rich"—argued that it is a grave and reckless category error to assume rich Americans represent "a monolithic, unchanging class." No, sir! Why, just factor in social mobility, for starters! A Federal Reserve study found that "less than half of people in the top 1 percent in 1996 were still there in 2005." Never mind that the individual composition of a plutocratic class has never been the point of the agitation against it; rather, what's at issue is *the scope of its influence*. Never mind, as well, that there's a great deal of difference between a 1 percenter sliding down to the 1.5 percent cohort and heading all the way down to the bottom quintile. For Wilson, it's enough to adduce the idea of mobility at the top, and presto: Algerism! "A business school student," according to Wilson, "may have little money and high debts, but nine years later he or she could be earning a big Wall Street salary and bonus." Admittedly, "there are people such as Warren Buffett and Bill Gates who are ensconced in the top tier, but far more common"—more common than two deliberately isolated examples, that is—"are people who are rich for short periods."

Phew! This is a surefire argument stopper—so long as you ignore the voluminous evidence showing that upward mobility in these United States lags behind the rates logged in such high-tax welfare states as Canada, Britain, and (shudder) Denmark.

Professor Wilson delivered some admiring asides on the sturdy meritocratic connection between higher learning and the spread of big-money jobs and argued, nonsensically, that leveling inequality could well entail banishing women from the workforce. But soon enough, he zeroed in on his real quarry: the shiftless poor. You see, the less fortunate among us have little to complain of, since they're afforded all manner of cheap consumer goods. "The country has become more prosperous, as measured not by income but by consumption," Wilson reasoned. "Income as measured by the federal government is not a reliable indicator of well-being, but consumption is"—and consumption is ever on the rise. "Though poverty is a problem," Wilson allowed in one of his more unguarded moments, "it has become less of one." (This, by the way, was an affront: the poverty rate had increased from 14.3 to 15.1 percent between 2009 and 2010, while the median U.S. income had dropped 2.3 percent over the same period.)

But that is no reason not to target the behavior of the poor as the real culprit behind America's economic woes. To redress the social ills besetting the poor, Wilson wrote, was a simple matter of "finding and implementing ways to encourage parental marriage, teach the poor marketable skills and induce them to join the legitimate workforce." This last missionary plea is especially ripe, as though Americans enduring the worst recession and contraction of the labor market in living memory were but perversely playing hard to get with a corps of would-be employers, and would be fully disciplined productive members of society if only there were some—any—way to "induce" them to do so.

Of course, in the stunted moral universe of Wilson and his cohort of policy intellectuals, the chief project is never anything so unwieldy and fraught as the achievement of economic equity; rather, the only surefire remedy for poverty—and the only path forward that doesn't involve the wholesale decimation of public resources and the certain demoralization of liberal social engineering—is the moral rehabilitation of the poor, even though no amount of moral improvement will ever revive the perverse natures of the "underclass" to the satisfaction of their scolding social betters in the right-wing policy world.

What's remarkable about Wilson's non-explanation of why wealth inequality is a virtue isn't so much its raw ideological self-delusion—that's the stock-in-trade of the conservative policy world. No, what's striking about these class-baiting excursuses in culture-preaching is that they are now the lingua franca of Washington's own hothouse class of political achievers, regardless of their notional party affiliations or ideological leanings. That's why, a week or so prior to the Wilson manifesto urging readers to focus their anxieties about wealth inequality on the misbehaving poor, the editors of the paper's daily op-ed section ran a piece by Democratic political consultant Bill Knapp advancing the identical argument. The Knapp outing bore the chipper sobriquet, "Middle Class Is Moving Forward, Not Backward"—and sure enough, Knapp, like Wilson, marveled at the income gains kicked up by the new knowledge economy and the explosion of the female workforce. Women have migrated into the labor economy at a 350 percent spike since 1960—evidence, in Knapp's curious formulation, that the United States is "creating more jobs than people."

Yes, there's poverty, Knapp concedes. But like Wilson, he takes brave contrarian aim at the social mores of the poor over and against any assessment of life chances parceled out by the labor or investment markets. "Politically incorrect as it sounds," Knapp insists, "poverty is driven by a lack of education and by single-parent households."

As for all the voguish talk of the 1 percent and the 99 percent also-rans, Knapp darkly warns that "an entire intellectual and political infrastructure is used to exaggerate and distort income disparity"—a flatly absurd and undocumented claim, but enough to reinforce the impression that this hack campaign consultant is the heroic Randian victim of a massive culture conspiracy, another decadent rhetorical tic of the policy right that has made its way across the partisan aisle. (Then again, one of Knapp's signature campaign clients is New York's billionaire GOP mogul-cum-mayor Michael Bloomberg, so, like all dispassionate apparatchiks in the D.C. orbit, he can lay claim to the precious credential of Third-Way bipartisanship.)

And like comrade Wilson, who argued that cheap consumer durables take the real sting out of poverty, Knapp seeks to seal the case for the eternally upward-tending U.S. middle class by taking sober inventory of all the cool stuff its members can now buy. After all, "83 percent of American adults owned a cellphone last May, up from 66 percent in January 2005." An allied spike in teen cell ownership over the same period augured especially well, our social prophet reports: "When more teenagers own luxury electronics, it means there are more families with disposable income.... The struggling middle class is getting their teenager cellphones, video-game systems and computers." Let them eat Nokia!

The structural identity of the Knapp and Wilson dispatches is striking, but the real payoff for D.C. policy thinkers here is the air of glib fatalism both writers share. You *could*, I suppose, try to do something about inequality, but such gruesome state interventions are bound to backfire, as the chaos in Greece now makes clear; Wilson fatuously noted that, yes, "Greece seems to be reducing income inequality—but with little to buy, riots in the streets, and economic opportunity largely limited to those partaking in corruption, the nation is hardly a model for anyone's economy." (Fatalists of the Wilson stripe of course can't be expected to note that however corrupt Greek officialdom may be, the policies of the neoliberal eurozone economy escalated the country's economic plight to crisis proportions: when market failures happen, state intervention *has* to be the cause.) Or you could, in theory, redistribute income to shift jobs and material benefits to the 12.7 million and counting Americans who are out of work, and the millions of homeowners facing foreclosure. But such measures might well upset the smoothest system of mass cellphone delivery in the history of human civilization—and besides, until less privileged Americans learn to breed and educate themselves properly, there's just no point.

Meanwhile, over at the other end of the economic spectrum, the *Post*'s editors sensed a different sort of political crisis brewing. The GOP primaries had drawn attention to Mitt Romney's fortune—the accrual of which stood pretty much as the former Massachusetts governor's sole remaining calling card for Republican voters. But Newt Gingrich derided the former Bain Capital pasha as an idle luftmensch, thriving on "Swiss bank accounts and Cayman Island accounts and automatic $20 million a year income with no work." So the *Post* dispatched political writer Marc Fisher to sort out the troubling finding that "Wealth Can Be a Political Burden" for rich candidates seeking to take their ordained place in the Oval Office.

Fisher offered a catalog of other candidates who'd been ensnared of late by the perception that economic privilege had left them out of touch with the sensibilities of the striving middle class—such as the 2004 Bush-Cheney ad showing John Kerry in full windsurfing regalia, and the televised image of Bush père's moment of awed befuddlement before a high-tech supermarket price scanner. And after revisiting the ample store of similar moments from Romney's primary campaign—from the $10,000 debate-stage wager with Rick Perry to the candidate's casual characterization of $370,000 in income from speaking fees as "not very much"—Fisher heroically unearthed a detail from Romney confreres and campaign hands to demonstrate that the candidate's nine-figure fortune had not insulated him from the struggles of real Americans after all. "Just last week," Fisher noted, "Romney and his wife, Ann, sent an aide to pick up their breakfast at McDonald's rather than shell out for an expensive hotel meal"—a flourish showing that the big-money candidate retains "a keen sense of the value of a dollar." It seemed not to occur to Fisher that most McDonald's patrons are unable to dispatch an aide to fetch their Happy Meals; but who knows, perhaps that's the next iteration of luxe entitlement awaiting the middle class once the novelty of the cellphone wears off.

Moving beyond these recondite readings from the Romney common-touch barometer, Fisher supplied a studiously noncommittal account of the careers of America's moneyed political leaders, with one academic source noting wanly that Romney's wealth is an "ambiguous" moral quantity in our public life, and another announcing blandly that "what matters most is the context of wealth." But Fisher gave the last word to the overleveraged billionaire and preposterous person Donald Trump, who reassured a Fox News interviewer who seemed skittish about this new populist clamoring against the natural political order that "ultimately, people want to be rich. And that's part of the American way."

Still, the *Post*'s excursions into the ambiguities of wealth had not yet exhausted the fatuousness of its position. What if some alert reader, not totally convinced by Fisher's Trump-style ventriloquism, still thought there might be something revolting about the methods of capital accumulation that our model citizens employ on the way to getting rich? And so editorial writer Charles Lane scurried to examine the forensics of wealth acquisition and determined, improbably, that the underlying issue is rentiership. As Lane laid out the question, questionable gains are those that come from rent—i.e., "any kind of income that people get by controlling existing resources—or exercising officially conferred privileges—as opposed to creating new wealth through labor or investment." See, any such rentier class would be out of step with the officially approved method of accumulation via innovation. The passive enterprise of rent-seeking rubs Americans the wrong way. Many of the 1 percent are indeed members of the privileged rentier class, Lane went on—lavishly credentialed high earners such as lawyers and (at the more productive end of the scale) doctors. Naturally, the beneficiaries of rent-seeking collectively implore the machinery of government to preserve their privilege: "Much political activity consists of trying to create, or keep, opportunities to collect economic rent. That's what lobbyists for various licenses, tariffs, tax breaks and subsidies—from the sugar industry to Solyndra—have in common."

In advancing these observations, Lane backed himself into something close to a heresy, certainly in the American sphere of respectable opinion, and definitely within the polite consensus governing economic coverage at the *Washington Post*. There are, in fact, some sorts of wealth that are unearned, and the arrangements netting them are inherently unfair. This simple insight, available to any ordinary person, shatters the simple equation of wealth and virtue that ensures the privilege of the 1 percent. So just imagine the furor if Lane had gone on to mention that the model of rentiership applies to people just like him, to the other wise men massaging copy into acceptable channels at the *Post*, and, indeed, to the rest of the name-brand Washington journalists who enjoy lucrative pay-to-play arrangements with the private sector, who collect five-figure speaking fees from trade groups, investment houses, and issue-advocacy shops, "controlling existing resources" and "exercising officially conferred privileges" while they manufacture and disseminate what passes for legitimate economic opinion in this time of national calamity.

Like most major newspapers, the *Washington Post* has spent the past decade saddled with a punishingly obsolete business model—in the first quarter of 2012, profits at the Washington Post Company fell by 7 percent from the first quarter of the previous year, thanks in part to a buyback stock campaign. (Anemic as this showing was, it was an improvement over the previous quarter's losses of 22 percent.) The Kaplan network of educational testing now accounts for 60 percent of revenues for the Washington Post Company. And as Bloomberg News notes, Kaplan "has come under government scrutiny along with the rest of the for-profit education industry." It seems that managers at the *Post* depend on a gruesome and extortionate form of rent-seeking activity for their livelihoods.

Nor is this awkward state of affairs without consequence for the newspaper's reputation. For-profit education institutions spent $11.9 million on lobbying in 2011, and for their money won the rollback of a proposed rule change at the Department of Education that would have greatly diminished the industry's $30 billion profit model.

Post Company CEO Donald Graham personally intervened with House minority leader Nancy Pelosi; the Kaplan group's own lobbying assault was captained by former White House communications director Anita Dunn. And to ensure maximum legislative compliance, a lead investor at the for-profit network collared Iowa senator Tom Harkin in a Capitol corridor during the height of the industry's blitz and told the lawmaker—who'd chaired several key congressional investigations into the industry—that he was determined to "make life rough" for him if the senator didn't dial down his attacks on the industry. "I took it as a threat," Harkin told the *New York Times*. "It was one of the most blatant comments ever made to me in my years in the Senate."

If these tactics sound, well, Nixonian, then you haven't heard the least of it. The *Post*-Kaplan connection is just one among countless symptoms of institutional corruption in the power centers of D.C. media companies, which routinely sponsor forums and other private get-togethers granting lobbyists and industry advocates access to reporters. *Post* publisher Katharine Weymouth notoriously was forced to cancel one pay-to-play venture, hosted salon-style at her own home at the height of the 2009 health care debate. Promotional come-ons for the gathering promised cozy confabs matching up the *Post*'s "health-care reporting and editorial staff members" with "your organization's CEO." The event was billed as nothing less than an "underwriting opportunity" for participants—i.e., a chance to ensure that *Post* reporters and editors shill for the lobbyist's policy agenda by placing said employees in the home of the woman who signs their paychecks. Participating companies would have shelled out $25,000 ($250,000 for the full Weymouth dinner series), and naturally would have expected more than an amusing pinot noir for the outlay.

None of this is meant to suggest that *Post* employees receive daily marching orders from the for-profit commissariat atop the company's publishing masthead. (Indeed, let the record show that I was a happy, and for the most part, a happily un-fucked-with, editorial hand at the *Post* from 2000 to 2004.) However, it is outlandish to pretend that a business model so deeply reliant on built-in conflicts, and so overt in its courtship of corporate interests, doesn't translate into a mindset of deference to wealth and power. Just think of how the *Post* of old would have reported on a government agency that hosted private gatherings with six-figure entry fees for the industry leaders it oversaw. Think of how Bob Woodward and Carl Bernstein, who broke open the Watergate story by heeding the simple dictum to "follow the money," might have reacted back in the day upon receiving word that the Republican National Committee had expended heroic amounts of cash to influence how congressional leaders came down on a key regulatory decision—and then presumed not only to assume a guise of utter impartiality but also to advise the public on the optimally prudent and mature positions to take on questions of regulation, wealth, and lobbying influence in the first place.

Then again, that's probably why the opinion-makers holed up in today's *Washington Post* ensure that it continues to be the primary source of sound advice on the socially ruinous moral trespasses of the poor: any honest reporter's investigation of the stubborn infrastructures distorting the debate over wealth inequality would lead to the *Post*'s own boardroom.

POSTSCRIPT

The foregoing dispatch was published before the Graham family announced in the summer of 2013 they would unload their flagship property to Amazon.com founder and CEO Jeff Bezos for a cool $250 million. But the web mogul's acquisition of this prestigious media brand seems unlikely to alter anything fundamental in the *Post*'s myopic handling of the premier social issue of our day. Indeed, if anything, the *Post* is likely to enter a golden age of rentiership under Bezos's watch.

Jeff Bezos, after all, has made his overcapitalized billions via a rent-seeking strategy of the first magnitude. He incorporated his retail empire in Washington state so as to shun steeper tax liabilities in traditional centers of e-commerce in California and New York. And after the 2008 meltdown, as state governments prepared at long last to entertain the notion of rolling back their generous tax giveaways to online merchandisers, Bezos embarked on a remarkable lobbying blitz through various state legislatures to ensure that the states hosting his state-of-the-art distribution and fulfillment operations would remain low-tax playgrounds for as long as possible. For cash-strapped states seeking to boost revenues with new sales taxes for online businesses, Bezos and Amazon's armada of lobbyists employed a classic strong-arm strategy: defer your tax plan just a little longer for Amazon, and we'll build new distribution and fulfillment centers in your state. The deals sailed through with deferential ease in states run by GOP legislative majorities, such as Texas, South Carolina, Tennessee, and Pennsylvania; the Democratic-run California assembly bargained the retail colossus down to one last Christmas season tax free before introducing new state sales levies. (So much, it seems, for the liberal War on Christmas.)

From diaper merchandisers to knife makers to shoe retailers, Bezos has campaigned to disable market competitors at the knees before enveloping them in takeover bids. As Amazon was negotiating with independent book publishers to acquire back-catalog rights before its ballyhooed launch of the Kindle e-reader, company executives were calling the initiative the Gazelle Project; Bezos himself had urged his management team to target small publishers—who would face likely market extinction without Amazon's listing for their back-catalog publications—in much the same way that rampaging cheetahs hunt down and devour a gazelle who's wandered away from the pack.

Captaining the *Post* shouldn't require Bezos's underlings to be quite so red in tooth and claw; even in its present enfeebled form, the paper commands around 60 percent market penetration in the D.C. metro region. Nevertheless, it seems a safe bet to surmise that a company founded on such rabid market-cornering practices is not likely to revert overnight to a more skeptical (i.e., journalistic) narrative template on the market's many routine miscarriages of social justice and maulings of economic equity. In short, the *Washington Post* as we've come to know it—the tireless celebrant of shallow consumer abundance, the monomaniacal crusader for the evisceration of social insurance and income support, the prim purveyor of the hallowed D.C. myth of permanent rule by a meritocratic elite—should flourish under Jeff Bezos's ever-watchful, tax-averse eye.

Omniscient Gentlemen of *The Atlantic*

MAUREEN TKACIK

Not long before *The Atlantic*'s parent company announced its swing into a profit-making business model despite operating in the most moribund corner of a publishing industry, I sat in a glass-paneled press room next to a small auditorium on the second floor of the Washington Newseum and took in the incipient profitability. All the unctuous little scabs who believe the future of words lies in rearranging them online would soon (inter alia) barge into the office of *Harper's* publisher Rick MacArthur to trumpet their e-vindication. But they evidently forgot to wonder how much of *The Atlantic*'s profitability owes to operating conferences, panels, and events like the 2010 Ideas Forum. These in-gatherings count as journalism only in the vague sense that they invite journalists to crowd into plushly appointed suites. At the Ideas Forum, *The Atlantic*'s own editorial staff was relegated to providing rapid-fire stenography services, to ensure the event was branded and promoted in real time on the website.

The din of younger colleagues tapping keyboards is never soothing, but sitting in the press room of the Ideas Forum felt like a human rights violation. What could anyone write about something so tyrannically dull—other than an angry elegy for the massacre of meaning? The average C-SPAN 3 segment is a crowd-pleasing cliffhanger by comparison. Mind flickering between rage and somnolence, I tried my best to keep awake by

From *The Baffler*, no. 19

writing notes. Here are some highlights, with names redacted to preserve the integrity of the tedium.

> [*New York Times* financial correspondent] rankles [Treasury secretary] with questions such as "What do you think is the most important thing the team has gotten *right*?"—there were two things, his interviewee insists—and occasional use of unauthorized verbiage like "re-regulate" to denote efforts to reverse the epochal dismantling of financial regulatory apparatus largely undertaken by the technocratic clique to which [Treasury secretary] owes his entire career.
>
> [Obama cabinet official], [Obama policy adviser], [billionaire CEO], [billionaire private equity tycoon], and [billionaire mayor] sing praises of [photogenic local schools chief whose extensive sackings of teachers and principals had been sufficiently unpopular with voters to have cost her boss the recent D.C. mayoral primary]. One refers to [recently released charter school propaganda-mentary] as her "Rosa Parks moment."
>
> [Billionaire CEO] expresses dismay that "laws are written by lobbyists."
>
> [Billionaire mayor] expresses indignation that some 40 percent of Americans do not pay income tax.
>
> [Prominent Democratic lobbyist and his lobbyist wife] emphatically deny the notion that the "deck is stacked" against [public interest] under current system on the basis that "everyone has a lobbyist... nurses have lobbyists, unions have lobbyists, everybody has a lobbyist. Everyone in this audience has an iPhone or a PDA because lobbyists created a competitive system [that] enabled this whole industry to grow; lobbying can be very good for consumers."
>
> [Prominent Republican lobbyist] waxes elegiac for bygone bipartisanship with an anecdote about his use of "surrogates" to obtain an implicit agreement from [former Democratic House speaker] to enforce a two-day limit on Congressional expressions of outrage over the decision of [former lame-duck Republican president] to pardon six

> individuals criminally charged in [high-profile byzantine secret arms trafficking/campaign finance/cover-up conspiracy] on behalf of his [former defense secretary and highest-ranking official to be criminally charged] client. An assurance in which Congressional Democrats guaranteed "two-day story" status to the controversy over a unilateral decision that effectively trashed a six-year investigation into [complicated conspiracy] to contravene Congress, could probably not, [Republican lobbyist] theorized, be a realistic deliverable for a client contending with the present-day "toxic environment" on Capitol Hill.
>
> [Centrist Republican senator] repeats the income tax thing.

Later it occurred to me that *The Atlantic* events are convened to attract and satisfy (by leaving slightly dissatisfied) a personality type I think of as the "omniscient gentleman," after a passage in Fyodor Dostoyevsky's *The Idiot*, which pits a modern-day Christ figure referenced in the title, Prince Myshkin, against a backdrop of "omniscient" name-dropping philistines whose interior lives and true intentions are a mystery to him. Encountering his first Mr. Omniscient on a train, he marvels:

> all the restless curiosity and faculties of [his] mind are irresistibly bent in one direction ...: in what department so-and-so serves, who are his friends, what his income is, where he was governor, who his wife is and what dowry she brought him, who are his first cousins and who are his second cousins ... The people of whose lives they know every detail would be at a loss to imagine their motives. Yet many of them get positive consolation out of this knowledge, which amounts to a complete science, and derive from it ... their loftiest comfort and their ultimate goal, and have indeed made their career only by means of it.

Omniscient gentlemen have for most of the last century held exalted status on Madison Avenue, where their facility with community quotidiana is recognized as the stuff of highly effective persuaders, influencers, tastemakers, connectors, and miscellaneous other prophets of consumer trends. *The Atlantic*'s special subspecies of omniscient gentlemen is the "thought leader."

This is not to say all people identified as tastemakers or thought leaders share the propensities of practitioners of the omniscient sciences, but in any sphere of influence, the more omniscient types are the ones more naturally inclined to keep up the thought leader lists, and assign themselves a place at the top of them. I know of one wretched hack who lists "Thought Leader" as his occupation on his Twitter profile; he recently scored a fellowship with the American Enterprise Institute.

Omniscience is the operating principle by which everyone understands everyone else in Washington, D.C. It is *how you relate*—the sort of Olympian free-associating that permits *The Atlantic*'s in-house thought leaders to cast America as Snooki, and "Jersey Shore" and "pessimism" as our ultimate obstacle to combating global warming.

The one thought-provoking moment I experienced following the thought leader summit occurred during the penultimate—and only officially controversial—panel of the Ideas Conference, in which Ahmed Chalabi, the former Iraqi exile/Jordanian bank fraud fugitive who planted many of the perambulatory news stories justifying the Iraq War, was interviewed by Sally Quinn, the recently deposed social columnist for the *Washington Post*. Quinn's history with Chalabi had been longer than most on Capitol Hill; her father had been a general in the U.S. Army and had helped create its espionage ring, the Office of Strategic Services.

Now both Quinn and Chalabi were—temporarily at least—social pariahs: she over a *Washington Post* column in which she purported to debunk a purportedly widespread belief that, with malicious forethought, she had scheduled her son's wedding on the same day as the wedding of her husband's granddaughter; Chalabi over his role in marshalling official misinformation that presaged the Iraq War and/or his possible employment as some sort of double agent for Iran.

Quinn wore a light beige pantsuit with a pink blouse that conjured the seventies. Back then she hosted an epic "pajama" party—Quinn's pajamas were lace and single-shouldered—for the newly elected con-

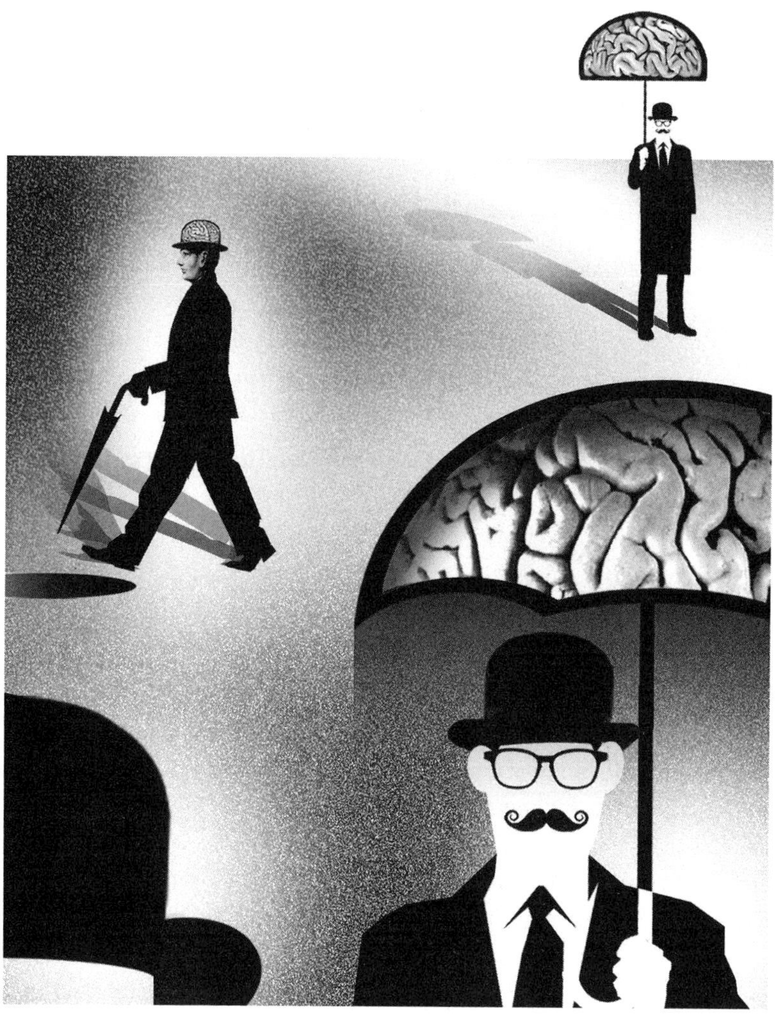

MICHAEL DUFFY

gressman scion of the Quinns' closest family friends, Barry Goldwater Jr., and thereby seduced (then *Washington Post* executive editor) Ben Bradlee into hiring/marrying her and leaving his second wife. In the moderate-pensive tone of voice with which you ask a close friend if there is something you are going to need to lie about on his behalf, Quinn asked Chalabi soberly about the nature of his relationship with

Mahmoud Ahmadinejad, expressing her disapproval of the Iranian president's subscription to 9/11 truther conspiracy theories. Chalabi laughed the whole thing off, noting "such views are commonly held in the region." This may have been the summit's first acknowledgement of a region outside the Newseum walls. But what stuck with me was Quinn's opening question/soliloquy:

> [You've] been pronounced dead politically and literally dead–physically–so many times that you can't count them. So how do you explain your survival? How are you still here? You've had assassination attempts, you've had death threats, you've been in, you've been out, you've been up, you've been down, you've been rejected by your political system, you've been rejected by the American political system. And still you're a member of the Parliament, you're now part of the political power structure in Iraq. What accounts for that?

Chalabi sat, placid and smiling and radiating a remarkable balance of the chakras. I am almost ashamed to say that in the moment I wondered idly about his astrological sign. Revisiting the moment a year later when he made headlines for defending the protesting Shias in Bahrain, I wondered whether anything distinguished him from the countless multiple-passport-carrying urbane mobsters who pass through the Capitol every few months for the ritual taxpayer shakedown.

Then suddenly it was over, and *The Atlantic*'s own godfather, David G. Bradley, was marching toward David Weigel, a young and prolific journalist specializing in Republican politics who had recently made a name for himself getting fired and rehired by the same media company within several weeks. For Bradley, this shift in nameplates apparently constituted a Chalabi-caliber show of resilience:

"DAVID!!!!! So good to see you!"

"Hello, David."

"David, you really came back swinging, didn't you!?!!! You were out for all of, what, a week??? But now you're back!!!"

"Well, I mean, it was actually a few weeks, and it really screwed up my health insurance..."

"David, I just want you to know I've been scheming ways to deploy you here for quite some time now! Now, of course I realize you may be enjoying your present ... deployment!"

"Well I mean, heh, I did just start ..."

"But David, let me tell you this. David, I know you think your mastery is politics. But I think ... I think your mastery ..."

Dramatic pause.

"... may be ... *mastery*."

"Oh uh, thanks ..."

"Do you know what I mean, David?" Bradley finished, gliding out the door. "It's the same thing with David Brooks. He thought his mastery was politics, but his mastery was actually, whatever he put his mind to. Think about it, David!"

And then he was gone.

David Bradley, *The Atlantic*'s owner, is inveterately omniscient and by all accounts almost pathologically a gentleman, which is odd when you remember—and you are bound to forget that when he is kissing the foot of some pimply blogger—that he has already monetized his unique skill set to the tune of nearly half a billion dollars. Bradley, however, seems to relish the courtship of mastery. As part of what he claims is a research project, he mails surveys to editors soliciting intel on local talent supplies, requesting that the editors rank on a scale of one to ten, or distinguish between "exceptional talent" and mere "talent," lists of names he has culled in prior efforts. He also scouts for career changers: one sad intern spent a summer in the mid-aughts compiling a spreadsheet indicating the location and employment status for every president and vice president of every extracurricular club to have graduated from any of the eight Ivy League schools in the previous decade. Bradley "spent more than 200 hours discussing his ideas with 80 journalists around the country," according to the *New York Times*, before he filled the magazine's editor in chief position with James Bennet, then the *Times'* Jerusalem bureau chief.

For all the ostensible objectivity and scientific rigor of the magazine's questing spirit, *The Atlantic*'s definition of talent seems to correlate to: a current fellowship at the New America Foundation or any of the other indistinguishably centrist think tanks, though preferably one with a brand (i.e., "Daniel Indiviglio is the 2011 Robert Novak Fellow at the Philips Foundation"); an ability to channel one's talent into the mastery of meritless and preposterous ("counterintuitive") arguments, deliberately obtuse rebuttals, and miscellaneous pseudointellectual equivocation/noise on topical issues; and proven senior-level mastery of aforementioned mastery as demonstrated either by radical shamelessness or the pious and deeply felt earnestness of a motivational speaker.

The New America Foundation was founded in 1999 by Michael Lind, Sherle Schwenninger, and Ted Halstead, who explained at the time: "My starting premise was that the old ideologies don't make sense anymore." Because, Lind elaborated: "You look at people like Daniel Bell and Irving Kristol ... you could make a living writing for magazines, really an upper-middle-class living, writing for purely intellectual magazines in the forties and fifties."

This was a stretch. Both Bell and Kristol were liberally subsidized by the CIA, which financed the Congress for Cultural Freedom, whose flagship "intellectual magazine," *Encounter*, Kristol edited in London and whose fancy international seminars were organized by Bell, who also worked a day job at *Fortune* and who brokered a deal with Henry Luce to promote in Time Inc. magazines (and thereby further subsidize) the intellectual output of CCF-affiliated intellects. The institutional network that supported those guys and their friends was not much different from the one that now connects up *The Atlantic*, the New America Foundation, and the Aspen Institute, keeping dozens of public pseudointellectual hacks in six-figure salaries. In lieu of the CIA, the funding for such ideas-synergy comes from corporations. Certainly, these think tanks are not *ideologically* different from those that hosted the cultural Cold Warriors of the fifties.

No one knows this better than Bradley, a man whose personal history comports so perfectly with the rigors of Cold War cultural combat that he may seem like a Manchurian magazine magnate, with his father, Gene Bradley—who enthusiastically endorsed, and possibly helped to invent, Korean War theories of mind control—resembling Angela Lansbury's character.

Gene Bradley's career as a professional Cold Warrior began before Winston Churchill's Iron Curtain speech, in a concentration camp in Linz, Austria. There, as an army press officer for General Mark Clark after VE day, he inspected the mass graves of emaciated bodies and "shoved it deep down into my mind," where, he later wrote, "it remained until I saw the movie *Schindler's List*." A new enemy kept him preoccupied, mostly at General Electric, where he served in a string of posts in what was the premier public relations struggle against the twin enemies of "Russia abroad, labor at home," as GE's CEO Charlie Wilson famously explained the company's messaging mission to Harry S. Truman in 1946.

After a stint at the famed ad agency BBDO and as a Pentagon flack, Bradley began at GE in 1953, just a year before his department recruited its most famous hire, Ronald Reagan, who toured the company's aerospace plants as a motivational speaker and eventually as an evangelist for the free-market system. Reagan's turn away from the ardently pro–New Deal politics he'd espoused as leader of the Screen Actors Guild was largely masterminded by GE's labor relations chief, Lemuel Boulware, a high minister of the open shop. Boulware made it his business to be best known behind the scenes—though he once bemoaned Truman's abortive veto of the anti-union Taft-Hartley law as another demonstration of the "economic illiteracy" that caused Americans to embrace socialism at home "while spending $20 billion in business tax money to battle communism abroad."

Boulware was a career marketing guru, and he saw unions as fundamentally a problem of "thought leaders." If a figure like Reagan could succeed in overthrowing labor leaders as designated opinion-makers, he reasoned, why, no one would bother joining a union in the first place. But thought-leading government, which was to be Gene Bradley's job, was a bit trickier, as it required a thought leader to mix in much more sophisticated circles and to drop all the boilerplate about the ills of big government.

In this mission Bradley excelled, founding *General Electric Forum*, a "defense intellectual" quarterly mouthpiece for decorated hawks to oppose the opposition to the military industrial complex; spending a year on loan to the Peace Corps under Sargent Shriver; and keeping enough distance from hard-core Boulwarism to earn an obligatory accusation of communist sympathies from the John Birch Society, according to the memoir he self-published in 2003, *The Story of One Man's Journey in Faith*.

The memoir is discombobulating reading, in part because this lifelong PR man is not the most reliable narrator, possibly also because his memory, in storing and accessing its inventory so selectively, has disabled some of the required capabilities. But if you focus on the omniscient sciences, some remarkable details shake loose. He mentions (in the context of a strange Vietnam War propaganda project) that one of his longtime closest friends was Frank Barnett, a Kremlinologist known mainly for heading a covert project to indoctrinate American soldiers using (inter alia) Birch literature in a bizarre project that had been deemed vital for preserving the national interest on the basis of a PR disaster that had roiled the Pentagon during Gene's tenure there in 1953: the incomprehensible defection of twenty-one American prisoners of war to Red China. He mentions the episode at the end of *Journey in Faith*, albeit in terms that bear little resemblance to reality. He writes:

> There is more truth than fiction in the substance of [*The Manchurian Candidate*]. This was revealed to me when I was an Air Force officer reviewing the studies that examined why so many American soldiers submitted to brainwashing by the communists during the Korean War and surrendered passively without a shot being fired. The research study that I read documented why the communists could succeed in brainwashing American GIs: because these American soldiers had never been taught the fundamentals of America. They had not been taught the facts of American history. They did

> not know our Constitution, our Bill of Rights, or American history, so when the crunch came, when pushed to the wall by ruthless interrogators, they had no core values to which they could hold. In truth they did not know why they were fighting, or even if America was worth fighting for.

In one of the many surreal chapters of *Journey in Faith*, Gene later attempted to influence—thought-lead?—what he saw as the perilously bereft civic "education" of the student left. The year was 1968, and the official story is that he was researching a *Harvard Business Review* feature—which he produced, although the research seems to have been rather more intensive than required. Gene describes consulting with the FBI, a connection made via "mutual good friends," and a deputy of J. Edgar Hoover's gladly inviting him to take a look at the Bureau's secret files on the student left; then traveling through Switzerland, Germany, and France "observing" demonstrations (though none are shared in the book or the story); and finally, and most bizarrely, leading a delegation of fellow businessmen in a "debate" with Students for a Democratic Society leader Carl Oglesby—hosted ("with the best of intentions but with a full measure of naïveté," he writes) by a concern called the Business International Corporation.

It seems likely that the 1968 summit at which Bradley "debated" onetime SDS president Carl Oglesby was the same SDS-BI meeting referenced in James Simon Kunen's SDS memoir *The Strawberry Statement: Notes of a College Revolutionary*. In the SDS version, the purpose of the meeting is straightforward. Certain unnamed businessmen who portray themselves as "the left wing of the ruling class" are seeking to "buy off some radicals"—purportedly because they're rooting for Gene McCarthy to win the presidency. The businessmen "see fascism as the threat, see it coming from [segregationist George] Wallace," Kunen reports. The idea is that heavy protests, which the businessmen offer to finance, will "make Gene [McCarthy] look more reasonable."

This stated fear and motive seems dubious. Gene, after all,

reported in the first chapter of his memoir how effectively he repressed his own fear of fascists. And the only people spooked by Wallace were those powerless enough to intimidate. Whatever the executives wanted from a bunch of college hippies, though, they were willing to both lie about and pay for. It's all too easy to see in retrospect that lopsided "debates" of this sort had accumulated into a political reality that, for the lifetime of a college kid in 1968 anyway, was inextricable from the concoctions of Cold War propagandists.

Just the year before, the National Student Association, the dominant campus activism network that had spawned SDS, had been outed (along with the CCF enterprises) as a CIA front. It would not be until the late seventies that the bland-sounding sponsor of the Oglesby-Bradley forum, Business International, would concede its own dual role as a CIA operation.

Nearly every page of *Journey in Faith* is bound to set off the intrigue detector of anyone who knows how the Cold War was won; names dropped include Treasury secretaries, CIA directors, senators, Iranian emissaries, shadowy KGB heavies, Henry Kissinger, Herman Kahn, and a Ku Klux Klan leader who converted to Christianity in jail after reading *Mein Kampf*. Gene Bradley's memoir is loaded with people who qualify as Triple A-List thought leaders—but it presents them without any narrative, context, or meaning that might leave the casual reader with any thought other than the obvious, *Wow, David Bradley's father was a big-time spook.* But Gene's odd foray into the student left might also leave readers thinking, *Wow, here's a vision of corporate-backed agitprop that can be unselfconsciously deployed in any setting or model of ideological conflict—no matter how unlikely or surreal.*

David Bradley was groomed for greatness. One day in the early sixties, admiral Stansfield Turner, the future CIA director who taught David in Christian Science Sunday School class, breezily told his mother that her son was destined to be president. After all, his favorite hymn, penned by Mary Baker Eddy herself, began:

Shepherd, show me how to go
O'er the hillside steep,
How to gather, how to sow,—
How to feed Thy sheep.

Gene, meanwhile, was bent on winning public distinction for his frail son, all but ordering him to embark on an all-but-winless career on the wrestling team at Washington's elite Quaker private school, Sidwell Friends, and stressing the mutability of personal identity as a key to success. "If you were to ask me, 'What has been the secret of David's success?' I would skip all the biographical data and simply say, 'David has worked to become the man he is today just as Marion Michael Morrison worked to become John Wayne.'"

Military intelligence professionals, the mind-cure faith, and a changeling, domineering father—it was the sort of upbringing that suffused Bradley's young life with a sort of spooky dullness. After watching Richard Nixon's resignation catch so many family friends financially unawares—and experiencing no small amount of personal disillusionment as a gung-ho intern in the Nixon White House—he decided to work on his war chest before going into politics, his first love. (Bradley's latter-day interest in politics, by the way, should not be taken to mean he harbors any definite political convictions; on the contrary, one of the professed sources of his admiration for writerly "talent" is his own inability to form an opinion on most political issues: "I define the middle," he has said.)

Upon completing Swarthmore, Harvard Business School, and a Fulbright scholarship in the Philippines (devoted to researching the mindset of the colonial Marxist guerillas), David returned to Washington to enroll in law school and to help Gene found a think tank called the International Management and Development Institute. When it came time for David to found his own business in 1979, he visualized a firm with all the affectations of a Washington think tank—down to the drab name, Research Council of Washington—but structured to turn a profit. He later renamed it the Advisory Board Company, which spun off the Corporate Executive Board, and those two generated a multitude of generic-sounding subsidiary Councils, Boards, and Forums. One of Research Council's first hires assumed from the classified ad that Bradley was operating a "front for a right-wing organization." It's still hard to say, at this late date, whether the joke was on that fledgling knowledge worker.

Whatever sort of organization was operating behind the fronts, its mission and culture were militantly corporate. Research Council grew quickly into a clearinghouse for corporate intelligence, offering modestly priced subscriptions to companies on condition of participation in their "best practices research" surveys. When Bradley filed in 1998 to cash out $150 million by taking Corporate Executive Board public, he was uncharacteristically blunt about his intention to sell out and leave the company altogether; investors did not seem to care, giving full credence to the prospectus's promise that the "Company does not believe that in-house research and analysis departments at individual corporations could obtain, at any price, similar information from other corporations about their management practices."

Or in other words: civilization cannot be sustained by propaganda and fraud alone. There needs to be available, at the right moment and for the right price, someone to take you by the hand and show you the "best practices" for dancing around the bullshit. At the core of David Bradley's corest competency is the grace with which he makes this pitch over and over again, as in the 2009 memo he addressed to *The Atlantic*'s editorial staff defending the magazine's off-the-record "salon dinners" for thought leaders:

> Perhaps the guests merely are being polite, but the uniform comment—on leaving or in thank you notes—is that they find no other place for such purposeful, engaged, constructive conversation across walls.... The decision to convene our dinners off-the-record was made at the outset....We were hoping to avoid the "canned remarks and rehearsed sound bites" that come with much public-policy discussion. My own view is that there is a great deal of constructive conversation that can take place only with the promise

that no headline is being written. Everyone—maybe even especially journalists—relies on this confidence in his day-to-day work.

Observe now the degeneration of a magazine that once published Henry James and Mark Twain into an elaborate loss-leader-cum-demand-creation mechanism for an event-planning operation whose chief selling point is the promise that you'll never read about it in the media, where certified thought leaders risk the loss of their health insurance for saying anything less than ultracanned and überphony. It is, indeed, a thing of mastery. Imagine the spike in eager inquiries that the in-house team choreographing *The Atlantic*'s secret dinner parties must have fielded after this memo.

And with this sort of triple-threat propaganda triumph in view, the otherwise baffling success of this once reputable magazine grows clear. Of course *The Atlantic* is a turgid mouthpiece for the plutocracy, a repository of shallow, lazy spin, and regular host of discussion forums during which nothing is discussed. It is, in every formal trait, *a CIA front*.

Well, how do you think their own retinue of thought leader enablers are able to sell so many tickets to all those fancy off-the-record dinners? Not by hiring the sort of "talent" who would be in any danger of talking to me!

Spook shop or not, *The Atlantic*'s soothing IV drip of frictionless, borderless, culturally agnostic thought-output plays a useful scrambling role in the context of unmitigated national crisis. A featured *Atlantic* contributor can be counted on—without interference from any known machinery of coercion—to wax incredulous when the current GE CEO Jeffrey Immelt, for example, pleads with the audience at a competing thought leader conference to spearhead a manufacturing revival.

The Bradley-subsidized chattering class instinctively knows to tune out altogether more articulate assessments of our plight, such as former Intel CEO Andy Grove's withering indictment of free-market dogma in a summer 2010 *Bloomberg Businessweek* cover story. Grove blamed the economic malaise on a sick cultural deification of "the guys in the garage inventing something that changes the world" at the expense of anyone involved in what happened afterward. His lament was the most eloquent tribute to the symbiosis of design and production and imagination and reality I'd read since Mao's 1937 essay "On Practice," which declared "man's knowledge depends mainly on his activity in material production." The thought leaders of our own political leadership class would never know about Grove's broadside, though—it was greeted by a Washington-wide wall of silence. (Indeed, the one wayward D.C. player who did take it to heart—former SEIU chieftain Andy Stern—was reduced to imploring unsympathetic readers of the *Wall Street Journal* op-ed section to search online for Grove's essay some sixteen months after it appeared.)

What mystified Grove was the assertion, voiced by the economist Alan Blinder and others, "that as long as 'knowledge work' stays in the U.S., it doesn't matter what happens to factory jobs." This was not only inhumane, Grove declared; it was idiotic.

But it is why the ideas, so-called, that inspire the omniscient gentlemen of *The Atlantic* are flat: their world is, literally, flat. Habitual "bipartisanship" has given way to a tendency to level the playing field between reality and fiction. And so in *The Atlantic*'s account of America's present crisis, Hanna Rosin wonders whether it was not deregulation or securitization that caused the financial crisis, but . . . Christianity; and James Fallows suspects America's awareness of its own decline is merely "our era's version of the 'missile gap.'" It's as though, in purging labor from the ranks of accredited thought leaders, they have eradicated thought itself.

Meanwhile, in China, Steve Clemons of the New America Foundation mourns the death of Steve Jobs with a breathless blog post about an epiphany he has just experienced while scouring the local thought leader horizon for signs of a counterpart to his late greatness:

> But one of the things I find odd is that the Chinese basically have a person who is their Steve Jobs. I don't mean someone who created

> a line of products that we have all become addicted to and which have changed our world—but rather a leader who saw a future, went against the tide, and used the levers of influence he had to gamble on a complete retro-fitting and relaunch of China. I'm talking, of course, about Deng Xiaoping.

Comrades: I hope that you want to throw up now, because I have run clean out of bile to waste on the mental morlocks who think up this sort of shit.

Irving Kristol's cofounder at *Encounter,* the British poet Stephen Spender, was the sole member of the CCF clique to be truly traumatized by the revelation that his beloved project was a CIA front. Then, in the early aughts, he was doubly insulted, via the revelation that George Orwell had on his deathbed listed his name on a painstakingly compiled list of "fellow travelers" whom the author suspected would conspire with the enemy in the event of a Soviet invasion—but only because he was "impressionable" that way. Natasha Spender later likened her husband to Prince Myshkin the gentle idiot. And I believe her, with one reservation: no one is too gullible to be unafraid of poverty.

As a child in China toward the end of Deng's rule, I remember hearing about the Korean War POWs. Without any ideological miseducation to obstruct or distort my perceptions, it seemed obvious that the most remarkable thing about the defectors was their willingness to relinquish their American citizenship to remain in a country that was so unbelievably poor.

Not until college would I begin to grasp America's own brand of poverty, and not until I spent the aftermath of the financial crisis among the bailout revisionists and inequality denialists of the omniscient D.C. elite would I recognize in myself the abiding fury the defectors professed.[1] Even as they so dearly missed ice cream, they elected to turn their backs on the demeaning propaganda machine that questioned their manhood, insisted they'd been brainwashed, and portrayed the Chinese enemy as robots programmed to commit gratuitous self-sacrifice in the service of world domination. Thousands of miles from home, they figured out that to be American in such an epoch was to get screwed over and defrauded by the self-appointed high priests of Patriotism. Somewhere along the way, someone had put it in their minds that they didn't need to take it—and it's a safe bet that he didn't sound anything like Mao.

NOTES

1 The whole topic of POWs in Korea is one of those historical subplots about which the facts were so utterly devoured by the accelerating avalanche of misinformation that they may have been irretrievably lost. At some point, the Pentagon shifted its initial explanation for the defection—Chinese brainwashing—to appoint a larger responsibility to the defectors' generally corrupt characters and barbaric behavior. By 1958 this low attack metamorphosed into an indictment of all American soldiers who served in the war; the report was leaked to a *New Yorker* writer who expanded the "findings" into a book, *In Every War But One*, which has since been pretty convincingly debunked. Strangely, when the writer Dwight Macdonald referred to that Pentagon report in an essay that same year in the CIA-founded literary propaganda outlet *Encounter*, it became the only piece the Agency itself killed from an issue. More significantly, the Worst Generation narrative was marshaled to justify many billions of dollars on both brainwashing research and practice—an area in which the Agency was already heavily invested. Later that year, microbiologist Frank Olson fell from a tenth-story window, a strange event that conveniently kept him from publicizing the details of the CIA's MKULTRA mind control experimentation. Most basic truths about that operation have been spun and shredded, brainwashed, and poisoned out of existence.

The Vertically Integrated Rape Joke

The triumph of Vice

ANNE ELIZABETH MOORE

Thirteen-year-old Milly Dowler, a perky schoolgirl from Surrey, England, never intended to be the undoing of mighty News Corp. The global media conglomerate—famously helmed by ex-pat Australian Rupert Murdoch—had, in Dowler's day, owned or held major shares in more than 250 separate media companies worldwide, including newspapers, film studios, radio stations, book publishers, and cable and television networks. But one spring afternoon in 2002, the tawny-haired tween set off a sequence of events that would end Murdoch's beloved company. (Spoiler alert: He gets his vengeance.)

That Thursday, Dowler, in her school's required mini-and-tie uniform, left campus with a pal, grabbed a snack, and disappeared. White girl in distress? This was *News of the World*'s beat. The Murdoch-owned British tabloid—his first media acquisition outside of Australia—was then in the midst of a salacious run of features outing accused pedophiles. The series started after the murder of eight-year-old Sarah Payne by a convicted sex offender in 2000; the paper's track record of publishing the names and photographs of rumored sex offenders without attribution or verification prompted police officials to denounce the vigilante-style coverage as "grossly irresponsible" and resulted in more than one violent attack on an innocent. Dowler's disappearance made the perfect follow-up, and the rag's coverage spawned so much media at-

From *The Baffler*, no. 24

tention that southern U.K. grade-schoolers were under claustrophobic parental supervision for months.

When Dowler's body was discovered a half-year later, the disappearance was reclassified as a murder. It would be six more years before police identified a suspect—and nine total before Levi Bellfield was convicted of the crime. An aggressive, pudgy man, Bellfield had a history of asking girlfriends to dress up as schoolgirls, of driving past bus stops and leering at tweens, of threatening blondes with violence, and of sexual assault. By 2011 he had already been convicted of the murders of two young women and the attempted murder of a third.

During the trial, the *Guardian* reported that the girl's voicemail had been hacked close to a decade earlier by a private investigator on contract with *News of the World.* Other phone taps emerged—of Prince William and Sarah Payne's mother, among many others. Scandalous headlines, even in the non-tabloid press, voiced the mounting public outrage over the intrusion of privacy the paper had committed against victims of violent crime. Blame kept finding new perches. Reporters were fired, and editors quit; executives got arrested. Police, and then members of Parliament, were implicated. Even James Murdoch—Rupert's son and then CEO of News Corp.'s Europe and Asia operations—was later revealed to have given a former footballer $1.4 million USD in hush money, proving that corruption and malfeasance went all the way to the top of Murdoch's empire.

By fall 2013 the *Guardian* had reported 79 arrests relating to alleged bribes of public officials associated with the scandal. Investigations into phone hacking yielded 24 arrests, and computer-hacking inquiries yielded 21. Yet even with 124 players implicated so far, the full contours of the scandal have yet to emerge. (Under British law, an arrest can come early in an investigation, well before charges are brought.) *News of the World* shuttered operations in 2011 amid the scandal's worst revelations, but parent company News International, now called News UK, has so far agreed to settle 130 of the 167 civil damages claims filed by 180 individuals. Total payout figures are not yet known, although a settlement to the Dowlers in the range of $3.2 million was discussed, and Murdoch has said he'd donate another $1.6 million to charity in their names. Last year a nearly $1 million settlement was paid to phone-hacking victim and songstress Charlotte Church. Metropolitan Police at one point estimated that News Corp. had tapped at least 5,795 phones over the course of its scoop-driven surveillance campaign, though the official count was later revised downward to 4,744.

Fallout from the phone-hacking scandal didn't end when *News of the World* did, however, and eventually the steady stream of sordid revelations cost Murdoch the chance to close on a takeover bid for BSkyB, a British satellite broadcaster he owned a stake in. More drastic action was needed, and Murdoch took it. This past summer, News Corp. officially split into two companies: the entertainment arm was dubbed 21st Century Fox, and the print-heavy news division became just plain News Corp (no period). The scandal would—finally—be referred to in the past tense.

In accord with Murdoch's agenda were the opinionistas, who quickly named a new culprit: society. The *Guardian* revealed in 2011 that within a month of Dowler's death a decade earlier, a *News of the World* reporter had played Surrey police the girl's voicemail messages. It was a crime, yet police did nothing. Some viewed the collusion between the Surrey cops and Murdoch's paper as a misguided quest for solidarity in pursuance of Dowler's killer; others suggested that the police feared reprisal from the media outlet. The lamentations came quick and served to normalize the illegal surveillance of crime victims for profit: the culture, all agreed, had changed.

Few held *News of the World*—or Murdoch in particular—responsible for implementing that change. Meanwhile, Murdoch's empire continued to do everything in its power to erode integrity both on the micro scale (via violations of privacy and bribes to cops) and the macro (by using relationships with top-level government officials to influence policy), although press coverage of the true criminal proportions of both trespasses can be hard to track down. (A search through the archives of the Murdoch-owned *Wall Street Journal*, for example, turns up only a smattering of hits about the allegations surrounding its owner.)

In a long litany of abuses of the public trust, this may not be the most damaging cultural shift that the Murdoch enterprise is responsible for. Yet it's impossible to overlook the similarities between the lurid upskirt journalism of *News of the World* and Bellfield's schoolgirl obsession. In the former, very young women's bodies were violated, both in the public imagination (on the pages of the tabloid) and in practice (through phone taps). In the latter, very young women's bodies were violated by a man who was serially raping and murdering them. During the period of public alarm over Bellfield's crimes, *News of the World* was offering most of the imaginable details (and then some) of sex offenders' predations on its front page, with a consistency, reach, and volume few other tabloids approached.

If Murdoch and crew capitalized on and cultivated a downward shift in the ethics of the U.K. police force and government officials, does it not stand to reason that they may also have lowered the U.K. standard of culturally appropriate behavior toward young women's bodies?

If so, we ain't seen nothing yet.

Edge Comes of Age

Culture may have changed; Rupert Murdoch's empire, in many ways, didn't. Following the split, the patriarch continued to run both newly created media entities—and as 21st Century Fox's first major acquisition in the wake of the scandal made clear, the illicit voyeurism that ended *News of the World* would remain standard operating procedure for the Murdoch machine. The entertainment division would simply do so with more hipster cred—5 percent of "edgy" Vice Media, in fact, which Murdoch took home for a cool $70 million in August 2013.

Jaded observers compared the Vice deal to News Corp.'s $580 million purchase of Myspace in 2005, just as the social-networking site began taking heavy hits from upstart Facebook. The money-losing enterprise sold to Specific Media and Justin Timberlake six years later for $35 million—6 percent of what News Corp. had paid for it—and Murdoch seems to have learned something about the Internet in

MELINDA BECK

the meantime. (*New York* magazine points out, for example, that he learned how to use email around 2010.)

Although Vice started as a print mag, the company found its niche online. The top story on Vice.com around the time of the 21st Century Fox sale was "Kings of Cannabis" (subhead: "You might not know who Arjan Roskam is, but you've probably smoked his weed"). Content-wise, this was a departure for Murdoch, whose portfolio of headlines at *News of the World* tended to implicate media stars and royalty, rather than readers, in drug use. ("Shamed TV star Leslie is caught snorting cocaine" and "Harry's drugs shame" ran the headlines on two such dispatches in 2002.) Yet Vice Media does sit on the young-ish end of the tabloid continuum, and as Andrew Neil, former editor of the Murdoch-owned *Sunday Times*, told *Frontline* of his former boss, "tabloids is what really gets him out of bed in the morning. . . . Not journalism—*tabloid* journalism is in his veins."

For Vice CEO Shane Smith, forty-three, the alliance with eighty-two-year-old Murdoch was a coming-of-age moment. The Vice operation started in Canada as a magazine called *Voice of Montreal*; founders Smith, Gavin "Godfather of Hipsterdom" McInnes, and recovering heroin addict Suroosh Alvi claim they went on the government dole in 1994 to fund the glossy, ad-heavy, free publication. (In one of the many examples of how Vice's brand of self-promotional authenticity doesn't hold up to scrutiny, the *Ryerson Review of Journalism* reported that the trio borrowed start-up money from their parents.)

Renamed *Vice*, the magazine became available in the United States two years later; the staff joined it stateside in 1999, first opening an office and storefronts in Manhattan, then moving operations to Brooklyn shortly thereafter. Today Vice Media's tidy empire claims magazine distribution in twenty-seven countries, print circulation of 1.2 million, and pass-along rates of 5.6 readers per copy. In sum, Vice claims a print readership of more than 7 million (although these numbers are self-reported), together with around 15 million unique web hits per month. The company is more than an ad rag and its companion site, however. It is, to quote from its own heavy-breathing 2013 press kit, a "360, MULTI-PLATFORM, VERTICALLY INTEGRATED, GLOBAL MEDIA BRAND"—including a record label originally launched with Atlantic Records; a book publishing arm; the marketing concern Virtue; an ever-evolving series of themed, sponsored websites; retail stores; and VBS.tv, a video partnership formed with Viacom and CNN.com, now going it alone as an online channel integrated into the Vice brand. (VBS was another, albeit more deliberate, example of failed authenticity; its letters don't stand for anything, but it does sound kind of broadcasty.)

Accounts of Vice's first nineteen years are not long on reliable narration. The juvenile company's early days are a hazy mix of pud-pulling and boundary-testing, limited in imagination only by an unformed frontal lobe. Founders might pin the absence of clarity on rampant drug use, but confusion about Vice Media often stems from straight-up lies: Smith is usually identified as their originator, but before departing in 2008, McInnes did his part to establish the venture on an unsolid bed of gaseous ooze, the aroma of which still clings to the company's stolid attempts at Serious Journalism. ("Eric Andre Told Us About the 300-Pound Stripper at His Birthday Party" is a headline story on Vice.com as I write this.)

The Gonzo Gambit

"*Vice* was built on lies," *Wired*'s Jason Tanz stated bluntly in 2007. These started as self-promotional fibs about big-media lawsuits and big-money investors—that the *Village Voice* was suing Smith and friends, for example, which never happened—but soon became journalistic fabrication. "They also published fake interviews with car thieves and hooligans who set homeless people on fire, and later ran a gag announcement that they had discovered Osama bin Laden in China's Pamir Mountains," Tanz writes. (I recently tried to parse a short video series on the Cambodian garment trade, but inaccuracies mingled so freely with false assumptions, leaps in logic, and inappropriate, sensationalistic footage of transwomen that a fact-check seemed futile.) If the content hasn't matured much, at least the company's response to allegations of prevarication has. Smith and crew originally distanced themselves from journalism; later they called the more ballsy falsehoods gags. Then Smith realized that "instead of talking about sneakers, we could talk about real issues," as he told Spike Jonze for *Interview*. That's when the stunts became "stunt journalism."

Lie becomes joke becomes stance: the evolution of form is mirrored by readers' decreasing attention spans in the Internet age. But the company's manic quest for a business model that distances creators and funders from the content engenders a lack of critical engagement among its consumer base; it also sidesteps the core practices of journalism. In this through-the-looking-glass world of brand-domination-through-truth-bending, the usual questions that govern an investigative reporting project can also be turned on the company proper: Who is accountable?

For Vice Media, accountability takes a back seat to accounts payable: the company's estimated total value, based on the Murdoch empire's buy-in, is $1.4 billion. The metric of success is "clicks" over "paper sales"—a clear, and discomfitingly natural, extension of tabloid news values into the digital sphere. Under this logic, nothing matters but the bottom line. However, the genius of the Vice model is that the bottom line, too, has been outsourced: Smith has acted as content supplier for a host of entertainment and journalistic outlets seeking to burnish their hipster accreditation, such as CNN, HBO, Warner Bros., and Viacom. This means that Vice Media's primary, if not exclusive, responsibility is to attract attention.

Accountability, Smith might say, is for crybabies. "Money isn't the report card," he told the *Guardian* in March. That's reserved for "clicks," both the motivator and the reward in a media ecosystem without broadcast licenses or cover prices—two outdated systems that, however ineffective, promote at least the appearance of media accountability to a viewing or reading public. The real goal, in Smith's words, is "putting your imprint on the world's cultural fabric"—a different game entirely. (Later, in *Interview*, he amended this goal, suggesting instead that the company's allegiance to the media profession was purely corporate in nature: "We're the same as Time Warner. We're the same as Bertelsmann or Viacom.... If anyone asks me what we are, we're a media company.")

Money may not be the report card, but that's only because it claims pride of place as the full-blown curriculum. Here's how Gavin McInnes chose to explain the set-up back in 1999: "This is the first time young people have had a revolution that involves them getting paid."

True enough. Even then, the glossy magazine was packed with ads, and distributed for free in retail clothing stores. The reader of *Vice* was always its commodity, but the social engineering behind the magazine ensured that at least some nominal part of the profits went into a big party the reader got invited to anyway. Who cares who was being sold out, so long as the revolutionaries were all getting lai—oops, *paid*?

White Supremacy as Usability Study

Nowadays, this payday-as-legitimate-media-enterprise structure is nakedly visible in Vice's marketing arm, Virtue Worldwide. None of that joke-or-journalism stuff here: Virtue simply offers Vice Media up for sale. A blurb from *Creativity Magazine* explains, "The major selling point of Virtue ... is that it already has a standing army of writers, photographers, artists and producers making cool stuff of their own, why not use them to tell your brand's story?" Below this—although no fees are noted—are listed all the imaginable services that a multimedia company could provide. (Including entire news-like sites that consistently favor the client's brand.) Also listed are capabilities such as "Focus Groups," "Usability Studies," "Experiential," "Street-Level Network," and "On-The-Street"—all fitting the general category of "Just Give Us Stuff to Hand Out to Our Cool Friends."

But before you call it a revolution (or even just punk rock), check out a few of the companies on the roster of sponsors and partners: MTV, Intel, the Ultimate Fighting Championship (UFC), William

Morris, Dell, media communications firm WPP, HBO, and media merchant bank The Raine Group. Vice Media is DIY only in the sense that forms for corporate control over content on this scale have not yet been invented, and about as "Fuck You" as a brand-new mass-produced T-shirt, available for $19.99 exclusively from Hot Topic. (Even this joke is stale; that's how little authenticity Vice Media inspires.)

Vice is, however, "edgy" as a marketing ploy, following an utterly predictable strategy to afford loud, mostly white, mostly dudes yet more license in culture to act out at will, to acclaim but little consequence. In practical terms, as any cursory search of the content at Vice.com will show, "edgy" means "racist" and "sexist"—sometimes by accident, although often not.

Take Dave Schilling's ongoing "This Week in Racism" column, which defends or decries various cultural moments elsewhere labeled racist. The listicles begin to point to a general American inability to articulate real fears around race, but the dos-and-don'ts approach to often nuanced instances of oppression serves to shut down cultural discussions of race that may prove fruitful, while evidently also providing rhetorical cover for the re-presentation of genuinely, unabashedly racist content. Vice's defenders will note that Schilling isn't white himself, and claim that the representation amounts to an all-encompassing racism—no one gets out unoffended—but the slurs that stick are not about white people, nor do they fully challenge the snarky white supremacy Vice has developed a reputation for parroting. In 2003 McInnes told *New York Times* reporter Vanessa Grigoriadis, "I love being white. ... We need to close the borders now and let everyone assimilate to a Western, white, English-speaking way of life."

In the interview—rumored to have led, ultimately, to his separation from the company in 2008—McInnes denounced the idea of sexual consent and suggested women want to be dominated. Such faux-edgy assertions amount to a rank misogyny McInnes recently made explicit in a spot on HuffPost Live. During the proceedings, he called a female panelist a "fucking idiot" who, along with the audience, refused to understand that women "naturally want to" stay at home to have babies instead of entering the workforce. Such views would be easier to dismiss as just another of Vice's triple-gainer brand of anti-anti-hip postures if the company's underlying dismissal of women's intellectual capacity weren't such a freely trumpeted feature of the site—and one reason the print magazine is banned from the occasional bookstore and college campus. Of the mere handful of women featured in Vice.com stories on Sept. 29, 2013, one is called "slutty" and another a "crybaby"; there is an offer to stage a mud-wrestling match between Nancy Kerrigan and Tonya Harding; and a photo of a girl approximately the same age as Milly Dowler accompanies a first-person tale of rape and abuse. (No phone tap necessary here.)

The hard-line masculine epistemologies that the site indulges so reflexively go hand in hand with real labor issues. According to one count, Vice features about 73 percent male contributors and about 27 percent female. Once you toggle over to the NSFW section of the site—that's its real name—content is rife with dudes' "stunt journalism" accounts of things they've done to humiliate sex workers. And recent allegations against Terry Richardson, the photographer credited with solidifying the magazine's aesthetic—overlit, underclad young white women simulating sexual pleasure, mostly, with Richardson occasionally stepping into the frame to give a thumbs-up—have him sexually harassing models. Jamie Peck, who sat for him when she was nineteen, wrote on *The Gloss* in 2010 that he'd asked her to remove her tampon so he could make tea with it; he then proceeded to remove his own clothes and request a hand job from her, while an assistant continued photographing the scene.

The mag's become known as the Hipster Bible for preaching a jaded worldview, and into such cynicism any combination of products may be injected and celebrated, for a fee. (The Vice-as-Bible meme also comes from another old joke, that the print version is everywhere, no one reads it, and you can't get rid of it.) Products, however, can't change what Vice is about—for Vice is about Vice, a media company for selfie-snappers. (Compare the gritty nekkid spreads and party shots to images in, say, *Playboy* or *Maxim*. The latter at least make a pretense of listing turn-ons.)

It's no coincidence that eighteen-to-thirty-four-year-old "urban trendsetters" make up Vice Media's target demographic, according to the media kit. These are the millennials, nudged into adulthood for legal boob-viewing purposes—the generation whose coming of age coincided with the removal of narcissism from the DSM-5. It's a generation that Pew Research describes as less white than their elders but about six times as pierced, and less skeptical of government but more so of people in general. (Vice Media's own skepticism led to the ousting of one female employee from a $250,000 social gathering she had helped plan.)

When Pew asked what makes them unique, millennials said: Technology use; Music/Pop culture; Liberal/Tolerant; Smarter; and Clothes. Previous generations gave values-based responses—Work ethic, Values/Morals, and Respectful—and every generation polled has said Smarter. So whether or not such answers make for an accurate accounting of "generational uniqueness," a difference is clear: millennials responded to a question that previous generations have understood to be about intrinsic principles of behavior with two different forms of cultural production. Three, if you count "apps."

We can read this as shallowness, or we can read it as millennials having gamed Pew's plodding model of demographic inquiry. Because they're right. *Every* generation's clothes, music, technology, and pop culture are necessarily unique. My generation just lost points on the test by spewing some values-based claptrap that Smith—exactly my age—disproves.

Millennials, in other words, want to make an imprint on the world's cultural fabric too, but the simple fact of managing to pin down that fabric and give it a thorough dye job seems to count for more than the substance of the design. Indeed, as I asserted in *Unmarketable* in 2007, the corporate adoption of independent modes of cultural production has left us with a deficit of integrity. The book was generally well received until spring 2012, when I got a flood of angry emails about it from young folks assigned it in a college course. My correspondents were appalled that I would delineate a meaningful difference between corporate and independent modes of production—and what's more, they were downright furious that I would hold the latter in higher regard. Couldn't I see, several young men some twenty years my junior demanded, that efforts to attract the largest possible mass of people by any means necessary were always virtuous?

This surely sounds harsh: some of my best friends, I swear, are millennials. And it's almost certainly the case that the millennial set's much-maligned displays of narcissism are rooted in other motivations. These are, after all, folks whose culture is created in large part by Murdoch's shifty maneuverings and Vice's kind of pseudo-journalism—not people, like Smith and myself, who recall a media environment before Jonah Lehrer, Mike Daisey, Jayson Blair, and @Horse_ebooks. We now live in a culture of increasingly hostile and invasive media, where getting consigned to an unsure economic future is a far more daunting prospect than getting caught in a lie. Another Pew study from 2013 showed that most teens take evasive measures to protect their privacy online: 58 percent of teens used codes to communicate on social media, and 26 percent deliberately posted false information about themselves to protect their privacy.

What I'm suggesting is not that young people are necessarily becoming more self-absorbed, as many have already, but that they may be abandoning truth-telling as a potential source of protection. I can't really blame them: we've fostered a culture where fact-finding is anemic, but consumer products are doing just fine.

Shane, Come Back!

It's hard to pinpoint the exact origins of the Murdoch-Smith bromance, but it likely began in May 2012, when Vice pranksters dispatched an unconvincing News Corp. exec look-alike and two dudes with slicked-back hair to disrupt a BBC interview on the Leveson Inquiry, the legal investigation into "the culture, practices and ethics of the press" sparked by the phone-hacking scandal. "We dressed a girl up as [former *News of the World* CEO] Rebekah Brooks and fucked around with the paparazzi this morning," @ViceUK tweeted.

The telltale slippage here that casually merges news organizations with celebrity-chasing photographers should be noted for the record, but whether the Vice crew perceives a difference is of little consequence. The more pressing concern here is which party emerged from the prank onto the moral high ground—for once, it was News Corp. A journalist might have used a stunt like the one Vice pulled to gather observations; even a half-decent satirist would have found a message to impart beyond self-promotion. Yet while the Vice hoax drew momentary interest by dramatizing just how little the members of the tabloid pack could be counted on to know who they're covering, the *détournement* ended there, adding only another layer of circus entertainment to the big-top-like proceedings.

Perhaps it enchanted the Australian expat. In October 2012 he tweeted from @RupertMurdoch that Vice Media was a "wild" and "global success" with "millenials *[sic]* who don't read or watch established media." The part of the avuncular mogul's pineal gland that controls lust for market share had clearly been engaged, and the long string of replies to his fact-finding tweet foreshadowed the pending investment in no uncertain terms. When, three months later, the Fox News Network hit a twelve-year ratings low and began hemorrhaging young adult viewers, the solution must have seemed clear. For Smith's part, the deal is a tremendous boon, offering untold new global reach to the Vice brand, with video distribution in the United Kingdom, Italy, Germany, and India through 21st Century Fox's Sky and Star networks.

Although separated by four decades, the two CEOs are not dissimilar. Following the acquisition of *News of the World,* his first offshore media outlet, Murdoch moved into the U.S. market in the 1970s, first with print, and then with broadcast and satellite television stations. He became a naturalized American citizen in 1985, a legal prerequisite to his purchase of the 20th Century Fox film studios and several independent television stations in major U.S. cities later that year. Media consolidation followed quickly: News Corp. affiliate stations then reached 22 percent of all households in the United States, and the FCC gave Murdoch on top of that a temporary waiver to operate both print and broadcast media in certain markets. Once licensing restrictions began to loosen—supported by op-eds in News Corp.–owned media—the affiliate stations combined to form the Fox Broadcasting Company in April 1987.

Smith brought Vice to the States just twelve years later, and the cultural fabric he intended to imprint at first blush seemed distinct. Smith learned to adapt soon enough, and it's a safe bet that Murdoch furnished an attractive role model. Murdoch wanted traditional power, and his political chumminess bolstered his media market shares, a lesson not lost on the Vice Media impresario.

With heavy lobbying and support from on-again-off-again pals like Mario Cuomo, News Corp. has regularly won the suspension of FCC regulations that would have impeded Murdoch acquisitions. Similarly, Murdoch's decision to hire former Nixon, Reagan, and George H. W. Bush senior media strategist Roger Ailes to run the Fox News Channel was well calculated (and, as *Gawker* suggests, may have indicated a longer-ranging GOP plan to create a free-standing media propaganda arm for the conservative movement). Smith has also begun hiring Washington insiders—though whether their chief mission will be to streamline the Vice mini-empire's access to new global markets or to influence domestic policy remains to be seen. (His agent, Ari Emanuel, is the brother of Rahm, the foul-mouthed Chicago mayor currently privatizing public services with astonishing rapidity.) How this new lobbying offensive will comport with Vice's recent hire of sixty new reporters equipped with Google Glass, who will "cover everything from Middle East war zones to health-care reform" (as the *Wall Street Journal* reported this November), is also unclear. In even more recent news, former News Corp. CEO James Murdoch, ousted in the phone-hacking scandal, just joined the board of Vice Media. It seems safe to assume that unseemly acts of corruption involving media moguls will probably be safe from Vice's roving lens.

The cultural impact Smith covets comes across in Vice-choreographed stunts, like Kim Jong-un and Dennis Rodman watching a basketball game together on HBO's dime. The stunts are presented as news, and phrases like "basketball diplomacy" have caught on to lend them the veneer of significance. But really, things have changed in the last fifteen years: Vice stopped inviting readers to the party.

Smith is now angling for a less traditional kind of power—the power to party anywhere and with anyone in the world. And don't underestimate it. For what's being celebrated is unchecked influence, and what we overlook in being told later how fun the party was is remembering to ask what really happened, or if indeed anything did.

There are plenty for whom the Murdoch-Smith party won't be much fun to hear about. That's because the surveillance of underage female victims of sexual violence really *did* happen, and clearly was News Corp.-sanctioned policy ten years ago. Harassment—verbal, from McInnes, and sexual, from Richardson—of young women continues among Vice alum today. The promise of Heineken and Ultimate Fighting Championship sponsorships that Smith brings to his partnership with Murdoch merely ups the stakes of such antics-slash-crimes. The rape joke has already been established as an all-but-official Vice brand. One posted on November 11, 2013, under "MILFs Anal Addiction," describes the attempts of an airline passenger to woo a celibate, born-again, teetotaling flight companion by getting her rip-roaring drunk, only to be cock-blocked by—get this—her daughter! And her parents! All Christians! Coitus coercion interruptus. Sad trombone.

You might not find this amusing; you might find it downright boring. That's because casual bigotry and misogyny for money's sake aren't new. They're being marketed to millennials now—the kids today!—but even that gambit has grown old and stale. ⚜

Party of None

Barack Obama's annoying journey to the center of belonging

CHRIS BRAY

In real life, the balls were rushed and exhausting for the Obamas to attend. They danced ten times to the same song, "At Last" by Etta James, hearing the same lyrics over and over. But the version shown on television was stunning, one of those rare moments when presidential symbolism, personal history, and the nation's emotions met and fused.

—JODI KANTOR, *THE OBAMAS*

Barack Obama's personal journey begins, and it is instantly made meaningless.

Sometime in the first half of 1966, Obama's stepfather was mysteriously forced to return to Indonesia from grad school in Hawaii. Lolo Soetoro went home to a long episode of political violence, the outlines of which are not substantially in dispute. Sukarno, Indonesia's first president, had tried to create political stability by balancing three competing political forces in the life of a new country: the army, the Partai Komunis Indonesia (PKI), and Islam. On the night of September 30, 1965, PKI members and leftist military officers attempted a clumsy sort of coup d'état that resulted in the murder of six right-wing generals and, accidentally, a lieutenant. The plot was a shambles: publicly incoherent, loosely planned, and easily suppressed. Suharto, the most powerful right-wing

From *The Baffler*, no. 20

general to survive the attempt, used the plot as a pretext to seize power and purge communists from Indonesia's political life. Within weeks, soldiers and militias were killing hundreds of thousands of people and removing thousands more to detention camps. In Jakarta, U.S. embassy officials informed their Indonesian counterparts that they were "generally sympathetic with and admiring of" the army's chosen course. American military planes rushed to supply radios to Suharto's headquarters to help his army coordinate the purge.

So Lolo Soetoro goes home, soon to be followed by his young wife, Ann, and her son, the future U.S. president. According to former *New York Times* reporter Janny Scott's *A Singular Woman: The Untold Story of Barack Obama's Mother* (Riverhead, 2011), nobody really knows even today what was happening at the time. "The details of the September 30, 1965, coup and counter-coup remain in dispute, as do the particulars of the slaughter that followed," Scott avers. Still, she concedes that a few things aren't shrouded in fog, such as the fact that "it is known that neighbors turned on neighbors." As a result of this nationwide outbreak of neighborhood violence, Scott concludes on the same page, "the army became the dominant institution in the country." Neighbors spontaneously turned on neighbors, driven by unclear motives to perform unclear acts; the PKI was destroyed; the army ended up in power. Mysterious events, clear outcome.

The Bridge: The Life and Rise of Barack Obama (Knopf, 2010), by *New Yorker* editor David Remnick, gives the story a touch of detail, explaining that Lolo Soetoro found himself in grad school "at a time when his country was enduring a horrific civil war." Seven dead on one side, hundreds of thousands on the other: *civil war.* Why were they fighting? "Suharto claimed that the violence had been initiated by leftists," Remnick reports, though he pronounces no judgment as to the veracity of the claim. The whole thing may have had something to do with the left and the right. Let's move on.

Placed by the authors in a murky setting, the narrative version of Obama's stepfather is assigned a murky role. "Lolo was in the army," according to Janny Scott's book, which shows him in uniform. Remnick, on the other hand, says Lolo "had taken a job as an army geologist," language that neatly elides the question of his personal agency.[1] Either he chose to become a geologist after a civil war, or he was forced to serve in an army that had recently engaged in mass murder and was still engaged in the indefinite military detention of political enemies. Apparently, these are small distinctions. He *took a job* in Suharto's army, sometime in 1966.

Whatever Lolo was up to, Ann and Barack were devastated and delighted to join him. Janny Scott has them living in a place where people are "unable to eat the fish because of decaying corpses in the water." On the next page, "Jakarta had a magical charm," and on the next, "the city felt friendly and safe." Jumping into this milieu of orientalist exoticism, Ann eventually got a job as an English teacher, where snacks were available in the teacher's lounge. There were, Janny Scott reports, many kinds of Indonesian snacks:

> They include seafood chips, peanut chips, fried chips from the *mlinjo* tree, chips made from ground rawhide mixed with garlic, sweet-potato snacks, mashed cassava snacks, sweet flour dumplings made with sesame seeds, sticky rice flavored with pandanus leaves, sticky black rice sprinkled with grated coconut, and rice cakes wrapped in coconut leaves or banana leaves, to name a few.

This is more detail than Scott has managed for the political events of 1965, in a story about a family that went home during a political purge so stepdad could join the army prosecuting it.[2]

Ann Dunham's occupational history is equally hidden behind this thicket of meaningless narrative. The English school, it turns out, was her *second* job in Indonesia. Here's Scott, again: "By January 1968, she had gone to work as an assistant to the American director of Lembaga Indonesia-Amerika, a binational organization funded by the United States Information Service and housed at the U.S. Agency for International Development" (USAID). The offices of the USAID were located at the U.S. embassy, by the way, where officials had communicated American approval of mass executions and arranged for the shipment of communications supplies.

Hints of the story Remnick and Scott are trying not to tell begin to slip out. Lolo Soetoro had served in Suharto's army, and Ann Soetoro was an employee of a thinly veiled Cold War federal agency, reporting to the American director of an organization with an office at the U.S. embassy in Jakarta. The naïf with a desk at the embassy had eyes, though, and she noticed some things. Ann "sensed the hauntedness of Jakarta," David Remnick writes, especially after she "came across a field of unmarked graves." And so the doe-eyed USAID employee ventured an innocent question to her husband: "She tentatively asked Lolo what had happened with the coup and counter-coup, the scouring of the countryside for suspected Communists and the innumerable killings, the mass arrests, but most Indonesians, Lolo included, were extremely reluctant to talk about the horrors of the mid-sixties." Remnick's phrasing presents all of its own answers as a preface to our discovery that Ann's question wasn't answered. Janny Scott's version of the story is a little less helpless. In this account, Obama's mother eventually "pieced together some of what had happened in Indonesia in 1965 and afterward from fragmentary information that people let slip." Somehow, a federal employee at the U.S. embassy managed to figure out some little bits about what had happened with that whole *political mass murder by the army* thing in the country where her husband was a soldier and her employer delivered military supplies.

And the lesson? Indonesia was where "Ann was Barry's teacher in high-minded matters—liberal, humanist values," Remnick concludes. It's where she taught him the values of "honesty, hard work, and fulfilling one's duty to others," where she lectured him about "a sense of obligation to give something back," Scott adds. It's where she "worked to instill ideas about public service in her son." Because Indonesia in the late sixties was the perfect place and time to learn about liberal humanist values and public service.

More recently, David Maraniss walked into this dark room and turned on the lights. His *Barack Obama: The Story* (Simon & Schuster, 2012), which tells the story of Lolo Soetoro and his family, sees the creepy significance of the political setting. Suddenly we have a version of Lolo who, sitting in Hawaii, knew that "the political situ-

RANDALL ENOS

ation in Indonesia made him especially vulnerable.” Whole layers of meaning open up, as Maraniss shows Obama’s stepfather amid dangerous events with precise language: “On top of all this, the Indonesian army, the military to which Soetoro still had civilian obligations, was involved in a bloody skirmish in Malaysia against the British.”[3] If he were to return to Indonesia, Lolo suspects he’d be “placed on the front lines doing reconnaissance work.” Throughout Maraniss’s account, a clock is ticking: “Soetoro knew that his time was running out.” Indonesian officials showed up at his university in Hawaii and sharply questioned him about his politics and his affiliations back home. He fought a losing battle to keep his student visa and was finally forced home by the loss of that visa in June 1966. When Ann arrived with her son to join her husband, Maraniss writes, “the extent of the political bloodshed in Indonesia during the purge and the brute power and force of the emerging Suharto regime certainly must have stunned and demoralized her." We've taken a sharp turn away from the world of delightful native snack foods.

But then Maraniss walks away from the politics that he sees so clearly. Serving the narrative conventions of American journalism about powerful figures, he works his way out of the detailed and careful story he's told, and instead tells the one he's expected to tell. Despite "all of the political bloodshed that Indonesia had just endured, violence triggered by raw power, fear, and political and ethnic hatred," young Barry Obama's classroom in Indonesia was somehow "a place removed." His teacher "spoke idealistically of the notion of tolerance." Floating above his setting, "Barry in Indonesia was not just an early coming-of-age story, but also the start of his coming to grips with race." Amazingly, in the most banal conclusion drawn by any of these books, life in Indonesia brought the future president symbolically "closer to his father in spirit than he ever would [be] again," a critical step in the formation of his personal identity. "He was also closer physically, only the breadth of one ocean away." *Oh, daddy, I am near you*. Something has dragged a sharp and engaged reporter away from the landscape he has carefully surveyed, back into the banality of a dismal publishing formula in which people must necessarily get to know themselves and feel better about their fathers. The established narrative conventions cannot be escaped.

Their Very Names Were Music

Political journalism in America operates as a kind of narrative cotton gin, cleanly stripping meaning from events. It creates the kind of magical world where no one is quite sure what happened in Indonesia in 1965, but the food was delicious and everyone walked away with a desire to benefit society through selfless public service. The overarching narrative premise, the bit of mechanism that strips out the politics, is that actions and conflicts are essentially personal.

A protagonist—a future president of the United States, say—is on a life journey or vision quest, struggling with the legacy of his mother, or of a historical father figure, or of an actual father, or some combination thereof. Villains appear, necessarily. They stand athwart the personal quest, for personal reasons involving bad personal character. Policy negotiations are spiritual and psychological tests: Will Barack grow into his destiny through bold action, or shrink from history with narrow vision? Is either eventuality due to the way he feels about race, his roots, his papa? What Barack Obama "proposed as the core of his candidacy was a self," David Remnick offers on the first page of his book, framing the nearly six hundred pages of portentous celebrity profiling that follows. Ron Suskind's *Confidence Men: Wall Street, Washington, and the Education of a President* (Harper, 2011) describes its subject as "this brilliant construct," sounding like an overawed Ivy Leaguer writing a seminar paper, and wonders whether this walking, talking narrative object can possibly "handle the waterfall of inchoate yearnings crashing down on him." In a closing chapter titled "Finding and Being Found," David Maraniss has Obama "on the way to his family's unimaginable destination, his own *el dorado*." In the *Lifetime* biopic, the role of Barack Obama will be played by Debra Messing.

Outside of the thing that passes for news on cable television, few journalists perform this dismal removal of meaning from politics more winsomely, with greater pretensions to wry knowingness and stylistic elegance, than Hendrik Hertzberg. In the introduction to his *¡Obámanos!: The Birth of a New Political Era* (Penguin, 2009), a collection of his *New Yorker* essays, Hertzberg parrots Remnick, his boss, with a description of Obama's "long apprenticeship as a student of himself." But Hertzberg makes sure to rub plenty of his own important self against Obama's student self, until you surely understand that they've met, they totally know each other, and oh my goodness, they are *mutual fans*: "I told him how much I admired his 1995 book *Dreams from My Father*, still the only one he had published." And then? "He told me that he and Michelle were big fans of the *New Yorker*." There are *three* shameless paragraphs about this encounter. (Hertzberg's wife and Obama's wife also dig each other, by the way.) Later, Hertzberg received an invitation to meet with the president during a conference for liberal bloggers, and he's happy to tell you about that, too. Follow an experienced journalist into a close discussion on important topics with a leading political figure, and learn from the hard-earned knowledge he brings to his analysis: "The discussion was off the record, but it violates no confidence to say that, as I suppose we all expected, he made a favorable impression on us." By not revealing the things that *I suppose we all expected*, journalism helps us to understand our world.

Every word in Hertzberg's book bridges the selves of the serfs with the selves of the political class. They complete us; they run for office so that we can feel, so that we can be personally redeemed and sanctified at our emotional core. Obama, in this, is like Mario Cuomo: "Both made Democrats, haunted for decades by a phantom of themselves as losers who are weak and glum, suddenly feel like winners who are strong and joyful. Cuomo was grand opera and Obama was the rebirth of the cool, a jazz formalist, but both were virtuosi. Their very names were music." Yes! Take a moment to say "Barack Obama" and "Mario Cuomo" out loud, so you can hear the operatic jazz mellifluence. In his speech to the Democratic National Convention in 2004, "Obama comes riding through the smoke and scoops up his audience like a hero sweeping a stranded damsel onto his horse." Hertzberg goes on, but I can't.

Little Faith in Government

On facing pages in Ron Suskind's *Confidence Men*, advertised as the inside story of how the Obama administration managed its way through the worst recession in seventy-odd years, Suskind introduces a guy named Billy Tauzin. On the second of those two pages, Tauzin is described as a steadfast advocate of the "unfettered marketplace," a description that closely follows Suskind's assurance on the previous page that Tauzin has "little faith in government acting as an arbiter" on health care matters.

So who is this limited government, pro-free-market fanatic? When Suskind first shows Tauzin in action, he's one of two people sitting near Larry Summers at a White House–sponsored meeting on health care reform: "A long-serving Louisiana representative who switched from Democrat to Republican in the 1990s, Tauzin had pushed through one of the most expensive pieces of legislation in American history: the Medicare Prescription Drug Improvement and Modernization Act of 2003. Costing $500 billion over ten years, it is considered by many to be a massive handout to the pharma industry, which in return hired Tauzin as their lead Washington representative."

So the "unfettered marketplace" is where the central government nakedly gives away hundreds of billions of dollars in handouts to private corporations, and people who don't believe that government should act as an arbiter in health care matters are the sponsors of some of the most expensive health care legislation in history, and free market purists work as corporate lobbyists in the District of Columbia, probing for the spigot. It's free markets and laissez-faire economics, a half-trillion public dollars at a time. Thank god Billy Tauzin doesn't believe in government intrusion in the health care marketplace, because just imagine what *that* would look like.

But Ron Suskind isn't an ordinary writer using words in order to describe meaning, any more than Billy Tauzin is an ordinary speaker using words to communicate a set of beliefs; no, Suskind is using words to police a story into established narrative forms, putting the competing players into their categories. Marketplace, free markets, regulation, deregulation, isolationist, pacifist, antigovernment, left, right, center, centrist, extremist, mainstream: these are Facebook words, telling readers about connections, positions, and identities rather than ideologies and actions. In political journalism, someone who believes in the "unfettered marketplace" is a Republican. That person need not believe in the unfettered marketplace, whatever that is, or act in its service. The phrase is not intended for that purpose.

Big books about national politics follow the same rules that Janny Scott and David Remnick bring to their stories about the Soetoro family's sojourn in Indonesia and how Young Barack was endlessly *becoming*. Suskind's book gives us, as the subtitle indicates, a story about "the education of a president," setting Obama's challenge against the test that George Bush failed: "He needed to grow, and he didn't." The nation is personified, too, and goes on its own personal journey, but it's sort of riding shotgun. As Obama rises to the presidency, Suskind says, "The ground was trembling from the streets of Chicago to the fertile fields of Kansas." Linked by trembling streets, the Chosen One is almost pornographically attached to the Body of the People: "It is a rare bond that allows a president and a nation to move as one. . . . Policies suddenly become not just what the president does at some adviser's behest, to score a political point, but who he—or, someday, she—is. It is then that president and public enter their shared moment." There are many such moments in *Confidence Men*, including an extraordinary analogy involving a school bus. It's on page twenty-four, if you haven't eaten lunch and want to read it for yourself.

Sometimes the narrative lens is a little wider than a single person, but politics still sinks beneath an aggregated personal journey in which a whole status group grows into its moment of destiny together. The model was laid down long ago by professional acolyte and melodramatic hagiographer of power Arthur Schlesinger Jr., with his sweeping narrative volumes on the Roosevelt and Kennedy administrations. Contemporary books like James Mann's *The Obamians: The Struggle Inside the White House to Redefine American Power* (Viking, 2012) take readers through the voyage of a class of Democratic foreign policy operators, the president among them, tracking them from the wilderness of the Bush years to the moment they could put on their cleats, take the field, and show the crowd how they could move the ball just like Republicans. While streets trembled on the fertile fields of Kansas, or something. They are all *becoming*. Of course, mapping all these personal journeys can be an exhaustingly circular task, as when Mann describes tedious think tanker John Podesta's tedious emanations about a tedious think tank called the Center for a New American Security: "In an interview in early 2010, Podesta confessed that he was a little disappointed with CNAS. It had started out in the political center, maybe slightly left of center, he said. But he felt it had drifted to the right after [Kurt] Campbell and [Michèle] Flournoy departed and had gradually become just another mainstream Washington defense institution." Understand? It started out in the *political center*, but it gradually drifted—a little to the left! a little to the right!—into the *mainstream*.

But the nonsensical language isn't meant simply to identify actors or clarify allegiances. Purporting to describe and explain, it ranks, excludes, and orders. Here's Mann telling the foreign policy version of Ron Suskind's Obama-finds-his-economic-bearings subplot. Experts are descending on Colorado for the annual meeting of the Aspen Strategy Group, and all the soup is just hot enough:

> The group spanned the spectrum of mainstream thinking about American foreign policy. They were, above all, respectable. Aspen participants were not too far to the left or the right; there was no radical critic of the United States such as, say, the late Chalmers Johnson, inveighing against American empire, and there was no isolationist like, say, Pat Buchanan or Ron Paul, urging that all U.S. troops simply be brought home. No, the visitors to Aspen share similar assumptions; they are senior practitioners, practical people who dwell within the realm of the possible.

They spanned the spectrum of people who share similar assumptions, representing the entire range of thought that you get when you keep critics out of the room. Everyone gets a voice but the actual left, the authentic right, people who say the word empire, and people who, being "isolationist," think the American military presence shouldn't span the face of the earth. All voices are welcome around the table, as long as they say more or less the same thing. It is, you see, a *centrist* forum, focused only on "the realm of the possible." If you think the "realm of the possible" shrinks when everyone allowed in the room to discuss the possibilities already shares the same assumptions, you've just shown why you're outside the locked door. Wear a jacket out there, hippie, 'cause the wilderness is *cold*.

They Are Married to Us, Too

Events and human beings outside the narrative frame of the personal journey toward the responsible center are incidental, sometimes mentioned but never fully perceived. Jodi Kantor's *The Obamas* (Little, Brown & Company, 2012), for example, is about the personal journey the Obamas are taking as a couple. The book scrupulously examines dilemmas like the one that opens chapter three: "The approach of the forty-third Super Bowl, with the Pittsburgh Steelers playing the Arizona Cardinals, raised a question in the White House: where would the forty-fourth president watch the game?" Here, too, we ride shotgun, as Kantor asks us to wonder not only about "the impact of the presidency on the Obamas' relationship," but also about "how the Obamas' personal dynamic had consequences for the rest of us." After all, she concludes, with the very last words that frame the introduction of her book, "they are married to us, too." We're like a whole national family of sister-wives, joined in mass matrimony. Just imagine how many in-laws we'll have to visit.

Pakistanis, on the other hand, take *their* places as the furniture our family casually rearranges in its living room. Some of the president's supporters thought he would scale back American drone strikes, but it was not to be. "The supporters," it turns out, "were wrong." Obama's personal journey as an emerging leader went elsewhere. Here's how Kantor's paragraph, describing the new president's first drone strike, ends: "Three of the other dead were children." Here's how the next paragraph begins: "The new first lady, meanwhile, was figuring out how Malia and Sasha could have playdates with their new school friends." One set of dead children backs up against a pair of live ones. It's jarring only if you're able to notice.

Meanwhile, fake problems are placed in the narrative to displace the real problems, like dead Pakistani children, that politicians and their journalist courtiers are not able to perceive. In a stunning passage that Ron Suskind surely didn't regard as stunning, we learn that an Obama campaign speech on foreign policy fell flat. As a result, Obama rushed to meet with a team of economic advisers, since "attention-grabbing domestic policies looked like the only way his campaign was going to generate forward motion." The campaign "had booked the room," Suskind explains, "for the next two hours." The advisers tossed around ideas, suggesting (for example) that high levels of unemployment among "low- to moderately-skilled male workers" could be addressed with a program to train them for work in the growing field of health care. Obama "shook his head": "'Look, these are guys,' he said," and they wouldn't want to take jobs as nurse's aides. Then, finally, an economist sitting at the table pulled something out of the air: "'Infrastructure,' he blurted out. 'Rebuilding infrastructure.' Obama nodded and smiled, seeing it instantly." This is how policy is made: people make shit up around a table to patch over a bad speech, and then go to Congress for a trillion dollars, maybe a little more, maybe a little less.

A few hours later, a bridge collapses—one bridge, in a nation of close to four million square miles—and the policy is vindicated. Here's Suskind again (observe the seamlessness of the collisions in these sentences, the way premises arise and are simultaneously refuted and sustained without ever interrupting the smoothness of the narrative): "It was government's responsibility to ensure that the physical foundations of the country, on which its economy and way of life rested, were sound. The bridges and dams, the electrical grid, the highways—the condition and upkeep of these things could not be left to the private sector and profit motive alone. They never had been. If government did not step up soon, disaster would surely ensue." So infrastructure had never been left to the private sector, because it had always been the government's responsibility, but the government needed to step up and start doing the things it had always done, instead of doing what it had never done and leaving roads and bridges to be maintained by the profit motive, which it had to stop doing despite never having begun to do it. Look again at the sentences on both sides of "They never had been," and see how all the claims fit together: absolute incoherence, total nonsense, and an established journalistic narrative.

To recap: Once, a group of Obama's campaign advisers, sitting around a table in a room that was booked for two hours, hit upon a new and sudden need to have the government start maintaining public infrastructure, and before the sun went up the next day, journalists were earnestly explaining that highways and dams could no longer be left to the private sector, pause, "They never had been," pause, *Government needs to step up*. All of these invented themes take perfect form in Noam Scheiber's exhaustingly banal *The Escape Artists: How Obama's Team Fumbled the Recovery* (Simon & Schuster, 2012), one of the finest pieces of raw stenography you could hope ever to read. The universe has given us Noam Scheiber for the same reason it's given us Hendrik Hertzberg: as an exemplar of a particular character type, in this case the earnest scrivener of conventional wisdom. Scheiber's résumé nails every point right on the head, from *The New Republic* and a fellowship at the New America Foundation to Oxford for a Rhodes scholarship. His personal journey worked according to design, training a young journalist to a state of impenetrable establishment credulousness. Scheiber types up a new Obama plan to spend $50 billion on "crumbling roads and bridges" as part of a package of "reasonable, centrist policies" that pushed against the "extreme demands" of Republicans, who, presumably, desire immediate American bridgelessness in which no one can drive anywhere because all the roads have returned to dust and the broken dams have flooded everything. There is oration, and it gets the requisite adjective: "Obama delivered . . . a speech as muscular as the American Jobs Act Sperling had crafted," Scheiber writes without laughing. If speeches are "muscular," does the phrase "bold action" appear? Reader, you know it does.

That Power to End Debate

But let's give them their due. Journalists like Ron Suskind, James Mann, and Noam Scheiber manage to notice policy and the significance of policy choices more than the career academic who has covered the similar "education of a president" narrative. In *Reading Obama: Dreams, Hope, and the American Political Tradition* (Princeton University Press, 2010), Harvard historian James Kloppenberg writes what might as well be a biography of Kim Jong-il on sale at Pyongyang airport. Every word is bold struggle and brilliant formation. Young Barack encounters many challenges, but

RANDALL ENOS

he is shaped by the strengthening fire; in one environment after another, "his exceptional intelligence enabled him to master difficult concepts that left many of his classmates floundering." That latter example specifically describes the future president's experience at, yes, Harvard Law School, where diminished cognition is apparently the norm and smart people really stand out. Fortunately, Obama has been able to cover the awkwardness caused by his genius with the social deftness that comes from his "unusual self-restraint and self-awareness," and his "vaunted poise," and his—okay, let's stop here.

Kloppenberg coughs out a book celebrating Barack Obama's

glorious philosophical pragmatism, his commitment to civic republicanism, his openness in thought and discussion. In this version of the heroic centrist melodrama, the Great Leader believes in a philosophy that demands "open-ended experimentation," citizen! He stands for "open-mindedness and ongoing debate." He is unique among politicians in that he insists upon "respect for one's opponents and a willingness to compromise with them."[4] Declaring the importance of all this open discussion and respectful exchange, Kloppenberg also writes back-to-back sentences like this:

> So incoherent is American public debate that Obama's critics simultaneously blame him for an economic situation he did nothing to cause and oppose larger infusions of money into the economy through much greater government spending, the only option that might address the problem. The impasse in which the nation finds itself stems directly from the American people's limited access to power—and their equally limited access to responsible sources of information about how the American economy works.

Does the professor who types sentences celebrating *open-ended experimentation* and *open-mindedness* notice that he also declares the presence of *the only option* for American economic policy? Does he notice that he pronounces dissenting sources to be irresponsible? Reader, he does not.

Oh, impassioned critic of our president who opposes the only allowable policy option, where is your openness, your pragmatic commitment to open-ended experimentation, your free-flowing debate, your modesty? Here, in any event, is Kloppenberg's: "Have the first three years of the Obama presidency made necessary a reconsideration of the arguments presented in *Reading Obama*? The short answer is no." This question-and-answer, from the book's paperback preface, drags its author into the realm of naked self-parody. "Since the book appeared," Kloppenberg writes with unembarrassable smugness that goes down like brandy in Cambridge, "I have heard from many people who have known Barack Obama at different stages of his life, and in very different circumstances. All of them have told me they think I have him right." What we have here, ladies and gentlemen, is professor James Kloppenberg of Harvard University saying he must be right because he's heard from "good friends" of the president's at Harvard Law School, not to mention from "a former head of a European government" too. Well, there you go. Sounds like the only person who hasn't confirmed his portrait of the president's "mature, penetrating mind" is the man himself; no doubt, the professor lies awake at night waiting for the call.

Reading Obama echoes another classic of the form, a ten-thousand-word *Vanity Fair* lament from September 2010 in which professional thumb-sucker Todd Purdum declared a similar concern over the kind of people who oppose whatever their betters declare to be the *only option* for public policy. "It used to be," Purdum wrote, starting with words that invariably signal idiocy ahead, "that news outlets had space to report or comment on only a fraction of any day's events. The pace of events has picked up, sure, but the capacity to assert, allege, and comment is now infinite, and subject to little responsible control." Later in the same article, Purdum quotes presidential adviser Valerie Jarrett, who does not appear ever to listen to herself speak, and who similarly laments the decline of the old days of responsible discussion: "Walter Cronkite would get on and say the truth, and people believed the media," she says. Yes, Purdum nods along, a thousand times *yes*: "Today, no single media figure or outlet has that power to end debate." What a shame.

Both Wall Street's Man and Obama's

Here I must pause to confess that I admire Ron Suskind's book, although I had to squint to feel it. At least I admire it more than do its critics, like Jacob Weisberg and Ezra Klein, who know that Suskind must have been factually wrong because his book about politics is full of pettiness, backbiting, and accounts of internal chaos and disloyalty in policymaking. This is the lament of the faithful, who know that politics is serious business and a public service. In any case, the critics are right that the book is a mess. For nearly five hundred pages, Suskind wages conceptual war on his own evidence, piling up proof about a set of premises while insisting on a whole other set of contradictory conclusions. But the evidence, bless its little heart, speaks through the author's fog, describing a set of policy arguments and their outcomes. Reporter Suskind overcomes Writer Suskind.

Here, at least, is a book about politics that has politics in it. We learn that Christina Romer—Obama's first chair of the Council of Economic Advisers—argued (along with several other key aides) that insolvent banks, including even the biggest of them like Citigroup, should be seized and wound up, their failures resolved through disciplined regulatory intervention. She lost to (in particular) Tim Geithner, who opted to "keep matters moving forward with as little disruption as possible," preventing a crisis of confidence in the financial system by endlessly throwing free money at it. Peter Orszag, meanwhile, argued for data-driven health care reform that would first aim to control costs, then use the savings to expand coverage. Instead, the bill that survived Congress "would be more accurately defined as 'insurance' reform than 'health care' reform," as Suskind observes, "since the centerpiece was mainly an expansion of the private insurance industry."

In a book written by someone who bothers to notice policy, *regulation* is a disputed thing of unclear boundaries and purpose: What is it? How will it work? What should it do? Whom should it serve? Look at the outcome of both of the major domestic policy disputes in the first years of the Obama administration. In health care, a policy initiative intended to reduce health care spending instead ended with a requirement that more people send money to private insurance corporations, while private health care corporations escaped any significant cost controls at all. (Somebody tell this to David Remnick, who crows about "the tens of millions of Americans who would now have health care," as though there's no distinction between an insurance mandate and the delivery of medical services.) In financial regulation, banks ran the table, and Suskind can write sentences like this one: "The government had handed $125 billion to nine banks, without conditions." While we have a national debate framed by a false choice between deregulation and reckless greed or more regulation and greater fairness, here are two instances in which more regulation produced more corporate income. The facts don't fit the debate; more remarkably, the debate won't fit the facts.

Neither will Suskind's book, which describes the "unfettered free markets" of the "deregulated post-Reagan era," and an "army of men" in government who held "an unshakeable belief in the miracle of the markets, the freer the better," and "traditionally antiregulatory Republicans," and the "general agreement" about the "lack of regulation" in finance. Describing efforts to legislate financial regulation after 2008, Suskind references the "sweeping" Depression-era regulation that it would be measured against: "There hadn't really been any since then, so the bar was low."

Right alongside all of that language, a reader gets Suskind's description of Alan Greenspan's "greatest historical influence," which was that he "helped to ensure that, in each crisis, the rollover of debts ... would be supported," creating "a flood of liquidity that altered the ancient, commonsense physics between price and value, confidence and pessimism." Two pages later, Suskind describes "Fannie Mae and Freddie Mac, guaranteeing roughly 80 percent of all mortgages, and for years encouraging the extension of debt to unsteady borrowers as part of [a] national bipartisan push to spread the 'virtues' of homeownership." A few more pages, and we learn that those two organizations, "and by association the U.S. government ... were the guarantors of Wall Street's business model and its vast profits," a business model assured by "government's role as backstop—final recipient of the risk being passed to and fro between investors in debt." Next, it's on to the bankruptcy reform legislation of 2005, which exempted repos and swaps, "like those soon-to-be-fatal credit default swaps," from the "automatic stay" on corporate liabilities on bankruptcy. After that, we hear about the "migration" of middle-class money from savings accounts to Wall Street, caused by "the government's 1970s creation of tax-exempt 401(k)s and IRAs." From there, Suskind turns to the Federal Reserve Bank's "cheap-money policies"; and then to banks "making money from the free money offered by the Fed, and sitting on the profits"; and then to AIG and "the government's total contribution to the firm" rising to "a stunning $170 billion"; and then to the stark declaration that "Washington was becoming Wall Street." See all the deregulation? It's almost like we didn't have any government at all.

Put it this way: In a book about the attempt to overcome the legacies of deregulation through the stabilizing and reasonable influence of the regulatory state, the pharmaceutical industry lobbyist Billy Tauzin is sitting next to Larry Summers in the White House, where everyone is somehow on a journey to the center. Describing the latest iterations of this regulatory-corporate fiesta, Suskind delivers the verdict of the asset manager Larry Fink, with an ellipsis from the original: "The president is much more of a centrist . . . in some ways he might even be called right of what used to be called center." I think that's supposed to be a compliment, delivered by a critic who was then "impressed," as Suskind notes, by an up-close encounter with the president to discuss the country's economic plight.

It's clear from all these accounts of the sensibly pragmatic exercise of power in Washington that the "center" is where corporations go to pick up their free cash. But at least there are no *extremists* at that center. You can just change the foreign policy names in James Mann's *The Obamians* to domestic policy names, and you will have exactly the same narrative on offer in Ron Suskind's *Confidence Men*. "Why is it that Democratic presidential candidates hold out the prospect of a new American foreign policy," Mann asks, "and yet often wind up with ones that are not fundamentally different from the Republicans?" Yes, *why is that?*

The Policy Executive as a Social Type

In October 2010 Kloppenberg described his work on Barack Obama's political formation to an audience at the U.S. Intellectual History Conference in New York. In his remarks Kloppenberg probed the sophistication of Obama's extraordinary mind, the depth of his philosophy, the seriousness of his engagement with the long roots of American political thought. In a story on Kloppenberg's talk, *New York Times* reporter Patricia Cohen wrote that the audience "responded with prolonged applause." A history professor in the crowd helpfully interpreted the enthusiastic response of Kloppenberg's peer group: "The way he traced Obama's intellectual influences was fascinating for us, given that Obama's academic background seems so similar to ours." The president is, like us, extraordinary. He went to college a lot.

Many critics have described the emergence of such insulated status groups among American elites, "the product of the cultural fragmentation that seems to characterize industrial and postindustrial societies," in Christopher Lasch's words. No fool for power, Lasch noted the separation of an emerging intellectual class from the society that produced it. As academic and political elites have evolved since then into status groups sealed off from reality and insulated from economic pain, they have substantially merged into a new kind of managerial elite. A Harvard history professor celebrates the ascendance of a Harvard Law grad and University of Chicago law professor to the presidency; and as the new president rises from one to another of these "strategic loci of social control" (in Lasch's words, again), he brings along other members of his social class. Professor Elena Kagan moves from the dean's office to the Supreme Court with only a brief detour to polish her curriculum vitae for government work; professor Cass Sunstein takes his desk in the new administration—as "regulatory czar"—not far from professor Samantha Power over in the State Department, who also happens to be his wife. Professor Christina Romer and professor Larry Summers wait outside the Oval Office for a meeting, the air thick with tension, in the same seats once occupied by professor John Yoo and professor Condoleezza Rice, while professor Steven Chu wraps up his discussion on energy policy. Wonderfully, Suskind describes "Summers's pride in leading the most academically accomplished, big-brained team since Kennedy's 'best and brightest.'" It worked so well the first time, didn't it?

As Kloppenberg casts a horrified look at all the irresponsible sources that burden the educated managerial class with incoherent debate, he sees himself. (And he likes what he sees.) As the professoriate continues, amazingly, to swoon over a Barack Obama who has been gratefully pronounced by the financial industry to be "much more of a centrist" than they had expected, they aren't seeing the object of their projected adulation. The highly educated class, the new kind of managerial elite, is protecting itself from self-knowledge. It's hiding.

Surveying the body of self-congratulatory, pragmatically centrist literature celebrating this self-congratulatory, pragmatically centrist administration, it's at last possible to understand the true character and scale of our plight: the nation is locked in an elite-made crisis—caused by regulatory capture, not by mythical deregulation—that has been extended and deepened by elite intervention constructed around further regulatory capture. The solution to that problem has been to batter at the chimera of deregulation. A failed elite class that finds itself unable to put its knowledge into effective operation instead speaks of that knowledge in a louder voice. It tells us, of course, that Barack Obama is a rare and magnificent genius, that he is a pragmatic centrist who correctly performs the only inevitable policy options, that he is one of us.

The Qing Dynasty died under the hapless guidance of men like these, men who had trained hard in Confucian principle and passed a brutally difficult series of exams to ascend to the highest ranks of a dying regime that they couldn't hope to save. We know so wonderfully much, and none of it works.

In this context, the center is a place of belonging, not a place of belief. It's therefore striking to note that, in a book that describes a battle between regulation and deregulation, left and right, Suskind describes one brief hopeful moment in Congress, a momentary coalescence among senators who favored tough limits on the size and leverage to be allowed to financial corporations. Congressional leaders opposed the measure, "But senators started signing on, as the most liberal members, such as Sherrod Brown and Vermont's Bernie Sanders, were joined by none other than Richard Shelby, the ranking

Republican on the Senate Banking Committee, and his party's leading voice in the chamber on banking issues; Nevada's John Ensign; and Oklahoma's Tom Coburn, arguably the Senate's most conservative member." You can appreciate how distressing this specter would have been to the White House, and to its dutiful class of mandarin apologists: Bernie Sanders and Tom Coburn were now in agreement on a key question of financial policy, burdening public debate with incoherence.

But then the *centrists* intervened, and left us instead with the mostly unfinished gesture of the Dodd-Frank Act, which solves the problem of too-big-to-fail banks by leaving them just as large as they are now. Fortunately, though, since it wasn't *deregulation*, Dodd-Frank could only have been a major victory for the *regulation* of the financial industry. To dispute that point is to be an *extremist*. A country that can't manage or mitigate the crisis of its failing institutions has at least found a way to avoid talking about it, five hundred pages at a time.

Disciplined, Satisfying, and Secretive

And yet the politics accidentally leak through. The narrative construct named Barack Obama is everywhere encountering boundaries, slamming into hard limits that prevent him from taking bold action to help us on our own journey at his side, even though our emotions have fused with his and we are married to him and his wife. In books that depoliticize political events, politics becomes an obstacle to Obama's performance of process rather than the process in which he is engaged. And that real process, the one he wishes to perform, is formidable indeed. "He had to clean up the financial crisis first," Jodi Kantor explains, "but then he would be able to move on to his real agenda, which included dealing with a rapidly warming earth and fixing a health care system so expensive it might eventually bankrupt the country." Oh, and he told his staff to get started on "an advanced smart grid to transport new forms of power across long distances," and he called leaders in the Middle East "to tell them he was committed to achieving Israeli-Palestinian peace in his first term." And let's also multiply some loaves and fishes, and can we reupholster the couch in the Oval Office?

But then the only reason Obama doesn't repair the global economy and reengineer medicine and change the temperature of the earth and toss up a new national power grid to harvest the wind and institute an immediate and lasting peace between Israel and Arabs is that people shamefully said no to him. His staff tells him that he can't just grab up land across the length and breadth of the nation to run his advanced power lines, but would have to negotiate for it with such intrusive things as "every tiny municipality along the way," pissants that they are. Here are the next two paragraphs in their entirety:

> I'm the president. Can't I get this done? he asked his advisers.
>
> Actually, no, they told him. The smart grid idea was scrapped.

Dunder Mifflined in his own office by uncooperative employees, Obama is similarly thwarted all over the imperial city by an inexplicable explosion of personal intransigence and meanness. Mitch McConnell, "a Kentuckian with large, calm eyes," is "conjured up" to twirl his waxed mustache and tie Penelope to the train tracks. "Where Obama was subtle and intellectual, McConnell was a tough, canny tactician who believed in brute repetition of anxiety-inducing messages about the mounting federal deficit, bailouts, and terrorist attacks," Kantor explains. The description of Obama as a subtle intellectual comes precisely one page after the one where he tells his staff to make an advanced smart grid appear, and then gives up when they tell him there are laws. But anyway, it's all just *narratives*: elsewhere in the book, Kantor writes that "the federal deficit was a stunning $1.4 trillion, the most red ink that post–World War II Washington had ever seen." Why does Mitch McConnell keep talking about the size of the federal deficit? Merely because he's a tough, canny tactician. The thing is simultaneously real and impossible to discuss as real, a dangerous reality and a narrative ploy that Republicans are playing as a game.

Crushed by Mitch McConnell's shrewd decision to pretend there's a federal deficit, Obama retreats to the rationality of state violence. "In comparison to the raucous noise of domestic politics," Kantor writes, "there was something disciplined and satisfying about secretive national-security work. There was no messy Congress to deal with, no stroking and horse trading with legislators, and certainly no Tea Party resistance." In short, Obama was "more at ease with the exercise of power than the exercise of politics."

Here it is, all of it: a world of personal will, without critics, without opposition, without irresponsible debate that tragically can't be closed anymore by a single paternal figure. Political events without political content or meaning, without politics. It is disciplined, satisfying, and secretive. Killing people overseas allows a leader to move past *politics* and achieve the satisfaction of *exercising power*. American journalists see the politics of their own place and moment as clearly as they see the political substance of Ann Soetoro's Indonesia, where young Barack Obama spent some time becoming.

Swing Sets

To my eye, nothing tells the story of our historical moment like the story about the swing set. It appears in Jodi Kantor's book, as the Obamas "stepped into new lives that seemed in many ways to belong to nineteenth-century regents, with a circle of staff whose size and degree of specialization seemed to rival that of a royal court." Remember that Kantor dwells on the limits Obama has encountered as his political opponents make slyly framed claims about federal spending and excessive debt. The president is confined in a political trap, bound by the inherent parsimoniousness and procedural paralysis of a government managed by political process. He also has "at least two valets to dress, groom, and pack for him, a navy steward to serve him meals, a maître d' and six butlers for the residence, and two personal aides for everything else." And then it's time to buy some White House swings for Sasha and Malia, and the staff leaps into action. "The staff performed their work with total seriousness:

when it was time to order a swing set for the Obama girls, rear admiral Stephen Rochon, the chief usher, traveled to the factory in South Dakota where it was being made to inspect it."

Trapped by its limits, unable to take bold action, pinching pennies, and frozen by political obstructions, the White House dispatches an admiral across the country to buy playground equipment for its children. The Obamas are helpless, living like nineteenth-century regents. The absurdity of our own historical moment is written clear as day by people who can't begin to perceive what they've written.

NOTES

1 Another, smaller problem: Lolo Soetoro was a geographer, not a geologist.

2 "Ann loved Indonesian snacks," Scott continues, offering some careful analysis of the *reasons* why she did. Surely she enjoyed the flavors of the snacks, but perhaps her delight was "compounded later by admiration for the enterprising people who made them." Then comes, and I am not making this up, another list of local snack foods, this one focusing on sweet snacks rather than the generally savory snacks of the previous list. "The snacks in Ann's department were the envy of other departments," we learn. There is a quote from an Indonesian acquaintance, describing how popular Ann's snacks were. There is a story about a bad snack that Ann did not like. *Lolo was in the army. It is known that neighbors turned on neighbors.* In a story about Indonesia in the late 1960s, you can learn a lot about the cookies and chips.

3 Compare this to Janny Scott's statement that Lolo Soetoro was later "in the army," or to Remnick's claim that Soetoro "had taken a job" with the army. We learn two critical facts in one tight sentence: Soetoro would become a civilian in a military position, and he didn't have a choice about it.

4 Here's the open-minded president on ABC News in early May 2012, compromising and respecting his opponents all over the place: "At a certain point, I've just concluded that—for me personally, it is important for me to go ahead and affirm that—I think same-sex couples should be able to get married. Now—I have to tell you that part of my hesitation on this has also been I didn't want to nationalize the issue. There's a tendency when I weigh in to think suddenly it becomes political and it becomes polarized. And what you're seeing is, I think, states working through this issue—in fits and starts, all across the country. Different communities are arriving at different conclusions, at different times. And I think that's a healthy process and a healthy debate. And I continue to believe that this is an issue that is gonna be worked out at the local level, because historically, this has not been a federal issue, what's recognized as a marriage." It's so centrist and responsible that it manages not to promise, offer, or suggest anything but the cool diffusion of *process*. If you're gay, we commit to talking about you some more.

POSTSCRIPT

In January 2014, Barack Obama gave a speech at Justice Department headquarters about a set of reforms he intended to apply to the National Security Agency. The topic had been hotly discussed, particularly in the wake of leaks by former NSA contractor Edward Snowden, and an attentive audience should have been more or less a given. A poll taken after the speech showed just how much America is still buying the Barack Obama product: "Half say they have heard nothing at all about his proposed changes to the NSA, and another 41 percent say they heard only a little bit. Even among those [who] heard about Obama's speech, few think the changes will improve privacy protections, or make it more difficult for the government to fight terrorism."

Like a *Twilight* sequel or a Lady Gaga album, the hysterically overhyped Obama presidency was bound to disappoint. The collapse of Obama's stature grew, first, from the president's obvious mediocrity of vision and indifference to execution. But the scope of the collapse was made possible only by the breathlessness of the buildup. We will not be free of this cycle anytime soon. Presidential elections are our most-marketed reality show, *The Bachelor* for 310 million would-be brides, and TV needs a big narrative. The solution, as always, is to look away as much as possible. We might be stuck with the shoddy product, but we don't have to gorge on the marketing.

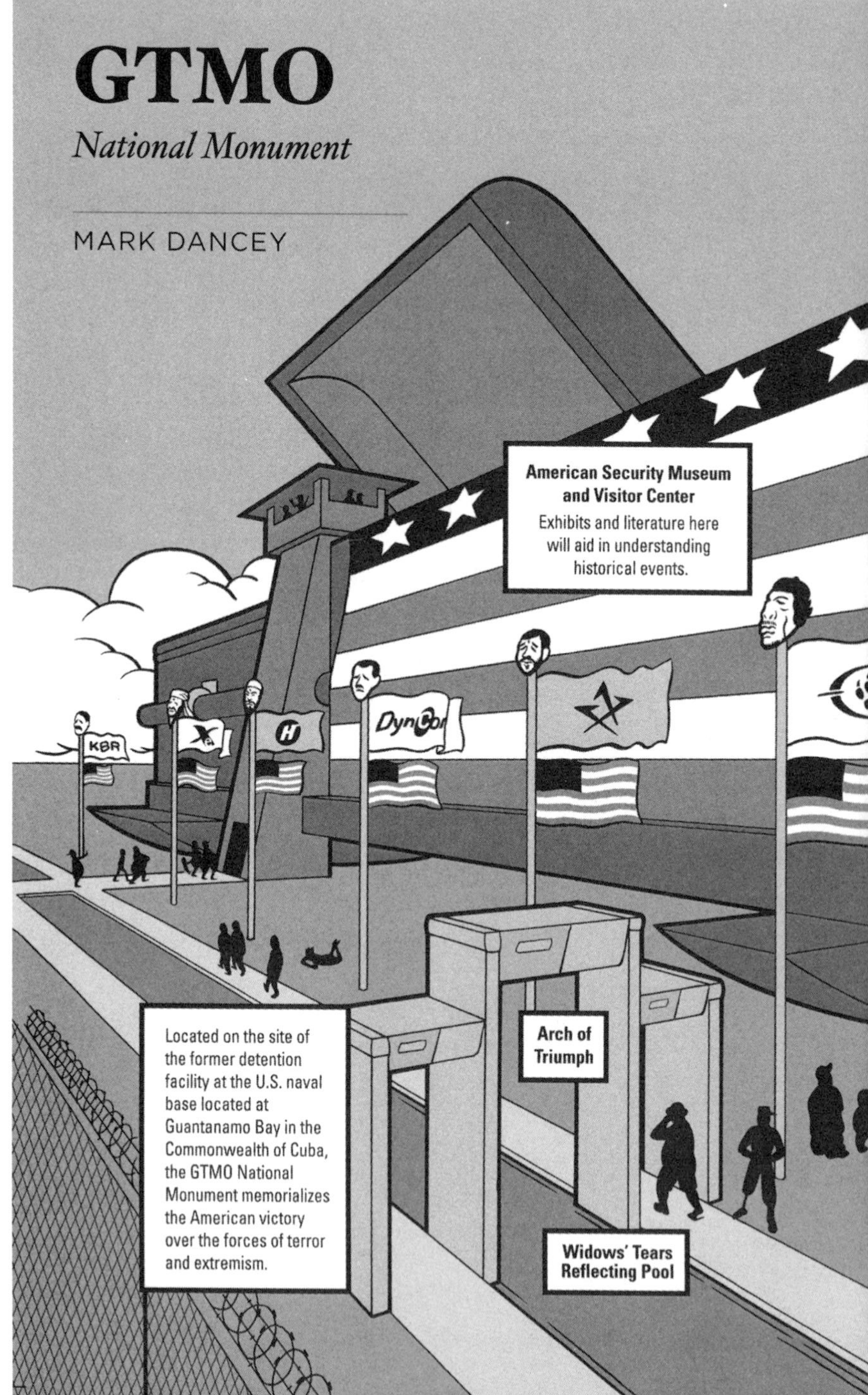
GTMO
National Monument
MARK DANCEY
American Security Museum and Visitor Center
Exhibits and literature here will aid in understanding historical events.
KBR
DynCorp
Located on the site of the former detention facility at the U.S. naval base located at Guantanamo Bay in the Commonwealth of Cuba, the GTMO National Monument memorializes the American victory over the forces of terror and extremism.
Arch of Triumph
Widows' Tears Reflecting Pool

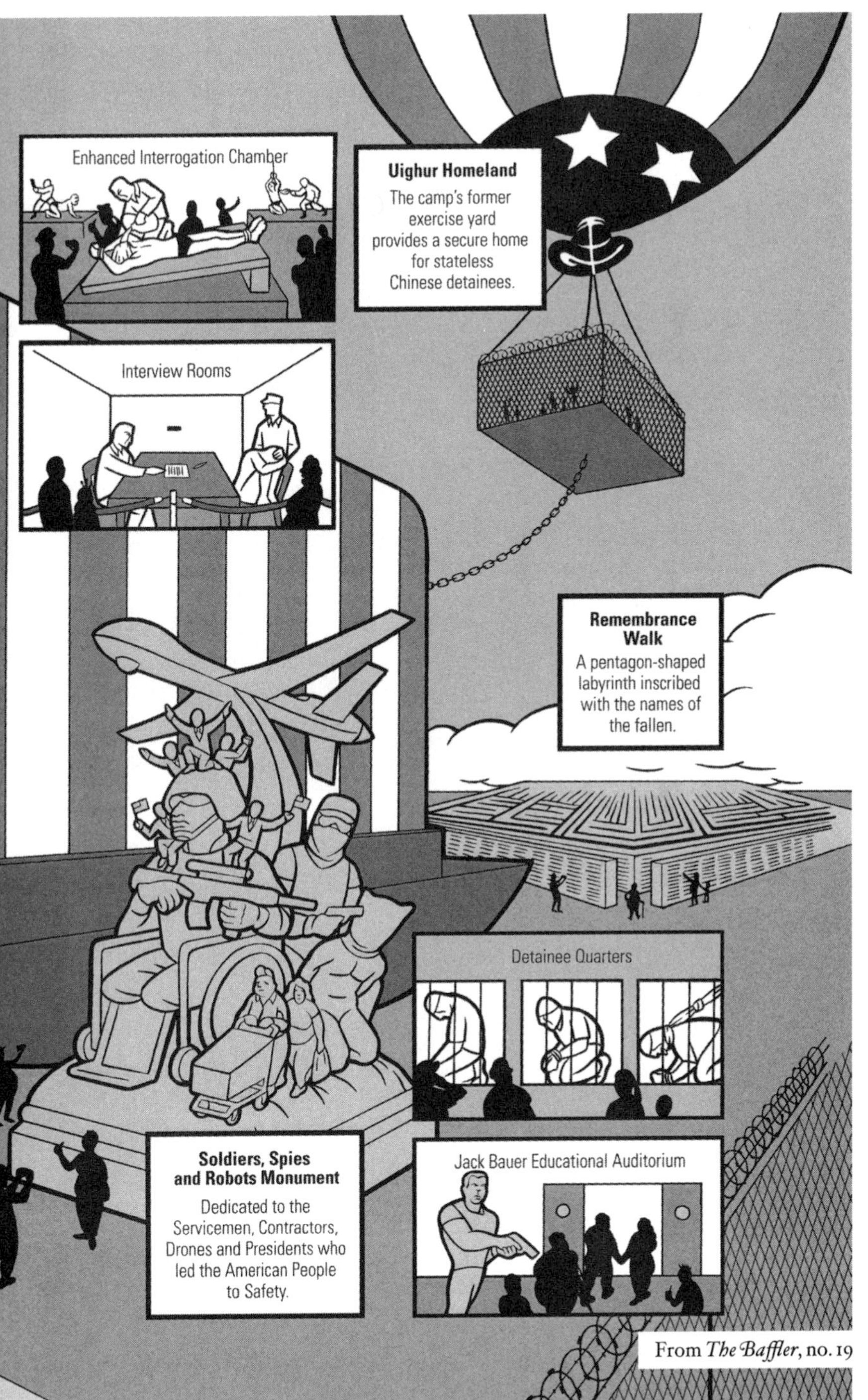

Enhanced Interrogation Chamber
Uighur Homeland
The camp's former exercise yard provides a secure home for stateless Chinese detainees.
Interview Rooms
Remembrance Walk
A pentagon-shaped labyrinth inscribed with the names of the fallen.
Detainee Quarters
Soldiers, Spies and Robots Monument
Dedicated to the Servicemen, Contractors, Drones and Presidents who led the American People to Safety.
Jack Bauer Educational Auditorium

From *The Baffler*, no. 19

ACKNOWLEDGMENTS

All the essays in this book were first published in *The Baffler* magazine, numbers 18 to 24—which means they benefitted from the editorial acumen (and occasional tender mercy) of Lindsey Gilbert, our managing editor, and Rhian Sasseen. When the book itself took shape, Emily Carroll made a beautiful index.

Kind thanks to David Mulcahey, Emily Vogt, and Conor O'Neil for their contributions to the cause.

Praise to Gita Devi Manaktala at MIT Press for being such a pleasure to work with.

No interns are used in the making of *The Baffler*.

CONTRIBUTORS

CHRIS BRAY is a sometime history professor and is writing a book about the history of American military justice.

MARK DANCEY is a Detroit-based painter and illustrator.

BARBARA EHRENREICH is contributing editor of *The Baffler* and author of *Bright-Sided*, *Dancing in the Streets*, *Nickel and Dimed*, and other books. Her memoir is *Living with a Wild God*.

SUSAN FALUDI is contributing editor of *The Baffler* and the author of *Backlash: The Undeclared War Against American Women*, which won the National Book Critics Circle Award for Nonfiction. Her latest book is *The Terror Dream: Myth and Misogyny in an Insecure America*.

THOMAS FRANK is founding editor of *The Baffler*. He is the author of five books, including *What's the Matter with Kansas?* and *Pity the Billionaire*.

ANN FRIEDMAN is a columnist for *New York* magazine's website. She lives in Los Angeles.

DAVID GRAEBER is contributing editor of *The Baffler* and the author of the *Debt: The First 5,000 Years* and *The Democracy Project*. He is senior anthropologist at the London School of Economics.

JAMES GRIFFIOEN is a writer and photographer. He writes the blog sweetjuniper.com and keeps a photo portfolio at jamesgriffioen.com.

A. S. HAMRAH lives in Brooklyn, NY, and writes about film.

HEATHER HAVRILESKY writes *Bookforum*'s Best Seller List column and *The Awl*'s weekly existential advice column, Turning The Screw. She's the author of the memoir *Disaster Preparedness*.

CHRIS LEHMANN is senior editor of *The Baffler* and its Dollar Debauch columnist, as well as coeditor of *Bookforum*. He is the author of *Rich People Things: Real-Life Secrets of the Predator Class*.

RHONDA LIEBERMAN is contributing editor of *Artforum*. Her Cats-in-Residence program debuted at *The Cat Show* at White Columns, NY, which she also curated.

ANNE ELIZABETH MOORE is the author of *Unmarketable: Brandalism, Copyfighting, Mocketing, and the Erosion of Integrity*, the comics editor of the *Los Angeles Review of Books*, and a monthly contributor of comics journalism to *Truthout*. She lives in Chicago.

EVGENY MOROZOV is the author of *To Save Everything, Click Here: The Folly of Technological Utopianism* and of *The Net Delusion: The Dark Side of Internet Freedom*, a *New York Times* Notable Book of 2011.

JIM NEWELL writes about politics for *The Baffler*. He's been a staff writer at *Gawker*, an editor at *Wonkette*, and a contributor to the *Guardian*.

RICK PERLSTEIN is an American historian and journalist in Chicago.

JOHN SUMMERS is editor in chief of *The Baffler*.

MAUREEN TKACIK is a financial journalist in New York City.

INDEX

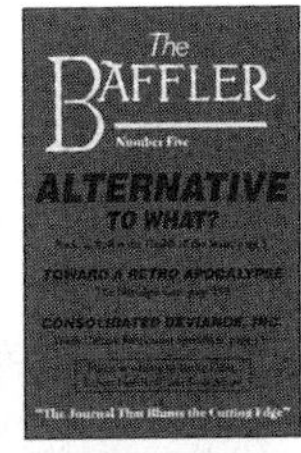

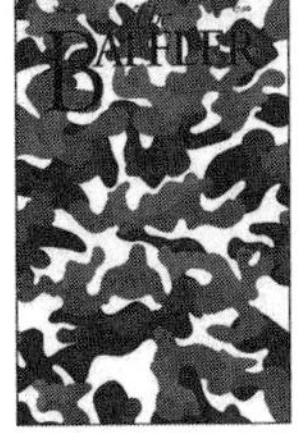

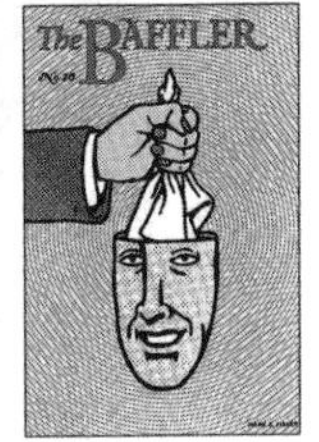

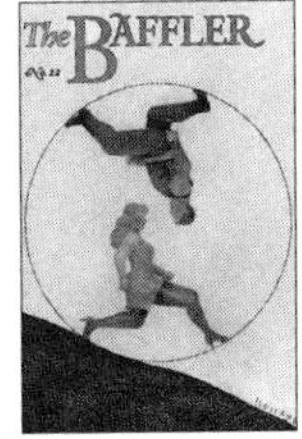

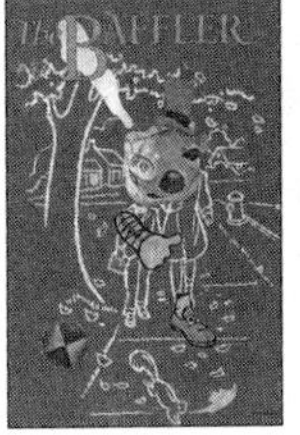

thebaffler.com

About *The Baffler*

The Baffler magazine stirred to life back in ye olde 1988 with a mission to blunt the cutting edge of culture.

Business leaders had declared the unregulated market to be the arbiter of all human striving, while the country's consensus makers had conveniently blathered on about the end of history, the tidings of eternal prosperity, and the wonders of creativity.

We said bubbles in the housing and finance industries resulted from an extremist New Economy movement that was doomed to fail, though generally deemed too smart to do so. We sounded the death knell of the traditional music industry a decade or so before it occurred, anticipated the dustups over unpaid labor in Information Age media, analyzed the right-wing backlash before it spun out its unmissable latter-day perversities, and never for a moment fell for the technology industry's corporate brand of nonconformity.

So when, circa 2008, the celebrated market wrecked the financial lives of millions of people around the world and knocked the consensus on its collective ass, we rebooted with a roster of new (and not-so-new) contributors and commenced firing off new salvos against a leadership class grown ever more brutal, deluded, and desperate.

Now that you have our most productively unconstructive recent essays between your eyeballs, if not in your hands, we beseech you to use them. Go and do likewise. It's fun.